Beulah's Song

Beulah's Song

A Love Story

WRITTEN BY

P. J. Rhea

First Edition 2025

Attributions

Interior Text Font | Minion Pro
Editors | Robbie W. Grayson III
Cover Design & Typesetting | Robbie Grayson III

Paperback ISBN | 979-8-3495-4254-1

Traitmarker Media, LLC
www.traitmarkermedia.com
traitmarker@gmail.com

From the Publisher

Beulah's Song: A Love Story is a work of dramatized fiction inspired by real events. While the narrative draws from true experiences, many names, identifying details, locations, and certain facts have been altered for creative purposes and to protect the privacy of individuals. Any resemblance to actual persons or events not explicitly acknowledged is purely coincidental.

This book is not intended to serve as legal, medical, psychological, or social work advice. Readers seeking guidance in these areas should consult qualified professionals.

The views and opinions expressed are solely those of the author and do not necessarily reflect the views of any organizations, agencies, or institutions with which the author may be affiliated. The publisher disclaims any responsibility for actions taken based on the contents of this book.

The intent of this work is to tell a compelling love story, honor the human spirit, and explore universal themes of resilience, connection, and hope. It is not meant to stereotype, generalize, or make definitive claims about the individuals or communities portrayed.

Traitmarker Media, LLC | *August 2025*

Table of Contents

Prologue

The package arrived on a Tuesday afternoon. Inside this heavy box was 110 copies of her published novel. The publisher had told her if she purchased at least 100 copies at the discounted price afforded to the author that she would receive 10 free copies to share with friends and family if she so desired. The suggestion was that the other 100 copies be sold to bookstores and used for book signings to promote her first published novel. She had dreamed of this experience for years, but the subject matter was not what she had expected her first attempt at writing to be.

Her heart pounded in her chest as she sat in the middle of the living room floor with the large box planted between her legs and a knife in hand to cut the tape. This had been a labor of love bringing this story to these pages. Her first novel but so much more.

She opened it and took the first copy out to examine it. The picture on the front cover was of a beautiful young girl with long auburn hair and pale blue eyes. Willamina was the name of the bravest person she had met to this day. How honored she felt to tell her story but also afraid of the fall out that was sure to come as a result of the secrets kept for so long. This book had been a well-kept secret from the family, and she knew some of them would be very upset that a secret kept from them would now become public knowledge. She knew some would be embarrassed and some would be insulted or may be angry at the truth but as she held up the first pristine copy only deep pride filled her heart: Willamina… a Young Girls Journal by Alexandria Stone.

I turned the book over and examined the back cover. There was a picture of the beautiful willow tree where the story began and on the inside of the back cover my own face stared back at me. I read about myself as if confirming it was really me.

Alexandria (Alex) Stone attended the Mercer University of Macon, Georgia where she studied Journalism and received her Bachelor degree in Liberal Arts and Sciences. I had begged my Nana to put her own name as the author or to at least co-author so she would get credit for her own story, but she had insisted it be my book. Her story but told in my words

Chapter One

The Summer I Didn't Ask for

You cannot be serious! I had spent almost every free minute of my last two years of high school helping with my grandmother. Oh, do not get me wrong. I loved her as much as any kid loves their grandparent, but it was so unfair that I was the only one to help mom take care of her. My grandfather had died years earlier and I was the only grandchild on my mothers' side of the family, so it became my responsibility to care for her. She had lived with us most of those two years and my life was on hold because my mother had to work and apparently my life was meaningless and dull, and I had nothing else to do.

Yes I cried when she passed away last month just a few short days before my high school graduation and yes I felt a lot of guilt for the relief that rushed over me when I realized my job of taking care of her was over but I'm still a kid and I wanted my life back.

Now two weeks into my summer break my parents announce that I am about to go stay with my Nana over the summer. My dad's mom lived several hours away from us but was close to the college I hoped to attend. Her housekeeper, Annie, was going to need the summer off to help her daughter after the birth of her first baby. Great! Just how I wanted to spend my summer. Taking care of another old lady. Yes, I loved her too; but to be honest I really did not know her all that well. We had gone to visit her on holidays several times but my mom, Martha had always preferred to spend them with her mom and my dad had not wanted to argue with her about it. My Papa Sam had passed away ten years prior and Annie came over during the day to help but went home at night to her husband and children. One year after Papa Sam passed away, Annie's husband passed suddenly, and she moved into Nana's house. It seemed like the perfect solution. Two widows taking care of each other. Annie had a bedroom and bathroom with a door that led outside to where her car was parked. Nana did not want her to feel like she was always on the job.

I would have my own room and bathroom upstairs not far from Nana's room in case she needed me during the night. I would have access to her car if needed and she even had a pool in the back yard of her house. I mean not a bad set up if you think about it.

Nana had given birth to four children. The first three were girls and then my dad came along after she thought she was finished having babies. William Samuel Stone, named after both his parents, was the golden child according to my aunts who still spoil him to this day. I am his only child. My father was only 26 when I was born in 1974 and he would have loved more children, but my mom only wanted one.

My cousins all have fond memories of Nana. I had been

left out of most of the gatherings at Nana's house since I've been old enough to remember but they all had stories to tell about how she would play with them in the front yard or build a fort in her living room. She had even taught them to climb trees. Something she apparently did a lot of as a child. And she loved to paint and draw so she would have sessions with them teaching them to paint. I had missed out on these sessions and had almost no memory of her except for the gifts and cards she was faithful to send every year and of course the week we stayed at her house when our Papa Sam died.

I have been told I am the most like her. She had shortened her name from Willamina to Willie because she hated the name. I had shortened mine from Alexandria to Alex for the same reason. She has always been a bit of a rebel and did not try to fit in. That was me for sure. I had auburn hair like her but had mine chopped off in a short pixie cut and colored it black to my parent's horror. My way of rebelling. I refused to fit the mold that was expected of me.

Nana was well known for her paintings. She was very talented and had sold many paintings to many businesses to decorate their establishments and had been commissioned a few times to do family portraits. She has also painted portraits of people holding office. She had been commissioned to paint 4 mayors and 2 governors, so I guess she is kind of famous. I cannot paint like her, but I am very interested in the art of writing.

I had submitted a few poems and short stories to our local paper and was the editor of our high school paper.

Maybe this would not be so bad. She did not have dementia like my grandmother who had just passed away. I was told she is in excellent health except for an occasional bout of vertigo. That was one of the reasons she did not want to be left on her own. *I can do this, I* told myself. Not only does it take care of my first year of college without my having to get an actual job this summer, but I will be miles away from my parents. Maybe once she is asleep, I can venture out and see what that little town has in the way of entertainment for an almost college girl.

In exchange for my companionship she had offered to pay for my first year of college. My mom was thinking of the money they would be saving, and my dad wanted me to know his mother and love her like he did.

"She is the best. She is fun and loving and I know you will enjoy the visit and getting to know her" he insisted.

"Okay, I'll do it," I told my parents. They were both thrilled for my mature decision and assured me I would love every minute. I was just hoping I would not be miserable and could at least meet a few new friends from the nearby college. Maybe get to know the area before classes started so I would have an advantage. I mean how bad could it be?

I was packed and ready to leave by the weekend. My parents drove me to Payne, Georgia to my Nana's, not only to get me settled but to pay her a visit. I know my dad loves her very much and I think he misses seeing her, but his job and my mom have kept him away more than he wanted to admit. My mom was fond of her but seemed to feel like she was in competition with her because of all her accomplishments and talents. Nana however did not feel that way at all and welcomed my mom with open arms always.

We had decided to bring all the things they had purchased for my college dorm.

Nana had plenty of room to store it for me and it would save us the extra work in a couple of months if I did not have to rush home to get it before classes started. We had toured the campus last year, so my parents did not feel that I needed them to be there when I moved in. They both claimed they wanted to avoid the tears that they knew would come if they had to leave me all alone in my college dorm. I did not say so, but I was a little hurt they seemed so ready to rid themselves of me. I wondered if my room would be turned into a craft room or exercise room. I could almost imagine that I would have to sleep on the pull-out couch in our den the next time I went home.

Nana lived in the house she grew up in. When Nana's father had died her mom had moved to be near her sisters. Her father had made it clear that once they both passed the house would belong to Willie but her mom said she didn't want to live there a minute more and signed it over to my Nana years ago. My Papa Sam had completely renovated the house to be exactly what Nana wanted it to be and that is where they raised their family and where she still lives today. She says she will not leave there until she goes to her reward.

It is an okay house and they have made a lot of changes to improve it but there must be something I don't know to make her want to stay here when they could have lived anywhere. All four of her children, including my dad, have begged her to come live with them. All have offered a lovely room in their house or to help provide a small apartment near them if she wanted to be on her own. She will not even consider it.

"This house holds too much for me to leave it" she would tell them. "My soul lives in this house and it is filled with my memories".

I did not see it. I mean it is just an old house. I did not realize it yet but soon I would understand why she could not leave.

When we pulled up to the front of the house my Nana was sitting on her screened-in porch behind a large canvas. My dad said she was taking advantage of the morning light.

Apparently, this was nothing new for her and would be a normal activity while I was staying here. I could not see her behind the canvas but as we started unloading my things my dad shouted to her.

"Hey mom, get your face out of the paint" and laughed at himself as if this were an old joke between them.

She stood up and walked quickly over to greet us. I had not seen her in at least five years, and I guess after dealing with my grandmother I expected her to be frail, sickly and… I guess old. She was none of those. I mean I know she is technically a senior citizen. On her last birthday she had turned 66 years old, but she did not look old at all. At least not old like I think of old. Not weak and bent over like my grandmother was. Nana was slim and straight as a stick.

She was not considered tall. Only five foot five inches but she held her shoulders back and walked with the grace of a model. Her hair was pulled back in a twist and clipped but a little messy with strands of hair falling loose around her face and neck. It was mostly grey but there was still some auburn. Her face had character. A few lines at the corners of her eyes and at her mouth when she smiled but she did not look old. She still had a sparkle in her eyes I thought was reserved for much younger people. My grandmother's eyes had always seemed dull and even vacant at times, but not Nana's.

She was smiling a broad smile as we approached the long porch and hugged all of us tightly. She seemed to be thrilled to see us and I noticed a tear roll down her cheek when she hugged my dad. She had missed him, and I knew he had missed her as well. She covered her canvas with a sheet and plopped her dirty paint brush in the can provided for them, then ushered us in the house straight to the kitchen for lunch. She had prepared sandwiches with chips and a pickle on each plate, a tall glass of iced tea, and a platter of sugar cookies if we needed a little dessert.

She also had watermelon in a bowl because she remembered how much I loved watermelon. That little act of kindness made me feel so at ease. Maybe I did not remember a lot about her, but she remembered me, and I could tell from the conversation between my father and my Nana that they had talked about me many times before.

She had tried to know me and keep up with my life when I was much too busy to notice.

My parents left early the next day because they had to be back at work on Monday. I promised to call every week and to come home for Christmas and bring Nana with me if she wanted to come. We shed a few tears as we all said our goodbyes but after only a few hours with her I could tell staying with her was going to be easy. She had a wonderful sense of humor and was a good listener. I did not get the feeling she would be demanding or controlling. I think this is going to be the easiest job ever!

My room was beautiful. Decorated in the most popular colors for 1992. She had given me the guest room at the opposite end of the hall from her room. It had its own bathroom which I had never had before. She had a desk with an electric typewriter brought in and she had purchased all new bedding including a brand-new mattress. I had my own phone on my bedside table, and she promised she was going to try and purchase a computer soon. My only concern was she was doing too much. After all, I would only be there a few weeks, and I told her so.

She looked at my parents with a questioning look and they had changed the subject rather quickly. I was not sure what they all had planned but the picture of my room being converted into something new popped into my head again. I am not going to panic. After all, I will be in the dorm in a few weeks and Nana is close enough that I can always visit if I do not want to go back home during the holidays.

Our first night alone started off a little awkward but we both seemed to relax after a little conversation. She explained to me what she expected from me while I was there. Mostly she wanted me to keep the house clean until Annie returned. I will handle my own room and bathroom and of course you will handle yours, but I also would like you to dust and vacuum once a week and keep the kitchen clean for me. I have a handy man that will come around a couple of times a week to mow and keep the pool clean. He does light repairs when needed and takes the trash to the curb for pickup on the days that is required. If you have any issues with anything around the house, we only must let him know and he is quick to get that taken care of. His name is Mark Armstrong.

She continued to tell me all the little details of the house and the routine she had for each day. She seemed so well organized and physically able that I wondered why she really needed me. I mean yeah, the house keeper was away for a few weeks but she could have hired someone to come clean a couple of times before her return and I'm no cook so I knew I wasn't there to prepare meals. Maybe she just wanted the company.

But the more she spoke of her activities, meetings, appointments and friends I did not think that was the reason either. She was a very busy woman. She was active and happy but there was something bothering her. She seemed to be anxious around me as if she had something to say to me but was not sure how to say it. She questioned me a lot about my views on things.

"So, Alex, tell me what kind of things you are interested in. I know you love to write. Have you written anything recently?"

"Not really since graduation. I did a lot of writing in school, but I know once I get into my college classes I will do plenty of writing." I mused.

She asked about everything. No one had ever seemed so concerned about my opinion. She wanted to know what my friends were like and if I like a certain type of guy. Some of her questions were odd but I tried to answer them as honestly as I could. One thing about my Nana. She was not judgmental. She seemed to be very open to different views and was accepting that not everyone had the same opinion and that was just fine with her. She also seemed very spiritual. My family has always gone to church, but it almost seemed like a habit we did not want to break. Not a heartfelt desire but just something you did. Nana loved her church family and loved God in a way that was real and noticeable but not pushy if you know what I mean.

"I read my Bible every morning. Feel free to join me if you ever want to."

She said it sweetly and with no sense of insistence. It would never be forced on me.

I would see her pray several times a day, but she did not make a show of it. If I had not been paying close attention I may not have even noticed. She did have a prayer before breakfast each day and asked for guidance for the day, but it was not long and drawn out, just matter of fact and on with your day.

I had been there 3 days and was starting to get a routine going. I had not seen the handyman but had seen evidence of his having been there. This morning the trash was placed at the curb and I had heard a lawn mower just as I went in my bathroom to shower, but he had finished for the day and was gone by the time I came down for breakfast. Nana was sitting there waiting for me and she seemed nervous.

"Is everything okay?" I asked.

"Yes sweetheart, I'm fine. Let us have a prayer and eat our breakfast. If you don't mind, after we clean up from breakfast, I need to talk to you about something."

I could not help but feel anxious while we ate. Had I done something wrong? She did not seem angry with me or unhappy with my job, but something was bothering her. She had been to the doctor the other day for a check-up. Maybe something is wrong with her. I did not want to lose another grandparent, especially one who I was just getting to know and who was so wonderful.

Once we finished and cleaned up, she asked me to join her in the front room. It was kind of a formal living room. No television, just a long navy couch and two burgundy chairs [1]in front of a window that looked outside over the porch. She had another room for hanging out to watch television and relax. We had watched a movie in there just last night. The fact that she wanted to talk to me in the front room made me think this had to be serious and I was getting worried. She sat down and patted the couch beside her.

"Sit down dear, here beside me."

When I did, she took my hand in her hand and swallowed so hard I could hear it. Then she took a deep breath and looked into my eyes.

"Alex, I'm afraid I have not been completely honest with my family. There are some things I have kept from them their whole lives but that needs to change. I struggled for a while trying to decide how I could tell them all I have hidden from them but then I thought of you. I have known for several years that you wanted to be a writer. I have read your poems and short stories and after talking with you for several days now I know my instinct is right. You are the one to tell my story."

I stared at her for several seconds, not sure how to re-

1

spond.

"ME? Why would you think I should tell your story? I mean, why not tell your own story. After all, it's yours to tell. I do not understand what could be so bad that you cannot just tell us all what it is. What are you… a criminal or something?"

I knew I was babbling on and on and making a complete fool of myself, but I did not know what to say. She allowed me to express my feelings, doubts and fears for several minutes and then she smiled at me and told me I would soon understand. She explained to me that she had written in journals for years. Since she was a very young girl. Had put down all her secrets on paper and hidden them away. She also told me no one had ever seen one of them. Not even Papa Sam. That she could not tell anyone as long as he was alive because it would have hurt him so much but now was the time. She hoped to live many more years but,

"I'm no spring chicken," she laughed "and I want this told while I'm still around to deal with the fallout."

"What could you possibly need to tell us that would be that upsetting?" I ask her.

She smiled a sad kind of smile.

"It would be easier for you to read the journals than for me to just try and tell the story. In the hallway upstairs just past my room is a door. If you open that door there are stairs that lead to the attic and in the attic, you will see a large, very old trunk. There are a lot of old clothes and a few pictures in it. Remove them and there is a false bottom in the trunk. You may need to take a screwdriver to pry up the bottom of the trunk but underneath you will find my journals. Bring them to me. I want you to read them in order and I want to be around while you read them so I can see your reactions."

Holy cow what could be in those journals that she kept them hidden like she was a spy or something. I just sat there stunned for a while not sure what to say.

"Dear if you rather not do this I will understand."

"Oh no Nana I want to do this" I assured her "I'm just a little shocked about all the secrecy."

"You will see why soon sweetheart...and I just pray you are the understanding girl I think you are."

I climbed the stairs slowly to the upstairs hall. I could feel her eyes on my back, and it made me feel anxious. My heart was pounding. What kind of craziness is this? *It is just a bunch of old journals, I told myself. I mean what could possibly be so bad.* I started making my way down the hall, past her door and to the stairs that led to the attic. I knew she was watching me, so I did not want to seem in too much of a hurry to find out the dirt on Nana, but I was almost overwhelmed with curiosity. *Had the hall always been this long? It seemed to take hours to walk those few steps.* Once I reached the attic stairs and knew I was out of her line of sight, I could move a little faster. The attic was dark, and I had not thought about a flashlight, so I was feeling around for a light switch.

"There's a chain hanging from a light in the stairwell, just reach up and pull on it to turn on a light" she instructed.

"Once you find that you will see a switch on the wall to your right at the top of the stairs. That lights up the entire attic."

I did as she instructed. The attic was full of dusty boxes

stacked on each other. There was an old exercise bike, a couple of old dressers, a standing mirror and a Christmas tree covered with a sheet but still covered in decorations. I moved through trying not to stir up the dust too much but still managed to sneeze several times. I was creeped out twice by spider webs. I am not a big fan of spiders. I also got a glance of my reflection in an old mirror hanging on the wall and almost jumped through the roof. *Why is it that places like basements and attics always feel like someone is hiding and ready to grab you?* I worked my way toward the back end of the attic.

There was a small round window on the wall facing each end of the house and small vents above them to allow circulation. I think those round windows are called Rose windows. They were for decoration and gave the false idea that the house had a third story. I think one was just above Nana's room. It appeared someone had used it as a place to sleep at one time. Maybe for when they needed an extra space for guest.

There was a small bed and a nightstand under that window that Nana kept covered with a sheet. It was the only area in the attic that had a solid floor. There were wooden slates in the vents that allowed a tiny amount of light to peek through and that is where she had placed the trunk. Under the vent toward the front of the house. The ceiling was not as high as a normal room and I bumped my head trying to rush over to it.

"OUCH" I yelled.

"Are you alright dear?" she shouted.

"Yes Nana, I'm fine. Just bumped my head but I'm okay."

Way to go Alex, I said to myself. *Knock yourself out and your Nana will have to attempt to climb those stairs and rescue your pitiful butt.*

I sat in front of the trunk. It was obviously very old. It appeared it was dark brown or maybe black. It was hard to be sure in the dim lighting of the attic, but it was covered in metal on all the seams. There was a lock, but Nana had given me a key to open it. The small stream of sunlight that came in through the vent seemed to almost spotlight the lock and you could see the dust dancing in the beam of light.

On my first attempt to unlock it my hand was shaking, and I dropped the key. It came so close to falling through a slit in the floor that I almost screamed again. I took a deep breath and told myself to just calm down. The second attempt was successful, and I heard the click as the lock let go of itself. I eased it off the latch and laid it on the floor. When I raised the lid on the trunk, dust swirled and caused me to cough and sneeze for several seconds but once I could focus, I saw a treasure trove of old dresses. I think I remember playing dress up as a young child on one of my few visits. There were hats and gloves and a couple of old purses. A young girl's dream of fun.

She had allowed us to play with this trunk many times and not one of us would have guessed it had a secret floor. I lay the dresses and accessories on the floor beside me. There were a few old pictures of people I did not know, and a few of this house when Nana was a child. It looked so different but enough the same that you knew it was this house. Once all the content of the trunk had been removed, I stared into it trying to see what would give it away, what would confirm this was not the real bottom of the trunk. But you absolutely could not tell.

I was fascinated by the clever way people had hidden

their treasures that day. I felt around with my fingers to try and open it but could not. I had forgotten my screwdriver, so I used the key. At first, I had no luck with it but finally in one corner I managed to get the key under the bottom and lift it up. There they were all neatly stacked about four books deep. Nothing fancy or leather bond as I had imagined. At least not the first few. They were just writing tablets like those used by children in school. They were ragged from use. It was easy to see they had been folded and stuffed away in hiding spots after young Willamina poured her heart into them. There was no writing on the outside of them with one noticeable exception. In small letters in the top corner of one of them was the name Isaiah.

Who was Isaiah? I had never heard of him. I wanted to start reading them that very minute, but I had promised not to read them without her. I placed them into the box I found nearby and placed all the things that had stayed in the trunk back in it. I did bring the pictures with me to ask Nana who they were. The box I used for the journals had been filled with a tea set and so I placed it in the trunk on top of the dresses before closing it. I locked it back and secured the key in my jean pocket.

There were several journals which made the box heavy. I had to take one step at a time while leaving the attic dragging the box along the narrow wood joist that lay across the floor. Once I got to the stairs leading out of the attic It was step, slide, and drop to the next step the whole way. Once I made it to the bottom of the second set of stairs, I pushed the box across the wood floor over to where Nana sat waiting. We looked at each other a little unsure of how to proceed.

"I'm really tired Alex, I think I need to lay down for a little while before we tackle this."

She quietly walked to the staircase, turned and looked at the box and at me then proceeded to go upstairs to her room. I sat there for several minutes just staring at the upstairs hall. I think I was hoping she would pop out and say, *Just kidding,* and come back down. I was not sure what to do. I picked up the journal on the top and started to open the cover, but my promise kept resounding in my head. I had *promised: cross my heart and hope to die,* that I would not read one word until she was beside me and ready to start. I had broken promises before. Flat out lied to my parents more than once. But I simply could not break this promise to Nana. It felt too important and she had all but told me I was the chosen one. The only person she had ever trusted with her story. I was not about to break that trust. I lay back on the sofa and closed my eyes, still clutching the journal to my chest.

Chapter Two

The Boy Who Saw Me Naked

"Alex. Are you asleep?"

In my sleepy state I heard a male voice calling my name. I must be dreaming, was my first thought.

"Alex!?"

My eyes popped open at the very husky sound of my name. This was not Nana calling me. Before me stood a man. He was young but possibly older than me. He had light brown hair that had a tight curl. His eyes were a beautiful gray and I could tell he was smiling by his eyes even before I noticed his sexy smile. As I took notice of his muscular arms, and his dark complexion I realized he wasn't wearing a shirt and I jumped up from my laying position so quickly It made my head swim and I think I screamed. At least I heard a scream and it did not sound like a man, so it had to be me.

"It's okay it's just me, Mark."

In front of me was a stranger in his swimsuit now touching my shoulder as if we were friends. I pushed his hand away and stood.

"Who are you?" I yelled at him showing more aggression than I had intended.

"I told you, I'm Mark." He smiled at me and put his hand out to shake mine.

"Am I supposed to know you? I have no idea who you are!" He appeared a little hurt but continued to hold out his hand. I did not touch it. Maybe if I did, he was going to grab me and pull me down. Was he there to rob us? Maybe to assault us. "NANA!" Had he hurt Nana?

I called her name about the time she walked into the room. Before I could respond he turned and saw her.

"Nana. How's my sweet girl?"

He walked over toward her and they embraced in a hug.

"You didn't tell Alex about me, did you?"

She looked over at me questioning my reaction.

"I most certainly did. I told her I had a handyman who came around several days a week to do chores."

Her grin was sheepish, and I knew then there was more to this hired hand than Nana had implied. For example, she had not mentioned how gorgeous he was or that he already knew me. She looked at me with big innocent eyes as if the detail had slipped her mind.

"Alex, this is Mark Armstrong. He is Annie's son and has been like a grandchild to me since he was a small boy."

He extended his hand for the third time and this time I shook it.

"Nice to meet you," I uttered politely.

"Actually, we have met before," he said, smiling at me in an almost flirty way. "I've seen you naked."

Nana laughed at the statement and told him to stop teasing me.

"What is he talking about?" I demanded and I stood there red faced and angry to be the butt of some joke I was not in on.

"When we were little kids," he explained. "You came to visit, and we played in a kiddie pool in the back yard. We were naked." He repeated it in a sing-song voice. "It was before Nana had the pool put in and we were both under 5 years old.... but I saw you naked all the same," he repeated once again while raising his eyebrows up and down for effect.

"Mark, stop teasing my granddaughter this minute," Nana scolded while laughing.

"Yes ma'am."

He turned to Nana again and told her he was done with classes for a short while and would be in the pool house if she needed him.

"Join us for lunch dear; I was just about to make chicken salad plates for Alex and myself. I know you love my chicken salad," she grinned.

"I would love to," he agreed, "let me go change first. I've been vacuuming the pool."

He turned to me to nod his exit when he caught sight of the journal I clutched in my hands. I had been holding it so tightly the whole time that my knuckles were white. Nana also noticed it and looked at me with suspicion.

"I didn't read a word, Nana. I promise I did not. I was just holding it when I fell asleep on the couch. Then, when this man frightened me," I spat out the words toward him, "I guess I was just clinging to it for...well I'm not sure for what, I was just clinging to it."

I had to admit; to myself at least, that my tone was a little sarcastic, maybe even hateful. Was I jealous of this guy for having such a close relationship with my Nana? I had really just come into her life and was getting to know her and here comes Mr. Pool Boy in his swimsuit looking all sexy and full of whimsical memories from his childhood spent around her house.

Once he had left the room, I looked at her for answers. I dropped the journal into the box with the others and we both went into the kitchen.

"Nana, what is the story with this Mark guy? Does he live here in the summer with his mom or something?"

She started preparing the lunch plates.

"Would you please get the bowl of chicken salad from the refrigerator dear?"

I retrieved the bowl, sat it down and began scooping it onto the plates where she had placed one large lettuce leaf and one slice of tomato. Each plate would also have a croissant and a pickle. Nana was big on pickles I had noticed.

"Nana, please before he comes back. What's the story with him?"

"Alex, it is not that much of a story. When Annie first started working for me, she had her daughter Rhonda. She is the one having the baby," she added. "Not long after that she found out she was expecting another child and was so worried I would let her go. I assured her she was secure in her job and because things were hard for them, I told her not to worry about childcare. She brought the children with her every single day. She would clean and cook while I played with the little ones. They were more like family than hired help to us.

Many nights her husband would come over to pick them up after working all day and the whole family would join us for dinner. Rhonda had no real dreams of college and was content to marry her high school sweetheart and work at his family's restaurant, but Mark had ambition. He not only wanted college, but he wanted to be a doctor. I told him if he would work for me until he was out of medical school and maybe give some free medical advice on the side," she laughed, "I would pay for whatever school his grants and scholarships did not cover."

I was a little shocked by her generous offer. I mean medical school was not cheap.

"Oh, don't worry dear. He is a very smart young man and it has not cost me what you might think. His first four years he had a full academic scholarship."

I could see she was so very proud of him and yes, the jealousy bug nipped at me again. She was making me stay here and care for her in order to pay my first year. Maybe my grades had not earned a scholarship, but I was straight B's while putting forth little effort. Okay not my best argument but I knew I could do better…would do better once I started my classes. I could not believe how important it was to me that she be proud of me. But it was very important.

"When his mother moved in with me and sold their little house, he asked me if he could rent a room from me. I told him he was welcome to turn the pool house into a little apartment if he kept it clean and well cared for. He agreed and has taken care of my property since then."

She finished the lunch plates and glasses of raspberry tea just as he walked in.

"Both of you sit. Mark, would you do the honors?"

He took Nana's hand, and both took one of mine, before he bowed his head and thanked God for our food. I was not expecting that at all. We began to eat, and he talked to Nana almost nonstop for the entire meal. Filling her in on the classes he had just finished and those coming up after a short break. He told her what he planned for the property over the summer.

"I'm going to paint all the outbuildings and the shrubs need pruning."

She clung to every word smiling at him and obviously loved him as if he were one of her own. I added a little to the conversation telling of my plans for college, but honestly it just did not seem to stack up to what he had to tell, and I got a little sheepish and quiet. Not me at all. When I did speak, he would watch me intently and Nana would smile at me as if all I had to say was monumental. I felt as if my mouth was moving but all that was coming out was *blah blah blah blah.* For some odd reason I was very intimidated around Mark. I felt so nervous and unsure around him….and I did not like it at all.

Once we finished our lunch, Nana walked out with Mark to look at the plants he had picked up from the nursery in town. They discussed where each group of flowers should go and what kind of mulch she wanted him to use. I stayed inside and cleaned up the kitchen. I also did some of the prep work for dinner later. I was learning a few things about cooking from Nana and surprisingly enjoying it. My mother would be so shocked. She would also be happy to know I had not colored my hair since I arrived. Because it was a temporary color, I would be back to my red hair by the time she saw me again. My black spikes had been a form of rebellion, but I honestly never liked it.

It made my mother furious which was the reaction I had wanted. Maybe that is why she was so ready to send me away. I grinned an almost devilish grin just as Nana walked in.

"I would love to know what put that look on your face" she mused. "What are you up to?"

"Nothing Nana, I was thinking how surprised mom would be when she found out I was learning to cook. And that my hair was growing out."

"I gather she will be very happy at both of those things?"

"OH, yes ma'am. She will be very happy."

That afternoon we worked together preparing our dinner. When she placed a third sirloin steak in the skillet, I assumed Mark would be joining us for dinner.

I hope he is not going to be here for every meal. Without meaning to, I let out a little moan.

"Are you alright dear?"

"I'm fine Nana…I had thought we would have dinner alone tonight…just us two."

I felt my face burn. How whiny was I? I sounded like I was 4 years old and did not want to share my toy. I looked over at her and she was struggling not to laugh which made me feel even more ridiculous.

"I'm sorry Nana. I guess you think I'm being petty and immature."

"No dear, not at all. It is flattering. Mark will not always be here for each meal. Today is his first day out of classes and his mom is out of town so I just wanted to give him a little extra attention. He is a very sweet young man dear. Just give him a chance and the two of you could be great friends."

Once we finished our meal Mark insisted, we took our dessert into the living room while he cleaned up. He had provided the dessert. Peanut butter ice cream with a drizzle of hot fudge on top. It was delicious. Once he was finished, he came in to tell us goodnight and thanked Nana again for the invitation. She told him he was welcome to stay a while if he wanted but I think he had felt my jealous vibe because he looked at me and then smiled at Nana.

"Maybe another time. I have a lot of work in the garden tomorrow and I want to get an early start. Good night ladies."

We put our ice cream bowls in the sink deciding they could wait until the breakfast dishes to be put in the dish washer. We walked to the den where the television was. As we walked through the front room, I resisted mentioning the elephant in the room. I did not bring up the subject of the box again. I decided it was best to wait until she gave me the go ahead. It was like Christmas time when there is a big beautiful package under the tree with your name on it. Like a gift you did not ask for and had no idea what it was, and you would walk through the room and just stand there looking at it. You could hardly wait to open it.

I had written in journals myself at times. I usually used them to vent if I were angry or upset. Occasionally I would write about something good that happened or someone I was crushing on at school, but never consistent with it. I also remember friends when I was in elementary school who would have those little diaries with the tiny key. They would guard them as if they contained the secrets to the universe but mostly, they contained day to day hum drum notions of what time they woke up, what they had for each meal, who they talked to on the phone or at school and what time they went to bed.

Most of them gave up on it after a few weeks of repetition and spent about a week feeling as if they were failures for not having more excitement in their lives. Surely Nana's journals were not hum drum daily dictations. I mean for one thing it was a big box with several journals, and secondly why keep them hidden and surrounded with secrecy if they were just normal boring stuff. We watched a few minutes of a game show. I felt like she was not really watching the show, but maybe working up her nerve.

"Alex dear, why don't we move back to the front room? I think we should start on those journals."

I jumped up before I could help myself, did a fist pump and let out a loud YES! Nana looked at me as if shocked but then burst into laughter.

"Yes indeed," she replied

We turned the television off and turned out all the lights except those in the front room. Nana got into her favorite chair and covered her legs with an afghan. I worked myself into the corner of the big couch that was close to her chair and pulled the box in front of us. Then I just looked at her and waited.

"Let me see which one is the first one," she said as she looked in the box. "Okay, here it is. I was probably fourteen when I started keeping a journal. This first one is mostly telling my family dynamics. Not really that interesting but it may help you learn about your heritage. Plus, it will give insight into how my parents could do what they did."

Okay, that sounded interesting. I was going to try to take a lot of mental notes and hope she would have no problem with me re-reading them later to remind myself of important facts. I held the journal in my hands and examined the outside cover. No clues there. Just a plan dark blue tablet much the same as those I had to use in school for each subject. She had not written anything on the outside of this one.

"I didn't write on the outside because I didn't want anything to draw attention to them if I accidentally left one of them laying on my bed," she explained without being asked.

I opened the tablet and examined the first page. She had written a description of herself and where she was in her life. Typical stuff for a young girls' journal.

DECEMBER 31, 1940

I was given several sketch pads and a few canvases for Christmas this year.

Somehow a regular tablet of paper was included with my supplies and I decided it was time to start keeping a journal. If I become a famous artist someday, people will want to know about my humble beginnings.

My name is Willamina Beulah Pettigrew. I am 14 years old and my birthday is February 3, 1926. I really hate my name and all my friends, and my father calls me Willie. My mother Francine and sisters Carolina and Georgia refuse to call me anything except Willamina. My mother said Willie is not lady-like and my sisters always agree with mother.

My father is William and I was supposed to be William Jr. but when I was a girl...well, Willamina. My mother thought it was a good compromise. My older sisters are twins. They are one year and one months older than me. They are my mothers' pride and joy. They cling on her every word and are very interested in fashion and social graces. Now that they are about to be 16 years old next month my mother is working on their debutante party. I am grateful to them because our mother is so occupied with their upcoming party that she hardly notices me.

I am okay with that because I have no desire for a debutante party. My idea of fun is painting and drawing. Because I am his substitute for a son… I get to wear overalls and a boy's shirt while helping the farm hands do chores. I also love to ride horses, so I often explore the large fields and woods surrounding the property.

I read the first journal almost halfway through as the little girl Willamina told all about her family tree, her likes and dislikes and her day to day routine on the ranch her parents owned. She talked of which teachers she liked and which ones she did not care for. She had an opinion about everything and at least in her journal had no problem saying what she felt. There were several pages dedicated to the planning of the debutante for her sisters. She was not at all happy about the dress she would be forced to wear for the occasion.

She explained how their father had insisted they learn the value of a dollar, so they were made to earn money for things they wanted. She did not mind doing that…but she was not happy that she had to use some of her own money to help pay for the dress she did not want in the first place. It just was not fair. Carolina and Georgia loved to sing and sew. Again, things their mother loved and was thrilled at her girls' interest. They would sew to make money but also would sing at weddings, funerals, and birthday parties for the more well to do families in the area.

Apparently, as far as Willamina was concerned their sewing was wonderful but their singing was not. Basically, she implied that their mother would ask people point blank if they would consider hiring her girls for their event and because of her family's status in town they were often unwilling to refuse. She also implied that people would try to avoid her mother for months if they had a wedding or some other special event coming up in order to not have them perform.

The journal was interesting but so far, I saw nothing that would justify the secrecy. I cannot imagine Papa Sam being upset by any of this. He probably knew most of this just because he had been in the family for a long time and just normal conversation would have provided him with this information about his in-laws. Maybe this was just going to be hum drum daily stuff like the little girl's diary's I remembered from my school friends. I yawned and Nana yawned in echo of mine.

"I'm sorry dear. Perhaps I should have just told you these things instead of making you read them. I was afraid you would think I was hiding something if I told you the first couple of journals were not that interesting. I promise they are not all like this."

She gave me the short version of the remainder of the first journal, and the second one. We ended with her turning 15 and decided it was enough for one night. We were both exhausted and ready for bed. I was still glad I had come to stay with her this summer. I loved spending time with her and getting to know her. But if this was our project for the summer...If I was supposed to turn this into a novel. Well we are in big trouble.

"Good night Nana."

"Good night Alex."

We had made our way up the stairs and after a quick hug I went to the right and she went to the left.

I readied myself for bed and was about to crawl under the covers when I heard a splashing noise outside. I looked out the window which had a clear view of the back yard and pool area. Mark was swimming in the dimly lit pool. There was an outside light on the pool house but other than that only the moon gave proof of his late-night exercise. It was not for relaxation; that was for sure. He raced from one end to the other swimming as if in a race.

Once he had completed several laps, he pulled himself up on the side and sat there for several minutes before standing up and going for his towel in the patio chair. I knew I had acted like a four-year-old child at dinner. He was a nice enough guy I supposed, but I was not sure how I would like his being around all summer. This was going to be my special time to get to know Nana and apparently, he was going to be in the way and besides; how could I ever hope to sneak out and explore the college town if he was there in the pool house. I would have to pass by his apartment to get to the car and he would probably hear me leave and tell Nana.

As I stood there silently complaining about him, I realized he was looking up at my window. I jumped back from the window and wondered if he had seen me watching him. My room was dark, and the sheer curtains were mostly closed so maybe he had not seen me. But if he did not see me, then why was he staring up at my room. *He was probably thinking about what a silly little child you are,* I complained to myself.

I attempted to peek out of the window again, trying not to stand too close to it. He was gone. I noticed the light come on in the pool house window and then after only a few minutes it went off and only the pale moon gave light to the world outside my window. I crawled under my cover and reprimanded myself for being jealous and petty as I began to drift into sleep.

In my dream-like state I also told myself that Mark Armstrong was not too hard on the eyes. Who knows, maybe he would give me a ride into town and show me the sites himself.

Chapter Three

The Girl Beneath the Willow

My alarm clock played its selected station to let me know it was 7 o'clock. Time to get up and shower. As much as I had looked forward to sleeping late this summer, I had promised Nana I would try to be down each morning in time for breakfast at 8 o'clock.

I walked downstairs and into the kitchen expecting to see her sitting at the kitchen table sipping her coffee and enjoying her bowl of cereal or her soft-boiled egg and grapefruit. She seemed to alternate between the two choices but did not eat anything heavy for breakfast. Just as I was about to sing out my *Good morning, Nana,* I realized she was not there. I looked in the sitting room, the den, and even went back upstairs to her bedroom but noticed she had gotten out of bed without straightening the covers.

Her robe and slippers were not on the chair in the corner where she usually left them in case she needed to get up in the middle of the night. I knocked on her bathroom door and it opened to a dark unoccupied room. Where was she? I ran to my room and looked out the window to the back yard. I noticed Mark working in the flower beds that surrounded the property but did not see her helping him. I made my way back down the stairs and noticed the front door was not shut all the way. I peeked out onto the porch and there she was. I remembered this was where we saw her the day we arrived. In that same chair at the end of the porch hidden behind a canvas.

"Nana? How long have you been out here?" I noticed she had her robe and slippers on, but also wore a painter's smock to protect her robe from paint smudges. I walked closer to see what she was painting. It was a beautiful painting of a large tree near a riverbank. A young girl sat under the tree and it seemed she was watching for someone. She looked sad. She reminded me of Nana as a young girl. Her auburn hair was long and was moving in the wind.

"That is such a beautiful painting Nana. Is that a Willow tree in the picture? And is that girl you?"

"Yes, to both," she replied. "That is me and my willow tree. A special place from my youth. I was inspired to work on my painting this morning, so I have been up since about 5:00. I love the light on my front porch when the morning sun rises."

She looked at the painting with the strangest expression in her eyes. A little sad or maybe just remembering her youth or something. You could tell the painting made her emotional. She took a deep cleansing breath and dropped her brush into the cleaning bucket to remove the paint from it. Once it was clean, she replaced it in the container with her other brushes, replaced the sheet over her painting and stood.

"I'm ready for coffee and" … she paused for effect….

"cinnamon rolls."

She gave me a big grin and marched into the house.

As we were cleaning up from breakfast, she explained that she had several errands to run and I was welcome to join her but it was not necessary if I would like to stay home and enjoy the pool. I protested just enough to sound like the helpful granddaughter, but the idea of sunbathing was too tempting to pass up.

Nana went upstairs to shower and dress for her trip into town and I put on my swimsuit and covered myself head to toe in sunscreen. As much as I would love to tan, I was a red head and had to be realistic. I grabbed a large towel, my sunglasses, a tumbler of ice-cold water and a book to read.

"Goodbye Nana!" I yelled as I rushed down the stairs. "Enjoy your trip into town."

"Thank you dear. And when I return perhaps, we can start on that third journal."

At that announcement I almost missed a stair and lost my footing. I grabbed the railing to steady myself. I had wondered when we would get back to them. The first two had been less than exciting. Do not get me wrong; It was wonderful to learn about my Nana as a young girl and to know more about her parents and siblings. I knew so little about this side of my family. But I had to face the fact that if the rest of them were like the first ones there was no way on earth I could write a book from them. She had implied the third one would get more interesting. I guess I will find out this afternoon.

I found a float in a little storage shed near the pool. It also had folding chairs and a few pool toys probably used when Annie's kids were young or when my cousins came to visit. I walked down the steps into the water and climbed on the float. I decided I would lay on my stomach to start out and once I had given that a good thirty minutes or so I would grab my book and lay on my back to even my tan.

This is heaven, I thought to myself.

I had a small radio playing music as I drifted around in the pool. I attempted to read my book, but the glare made it hard, so I tossed it back in the chair near the pool. The sun was warm, and I was enjoying my favorite song when I heard noise from the garage. Mark was apparently going to mow the yard. *Did he have to do that now?* He started up the very noisy mower and headed to the front yard.

"Thank goodness!" I mumble under my breath. The front yard was huge so he should be out of sight and sound for a long while. After a long lovely session on my stomach I paddled over to the stairs to get a good drink of cold water and to re-apply my sunscreen. I mounted the float again this time on my back. My plan was to lay here another thirty minutes, take a quick dip to cool off, and go shower so I would be ready to get started when Nana returned. I might even start things for dinner. She had said she would be having lunch in town so I knew she would be gone at least until late afternoon or early evening. I was drifting around the pool and contemplating the meal I wanted to prepare so I never noticed the sound of the mower suddenly ending and the garage door closing. The water was calm and cool as my hands hung off the edges of the float and I was so relaxed I thought I might easily drift off to sleep…. when *SPLASH!* A wave of water knocked me off my float and I was plunged into the water. I fought my way back to the surface, coughing and sputtering water from my nose and mouth. My hair was plastered over my face and my sunglasses had dropped to the bottom of the deep end of the pool.

"Are you out of your mind!" I screamed "You jerk!"

I was so angry and so overreacting. Back home if some guy had done that I would have laughed and splashed him. But for some reason it had just rubbed me the wrong way for Mark to do it. I found myself feeling uncomfortable that he had seen me in such a disheveled state. My hair wasn't at its best right now anyway with the black color not completely faded out and the spiked cut I had gotten to irritate my mom was not my most flattering look when it was dry...but wet...pitiful. I had not showered this morning and yesterday's mascara was now under my eyes. I dove to the bottom to retrieve my sunglasses and when I came back to the surface he was gone. I noticed the light come on in the front room of the pool house and then he closed the drapes. *I do not care if he is mad or not,* I mumbled, but I really did care.

I made my way to my room feeling like the biggest idiot on the planet. The steaming hot shower helped to melt the anger away. Not the anger I had expressed to Mark but the anger I felt toward myself for reacting the way I had. Like a spoiled child who could not take any teasing. I was not that person. I was the fun girl who could take a joke as well as dish them out. I was going to have to apologize to him for the way I acted. I just wished I knew why it had bothered me so much. Why did this guy get under my skin so quickly?

Once I had cleaned up, I made my way downstairs to the kitchen. I was startled again when I walked through the door and found Mark leaned up against the counter eating a sandwich of monumental size. Did he have to do everything over the top. This sandwich had several layers of meat, bread, and condiments. I would have never been able to get my mouth around it, but he was having no problem. I realized I was looking at him with disdain… again. He took the last bite and drank the remainder of water from his glass. He placed the glass in the dishwasher and tossed his napkin in the trash can under the sink. He started to walk away without a word but then stopped before opening the door that leads outside and turned to face me while still holding the doorknob.

"I'm sorry I caused you to fall off your float," he said. "I didn't think it would make you mad. I was just horsing around but I will know better than to do that again."

I just stood there looking at him. I did not say a word. What is wrong with me? I should have said, *No problem, I over reacted. It was funny. And, by the way, that was some awesome sandwich you made.* But no; I just stood there and stared at him like he was speaking a foreign language and I had not understood what he was saying. Finally, after a minute of silence he rolled his eyes and walked out of the door. *What is freaking wrong with me*, I yelled in my head. What is it about Mark that turns me into a crazy person? Do I really resent him that much for being here? That makes no sense at all. As I continued to battle the voices of reason in my head I glanced up and found Nana standing in the doorway watching me.

"Are you alright dear? You seem upset about something."

"It's nothing Nana," I lied. "Just trying to decide what I needed to do to get tonight's dinner prepped."

I could tell from the look on her face she was not buying a word of it, but she did not pursue it any further. One thing about Willie Stone, she could read people and she knew when it was best to let a subject drop. At least for now.

"I had a large lunch so I thought perhaps we would just have salads tonight and maybe some fruit. How does that sound dear?"

"That sounds perfect Nana. I think I will make myself a sandwich for now and once I finish eating that I will cut up the vegetables for the salad and store them in the refrigerator until tonight."

"That would be nice, and I will make my raspberry vinaigrette and slice some watermelon so that when we are ready to eat later it will only require putting everything on a plate. So, did you enjoy the pool?"

I started to just say yes and leave it at that, but what if Mark tells her about what happened. Then she will think I do not trust her enough to tell her the truth. Or she might think I am one to hide things and cannot be trusted myself. Or maybe she will just conclude that her youngest grandchild is a cuckoo bird.

"Nana, I'm afraid I made a fool of myself in the pool"

She looked confused by my announcement but did not comment. I proceeded to relay the entire episode of events.

"Nana, I acted so childish. I can't explain it but he just brings out the worst in me."

She looked down toward her feet and I think she was trying to hide a grin.

"You did not overreact dear. He should not have startled you like that. I can talk to him about it if you want me to."

"OH, NO, MA"AM!" I all but screamed at her. "I really do not think that is a good idea. He apologized and it's not that big of a deal"

If she were to complain to him about his actions, I would never be able to face him again.

"Okay then if you're sure. I will let you handle it. But sometimes we react to things in an unexpected way because we want to make a good impression."

I knew what she was getting at and that was far from the truth. I decided if I protested too much, she would only feel more right about her assumption, so I changed the subject. We chatted about her morning and her friends. She told me about the restaurant she had eaten at for lunch and insisted we needed to eat there soon.

"You would love it!" she promised.

We sat on the front porch for a little while and I kept glancing over toward her covered painting. She asked me if I would like to see more of her paintings.

"Absolutely I would love to see them." I said.

She had me follow her into the room down the hall from the den. I had not seen the entire house even though I had been with her for several days now. The room was probably an office or library when my Papa Sam had been alive, but now it was like a small gallery where she stored her finished paintings. Some of them were of flowers in vases, or ocean scenes. A few were of people who had commissioned her to paint a portrait of their family or child, but she still had just a little more touch ups to do before delivering them to the families who had posed for them.

But most of them were of the same location. Just like the one on her front porch. Different versions of the tall willow tree near a stream. The one on the porch had her in it as a young woman but most of them had no one. The only real difference was that the seasons changed, and some would include an animal or a different skyline. In some the sky was dark and cloudy as if a storm were coming and in another the sky was so blue you could almost imagine standing under it looking up. She was certainly obsessed with that place.

"They are all so beautiful Nana. You are so talented. Why do you hide them all in this room? Why not display them throughout the house so others can enjoy them?"

"Thank you, Alex. You are so kind to say that. Well some are for others who have paid me to paint for them but either I have not released the finished painting yet or some have simply not come by to pick their painting up. For example, the large one of the ocean scenes is for a woman who is re-modeling her home and needed me to hold on to it until all the other projects are complete before she has it picked up. Oh, and the one with the three little blonde headed girls is a surprise birthday gift so it must stay here until the day of the party.

"What about all the others Nana? Why are so many of them of the same place? The one you are working on now is of this same willow tree, isn't it?"

"You are correct," she admitted. "Alex, this place and this tree represent a very important part of my life. I have had others ask me this same question, but I would always just tell them I did not know why I did the same painting over and over. I would tell your Papa Sam it was just my favorite part of our property."

"You mean the tree is on your property? Where is it? I haven't seen it."

"It is beyond the fence that we placed to mark off our yard. We built the fence just past the pool house and garage, but we have several acres past the fence that are grown up fields now. I sometimes rent them out for the local farmers who want to grow and cut them for the hay, but it would be too much to care for if we wanted the yard to extend to the end of our property. I don't think Mark would ever finish mowing," she explained.

I studied the portraits for several minutes and walked over to the window hoping to see it from there.

"You can't see it from here. But soon you will understand why it is so dear to me."

I turned and looked at her. She had that thoughtful, half sad look on her face again and now she was looking at the paintings as if seeing herself in them. She reached over and touched the tree in the one closest to her and smiled.

"The journal," I asked.

She nodded.

"Let's go make our salads Alex, and then you can hear more about that tree.

Chapter Four

Isaiah

We finished our dinner in record time with little talking. Then we cleaned the kitchen also in record setting time. I had noticed that Mark did not join us for dinner tonight and could not help but wonder if it was because of my behavior or if he would be coming over while I was in the middle of reading a journal. I felt as if Nana did not want him or anyone else around when we were looking at them. As if she could read my mind, she told me Mark was helping a friend who was adding an addition to his house and would probably stay there tonight rather than drive back late.

We took our usual places in the front room. Nana got settled in her armchair with her afghan over her legs and I made my seat in the corner of the couch close to her by placing pillows around me. Once we were both comfortable, I waited for the go ahead from her. She did as the first night and took a deep cleansing breath before handing me the journal. The only thing that distinguished it from the first two was the word *Isaiah* she had written in the corner of the cover.

"I wrote that name on the cover many years after I wrote in the journal. I wanted to be able to find that one without having to look through all the rest," she gave a little smile.

I looked at her to be sure she seemed okay for me to begin and she nodded the go ahead. I ran my hand over the cover and hesitated for just a minute. Took a deep breath and opened it to the first page.

May 26, 1941

It has been a hot Monday working in the house with my mother and sisters. I would rather be helping with the chores around the farm, but we are expecting company this Friday and mother wants the house cleaned from top to bottom before they arrive. We are washing all the bedding and hanging it out to dry on the line out back. Every window is open, and we have fans in every room, but the heat is unbearable.

I do not understand why we must clean the upstairs. The company is a preacher who is holding a gospel meeting in our church and every night a different member is expected to feed him supper and give him lodging for the night. Our guest room is downstairs, and he would have no reason to even come up the stairs, but you would think he was going to put on a white glove and check every inch of the house. I hope I can go to the stream later and get cooled off.

With going to the meeting every night, I have had no time to work on my drawings and my father had given me permission to miss tonight because four people had paid me 25 cents each for a picture to hang in their living room. That was a dollar just for doing the one thing I loved more than anything. They had left it up to me what scene to draw. Except for Mrs. Barkly. She wanted flowers. A field of flowers she had said. I do not know why I can draw like I do but it comes so easy for me. Our house help Millie said it is a gift from God and I should always use it for good. I just use it for fun and for making money. I could draw from memory and didn't need to be at the place I was trying to replicate but I told my father I needed to be there in order to draw because he would let me take the horse out late in the day to work on my art as long as it was to be sold. The for-fun work I could do from home.

I also loved to paint but most of the time I did not have paints unless someone paid me to paint something and they would provide it for me. I could not afford it on my own and father, who had money, would not provide it. He insisted we (my sisters and I) learn the value of a dollar and so the only time he provided me with art supplies was for Christmas.

My mother was not at all happy that father had given me permission to miss the service but she knew he had the final say on the matter and he was one to always do the job you agreed to and on time. Honestly, I had finished three of the four and had a good start on the last one, but the stream was calling my name and I really felt that God would understand.

I normally took my horse but it had been such a miserable hot day and I knew I would have to brush him once I returned because he would be so hot, so I decided to just walk the half mile to the stream. I put on the overalls I usually only wore for farm chores and put my hair in a cap. I did this for two reasons. It was cooler if my long hair was up off my neck. The overalls would be better if I happen to end up in the water because I would not have a muddy dress to explain to mother.

When I got to my favorite spot the first thing I did was jump in and cool off. The water felt so wonderful and I could have stayed there forever but I knew I would have to show father the work I had finished once they returned home so I had to get busy. I had hung my overalls and shirt on a branch and jumped in the water in my bra and panties. This was our prop-

erty, and no one was ever this far down the stream. I dressed and put my wet hair up in the cap. I had tied my art supplies in an old flour sack I used to keep them in when I rode my horse.

I used the rope on it to tie it around my waist and proceeded to climb one of the tall trees. I loved to sit in its branches while I was drawing. I had placed a plank up there almost a year ago to sit on. It was placed between two large branches and made for a nice seat. I could see forever from up in the high branches and I could also feel the cool breeze. I had no doubt that my mother would have a heart attack if she knew I climbed any tree let alone a tall one over a stream. I just had to be sure I never fell out and if I did...well it had better kill me or she would once she found out.

I had been in my tree for a while and without meaning to, I drifted off to sleep. I was startled awake by someone singing. When I opened my eyes, I discovered it had grown dark. I knew I was going to be in such trouble and started to climb down when I heard the singing again. From my perch I could tell there was a man in the stream. The moon was partially hidden behind clouds and I could not tell much about him at first. He seemed to be bathing and was singing to the top of his lungs. I guess he did not figure anyone was around. I mean you usually did not find girls hiding in trees at night. His voice was like silk. I had never heard anyone sing so beautifully. The good Lord knows my sisters did not and I had never heard anyone who sounded so beautiful.

He was singing hymns like the ones I had heard in church. Maybe it was the traveling preacher. But I thought the preacher was an older man. Mother had said he was around fathers age and had a wife and children who did not always travel with him. This was definitely not the preacher. I noticed he had a small campfire a few feet away near the old willow tree that sat beside the stream. I loved that tree and had drawn it a few times. Its branches were like lace hanging down from a lady's dress. They flowed and moved when the breeze would blow, and I had sat under it many times while reading or drawing. I had even hidden under its skirt of leaves a few times when someone would be out looking for me.

The man started to climb out of the stream and as he took the towel from a branch, I realized he had no clothes on. I gasp and closed my eyes for just a second. I noticed he was being still and listening to see if he heard something. If I had not been in the tree, I think he would have heard my heart beating in my chest. What was I going to do? Here I am stuck in a tree with a naked stranger just below me. After he dressed, he went over to his fire and unrolled a blanket. He rolled up a shirt and made a small pillow with it then settled down for the night.

Once I thought he was asleep I began to slowly make my way down the tree. I tried not to make any noises, but I was shaking so much it sounded like a storm wind blowing and rustling the leaves. When my feet finally hit the ground, I ran like a rabbit down the familiar path and back home. Lucky for me I know this area like the back of my hand and could find my way with only the little bit of moon light. And lucky for me my parents had been delayed at the meeting because so many people had responded, and the prayers and baptisms had added a good hour to the already long service. I got to my room and changed clothes just as they pulled up to the house.

I crawled in my bed and when they peeked in on me, I pretended to be sleeping. I was glad they didn't come over to check on me because if they had gotten close, they would have noticed that I was wet with perspiration and that I had forgotten to remove the cap that held my long hair. Somehow, I was going to find out more about this mysterious man with the beautiful singing voice who had trespassed onto my parent's property and had been swimming naked in the cool stream. But who could I ask? Certainly not my parents.

May 28, 1941

Yesterday it was almost impossible to keep my mind on my chores. It was day two of cleaning this house this week, and my job was to take every rug outside and beat them silly with a rug beating tool. It looked like a fly swatter made of woven straw but much larger. I had never realized just how many rugs there were in our house. And they were many different sizes. Millie, our house help, had to help me carry the bigger ones. When she was not helping me, she was cleaning windows. My sisters had the easier jobs such as cleaning the silver or dusting furniture. They whined the whole time as if they had been given the most demanding chores of the day. As I beat on those rugs, I was also trying to figure out the stranger from Monday night. I just had to find a way to see him again if he was still there. For all I know he has moved on and will forever remain a mystery, but my gut said he was still there. I had until Saturday to come up with a plan. My mother was not going to allow me to miss another night of the meeting and during the day I was under her scrutiny doing household chores.

June 01, 1941

It is Sunday night and I could hardly wait to pull out my Journal and enter my news. Yesterday I put my plan into action. I decided that until I knew more about him, I needed to be sure he did not spot me. I waited until my parents assumed I was asleep. To my knowledge they had never checked on me after I went to bed unless I was sick. I cracked my door and listened to the house for several minutes. I could hear the muffled sounds of my sisters sleeping. They both snored but would never believe me when I told them. I could hear my parents talking quietly in the parlor at the front of the house. They had the radio playing softly and I knew they were having their time to unwind before bed.

I dressed in my overalls and shirt just like before, and put my hair in a tight bun on top and covered it with my cap. I put my sketching pad and pencils in my sack and tucked it into my front bib of the overalls fastened with a safety pin. I had hopes of making it home before my mother and my father were stirring around. Sunday morning was one of the few days it would matter. Any other morning and they would assume I had gone out to the barn early, but not on Sunday. My mother would have me up to gather eggs for breakfast and to prepare to attend church.

I messed my covers up a little so it would look like I was sleeping just in case they looked in on me. Then I eased out my window. There is a large tree beside our house that is directly beside my room. Once I got out on the roof all I had to do was climb onto the large branch nearest my window and work my way down. The moon last night was as bright as I had ever seen it so I would have no problem following the path.

As I approached the stream near the willow tree, I heard the beautiful singing like before and stopped in my tracks. I had to make sure he did not see me. The clothes might fool him from a distance but up close there was no question I was a girl and I could not risk him seeing me just yet. I made my way up to the tree where my seat was waiting for me. He was sitting near his fire reading something. His back was to me and I could not really tell anything about him. He had an old hat that hid his face.

I started to climb but made sure I used the side of the tree out of his vision so if he were to hear me and turn around the tree would hide me. Once I made it to my perch, I got comfortable and pulled out my pad and pencil. I began to sketch him. I had drawn the Willow tree a hundred times so that was something I could fill in later, but I had never drawn a man who was not in a family portrait. He was in shadow but just his silhouette was fascinating. He seemed tall and his shirt sleeves fit tightly to show he was muscular. I was trying to see what he was reading but could not tell from this distance. He hummed and sang a lot and it was so beautiful. He had a voice like an angel.

He stood and stretched once. Looked in my direction but said nothing. He moved into the curtain of the willow tree and the next thing I heard was the water as he jumped in the stream. He remained in the shadows and I strained to see him. Once I almost fell off my perch and caught myself, but I made a little noise and was terrified he would hear me. He swam around enjoying the stream for a few more minutes and then climbed out in the same hidden spot he had entered. While I sat there quietly working on my drawing and waiting on him to re-appear, he spoke.

"So, what is your name?"

I said nothing. I don't think I was breathing.

"I noticed you the other night and wondered if you would come back. You are welcome to come sit by my fire and visit for a while. What did you say your name was," he asked again?

"Willie," I replied so low I doubt he heard me. I cleared my throat "Willie," I repeated.

"Isn't it late for a young boy such as yourself to be out alone.

Do you have family? If you're hungry I would gladly share what I have."

Oh wow. He thought I was a boy. I was so relieved.

"No sir, I'm not hungry. This is my father's land and I wondered who you were and why you were trespassing."

As soon as the words left my mouth, I hoped I had not angered him. If he were a criminal, he might think I would turn him in so he would need to shut me up.

"I don't mind you being here," I added. "Just curious is all."

"My name is Isaiah Reed," he informed me. "I have been hired for the summer to help your neighbor with chores. He had nowhere for me to sleep so I found this wonderful spot to rest from my day. I was told the property line was hard to follow because the stream winds in and out through the two properties. Do you think your father will be upset?"

Actually, from what I was told the willow tree is on my father's land but the tree I like to sit in is on our neighbor Mr. Carlton's land, so I guess it is okay as long as neither man investigates too closely.

"No, he won't mind, I lied." "I'm not hungry but thanks for the offer, and If it's all the same to you I like sitting in my tree."

Isaiah and I talked for a long while. I had to be very careful not to say anything that would let him know he had mistaken me for a boy and I was going to have to go soon to make it home before my absence was known. He gave me the opportunity when he said he really needed to get some sleep so he would be ready for the hard day working in the fields. He did mention that he did not like working on the Lord's day, but Mr. Carlton had not given him a choice. This told me he was probably a Godly man or at least a good man. He was laying on the blanket he had tossed over a pile of leaves and straw.

The fire had dwindled down to embers and soon I could tell he had fallen to sleep. I eased down from my tree perch and took off running like a rabbit. I made it home in time to be found in my bed. This would be a difficult day without any sleep. I often struggle staying awake during Brother Roberts sermon, but today it would take a true act of God.

I hid in the barn loft after lunch and chores to steal a nap. If anyone comes looking for me, they will think I am off somewhere drawing a picture. After all that is what I am usually doing. But I wanted to rest up so I could go talk to Isaiah Reed again tonight.

I looked at my Nana and raised my eyebrows.

"You were a sneaky rascal as a kid."

"I guess I was," she said with a little grin.

I continued to read for several more pages and found that their visit was almost a nightly thing. She found herself looking forward each day to her time with Isaiah. She had not fully seen him because they always had to visit at night, and she had still refused to leave the safety of her tree. Once when the stars were bright enough to highlight his form, she found herself drawing like mad to capture his beautiful body as he stood in the stream with the water barely covering him. He was still under water from his hips down, but it was more than she had ever seen. He had been naked the first night she discovered him, but it was so dark she only really saw an outline of him for a few seconds. The end of the third journal pointed out that Isaiah had been born near here, but his parents had taken him and moved to Washington D.C. in order to have more opportunities. His grandmother was the one who told him about Mr. Carlton needing workers and he planned on working for him a few months and then enlisting in the Army. He hoped for a chance at a better life. He also wanted his music to be recognized. He hoped someday to entertain people with words from his heart.

"Nana, he sounds really wonderful. How long before you told him the truth about who you were?"

"That is in the next journal. Are you tired yet? We can start it tomorrow if you would like."

I studied journal number four for a few minutes.

"Let's take a short break. Go to the restroom, get a snack and a good stretch. But I think I would really like to read just a little more if you are up to it."

She smiled and gave me a pat on the leg.

"I'm up for it."

I was really hoping Willie was going to tell Isaiah that she was a girl. I could not wait to see his reaction. I had a gut feeling there was a chance for romance in this story, but Nana had not given me a single clue either way. We both took care of the personal business and agreed we might both be more comfortable if we put on our pajamas. Once we both came back downstairs, we grabbed a bottle of water and a cookie to re-charge. I picked up the next journal and began.

JUNE 14, 1941

It is a Saturday and except for Sundays I have managed to visit Isaiah everyday this month. I cannot wait until I talk to him tonight. He is the dearest man. I find myself thinking about him all day. I keep the sketches of him in a secret spot in the barn not only so I can look at them throughout the day but because I could not risk my parents seeing them. I had drawn several of him but always from behind or sitting under the willow tree. Because I could only go out at night, I had never seen his face.

I desperately wanted to see him up close. There were times when I was drawing him that his body made me feel strange deep in my stomach. I would have trouble breathing and the desire to touch him was strong. I wanted to run my hand over the large muscles in his arms and along his back. And I must be honest. I wanted desperately to kiss him. How could I possibly feel like this for a man I had never seen face to face. He did not even know I was a girl. Soon I would have to be truthful.

I had told him a lot about myself, but I had lied about many things that would reveal the truth. I got to my tree early and he was not there yet. I walked over to look under the willow to see what he kept there. His blanket, a few cans of beans and a Bible. So that was what he was always reading. I heard singing down the path and knew he was coming so I ran over to my tree and climbed it quickly. I was trying to turn myself around to sit on my plank, but my sack had caught on something and I was off balance. My feet slipped and I started to fall. As Isaiah walked up, he was surprised to see me hanging from the big limb struggling as I tried desperately to get back up in the tree.

"Willie, hang on, I'll climb up and help you!"

"NO," I protested. I am fine. Just give me a minute and I will get back up on my limb."

He watched patiently but started making his way out into the stream. He knew if I lost my grip, I would land in the water. I struggled for a few more minutes and then my cap fell off my head. He went to catch it but of course when he looked up, he saw my long red hair. I could not hold on another second and found myself falling toward the water below. Isaiah tried to grab me in order to brace my fall. The water was about chest deep on me but not deep enough to safely jump…or fall…from that high in the tree. The impact caused us both to fall and go under water. We both jumped up quickly and just stood there staring at each other for several minutes. I think we were both equally shocked at the person that now stood in front of us.

"Willie, you're a girl!"

I was looking into the beautiful shocked eyes of a tall black man. He went from shocked to what appeared to be worried, but the light was only on part of his face, so I wasn't sure. I held my hand out and started to introduce myself properly.

"Willamina Pettigrew. I'm pleased to meet you."

He bolted. He grabbed his few belongings and made his way up the path toward Mr. Carlton's barn. I just stood in the water for a long while not sure what to do. I should have told him sooner. He is angry because I was not honest with him. I understand that but I was not expecting him to leave. I crawled up out of the stream and started the journey home. I cried the whole way. This is not like me. I do not cry. I had ruined my chances to know him by my lies. Suddenly it hit me like a slap hard in the face. I was all upset and crying over this man I had grown very fond of. He was a black man!

JUNE 22, 1941

It is Sunday. I knew I would not see him today because my parents would never allow me to go anywhere. If I were to sneak out of my window tonight would he even be there? Would he ever speak to me again? I have been hiding in the barn like I always do after lunch on Sunday. This Sunday I was not taking a nap. I had not slept last night but I could not sleep. What could I do? I knew it was not appropriate for a white girl to be alone with a black man, but I did not care. I missed him and I wanted to make sure he did not hate me. I decided to take a chance and rode my horse to the willow tree while it was still light outside. No reason to hide in the dark now.

Isaiah was not there. I saw no sign he had returned after last night. His blanket was still gone along with his belongings. I rode around the area looking for any evidence he had made a new camp. As I rode along the path next to the stream I came upon a small house. It was old and worn but I could tell someone lived in it. There were clothes on the line in the back of the house and flowers had been planted all around the yard. A girl walked out on the porch and looked at me. It was Millie. Our hired help was here. It suddenly occurred to me that I had never questioned her about her home. I knew the one day she did not come to work for us was Sunday and of course she left late in the day, but I had never wondered where she went.

"Miss Willamina, Is that you? What are you doing out here? Are you lost?"

"Hi Millie. Yes, it is me. I was just riding around looking for someone and came across your house."

"Who you looking for way out here," she asked?

I was not sure I should tell her. If she knew him it could get him in trouble. If she decided to tell my parents, it would get me in trouble.

"It doesn't matter, I don't think he would be this far out."

Before the sentence was completely out of my mouth Isaiah walked out on the porch and stood beside Millie. I did not have to tell her that he was the someone I was looking for. The way we looked at each other was enough to answer the question of who. She looked at Isaiah and then at me more than once then gave him a look that I would guess meant…WHAT HAVE YOU GONE AND DONE? Then she turned and stormed into the house.

"Is Millie your girl," I asked? He looked down and almost laughed.

"No, she is my cousin. This is my grandmother's house."

As he was saying it an elderly woman came to the door and peered out at me. Then she gave him a worried look and one of those eye warnings that moms and grandmothers give before walking back into the house.

"I'm sorry Isaiah. I didn't mean to lie to you but when you assumed I was a boy I just thought it was the only way you would talk to me."

"I should have known," he mused. Some of the things you said made me think you were a really confused little boy."

"Like what? What did I say that gave me away?"

"I don't know. Just the way you would describe things and you would sigh and giggle at times."

I blushed.

"Oh well, I tried to think boy, but I guess I wasn't doing a very good job. Isaiah, I have enjoyed our friendship and I would hate to lose that. I hope you will accept my apology. I hope we can still have our long talks because I would really miss them."

"I do accept your apology. As for the continued visits I'm not sure I can do that."

He looked at me as if I had betrayed him like no one ever had before. He did not look angry. He looked hurt. He looked sad.

"Willie. Or should I call you Willamina?"

"No, my friends call me Willie. I hate the other name."

"Well, Willie, do you realize that if the wrong person saw me talking to you the way we were? Being all friendly and telling

each other our feelings and beliefs like that. It could cost me my life."

That hit me like an arrow in my heart. I had been selfish and careless with him. He was right. I had heard the horror stories of how some blacks had been treated. But I did not know he was black. I had never seen him in the daylight or up close.

"Isaiah, I didn't know I was putting you in danger. It was always dark when I came to visit, and I could not tell. Your speech did not give you away like the Negroes I know. The ones who work for us".

My voice faded as I said these words and I looked toward the door to see if Millie was listening.

"I didn't realize you were black, so I didn't know I was putting you in danger," I repeated.

"I have been blessed with a little more education than my cousin, but I can see where you may not have known. I believe you when you say you did not know. After all, I thought you were a boy. A big sissy, but a boy," he broke out in a grin.

I had to laugh at the mix up myself.

"So maybe I'll see you again under the willow tree?"

He never really answered the question but gave me a nod that could have meant yes. Or it could have meant, No, do not come back," or it could have even meant, "I am not sure myself so let me think about it." I guess when I go back to the willow tree, I will get my answer.

"Nana, did he forgive you? Was he there when you went back?"

She only smiled at me. She stood up and placed the journal we had just read from back into the box. She closed the flaps on the box as if to signal we were done for the night, kissed the top of my head and walked toward the stairs. I watched her without moving or speaking as she made her way up the stairs and turned to go to her room.

"Goodnight Nana."

"Goodnight Alex. I love you."

"I love you too."

I think that was the first time, as an adult, I had said those words to her.

I hope Isaiah forgave her.

I don't know why it mattered to me so much, but it did. It just felt right somehow

Chapter Five

The Sacred Clearing

My eyes opened and the first thought I had before ever raising my head off the pillow was that Nana and I had one more thing in common. The young Willie of her journal had to wait and see if Isaiah would ever speak to her again. Sure, Nana knows the answer to it, but I would have to wait and find out. And I had made a complete idiot of myself in front of Mark and would have to wait and see if he would speak to me again. Why I even cared was the real question. He was important to Nana so for that reason alone I needed to try and get along with him. But beyond that I found myself concerned with his opinion of me.

I realized I was dwelling on him a lot. Not just his being angry with me but I was dwelling on HIM. His beautiful gray eyes, his dark hair and those muscles had disrupted my sleep more than once. And as much as I hated to admit it, he was a genuinely nice guy. He was kind and helpful to Nana and had *tried* to be nice to me, but I had my 'mean girl' wall up and pushed him away. I decided I wanted coffee before I took my shower, so I put on my robe and slippers and made my way to the kitchen. When I walked through the front room, I noticed Nana was painting on the porch again. She loved the early morning light and I think the solitude. I pushed through the door that led into the kitchen, but it stopped midway when it hit something. I heard something hit the floor and then the sound of someone sucking air through their teeth followed by a groan.

I peek my head in to see Mark covered in his breakfast cereal and the coffee mug pouring onto the floor as he tried to balance the bowl and cup in his hands without dropping them. The thing that I had heard hit the floor was a small plate that had contained toast. The toast was on the floor and the milk from his cereal along with the coffee were dripping onto it. I started to laugh but when I noticed his face, I decided it was not a good idea.

"Oh Mark! I am so sorry. I had no idea you were in the kitchen. Let me clean this up," I said as I frantically started picking up the toast and plate on the floor.

I was on my knees trying to scoop up the mess when I realized the milk was dripping from his bowl to my head. I looked up toward him and a blob of cereal hit me in the face. This caused me to slip and so I turned and sat down in order to clear the cereal from my eyes and realized too late that I was sitting in the spilled coffee. I was prepared to be furious but when I looked up at Mark's face again, he was trying to muffle laughter. Despite the effort to control himself his eyes were watering and his face was red.

He finally lost the battle and burst into a laughing frenzy. His laughter was so out of control that all he could do was sit down beside me in the coffee while still clutching the bowl and mug. I stared at him for a few minutes and then started to laugh at myself. We both sat there soaked and dripping milk, cereal, and coffee laughing uncontrollably. Nana had apparently heard the ruckus and opened the door to see what was going on. When she saw us sitting there like that she also had to laugh. She did not ask a single question but simply shook her head and said we kids needed to clean up our mess. She walked out and went back to her porch to paint. I loved her so much for that. For not getting angry or shaming us. Just told us to clean it up and left the room still laughing.

"We will Nana," Mark said

"Okay Nana," I had said at the same time.

We sat there a few more minutes gathering our wits.

"I'm sorry Mark. Sorry for this and sorry for my crazy behavior at the pool yesterday. I am usually not such a sour hateful person. I don't know why it made me so angry, but I overreacted, and I want to apologize."

He looked in my eyes for a few minutes longer than I had expected and I started to feel a little awkward.

Just say something already, I thought.

"It's okay. I should not have knocked you under. Sometimes I can be a big kid. I'm sorry about the cereal too," he added.

"I'm the one who came in and knocked it all over you."

"True, but when you looked up at me while cleaning up the toast, well I kind of deliberately tilted the bowl and dumped the blob of cereal in your face…on purpose,"

He grinned sheepishly and waited. I looked at the floor at the small pile of soggy cereal, picked it up, and proceeded to throw it in his face. It was on then…all out food fight in the kitchen floor while both of us laughed hysterically. It took us an hour to clean up the mess that should have taken ten minutes. Once we were done the air was clear between us. We both felt cleansed of the tension that had settled between us and all seemed right. But we, on the other hand, were a mess.

We parted ways to our own showers to clean up. He left out by the back door from the kitchen. I went back through the front room toward the stairs. When I passed by the window, I noticed Nana was still painting on the porch. She was grinning so big and she looked up at me and nodded approval. She somehow knew things would be much better now between Mark and me. That was important to her, so I was happy about it too.

After my shower I made another attempt at coffee and breakfast. Nana and Mark were at the small breakfast nook sipping coffee and eating cereal.

"Want some," Mark asked with a smile.

"No cereal for me. I have had enough cereal today, but coffee and a toaster pastry," Yes?

I made my coffee with the flavored creamer Nana had gotten me and put the pastry square in the toaster. Then I put the icing from the tiny packet on it once it was warm. Nana and Mark were finished eating by the time I sat down and were discussing the things she needed him to do the rest of the week. She then turned to me.

"I think I need to take you on a tour of my property today. You can see what is beyond the pool house."

I knew she was telling me she would show me the willow tree but did not want to say that in front of Mark. He looked a little confused as to why she would want to show me the grown-up fields beyond the pool house, so I assumed he had never gone much beyond that point himself.

"You want me to go with you ladies? Maybe drive you in the golf cart to save having to walk the whole way," Mark asked.

"No, I do not but thank you for the offer. I think Alex can drive the cart and we will be just fine."

Nana winked at me and I smiled and took a big bite of my pastry. I was excited. Yes, it is just a tree. But I had a feeling that as we went further into the journals it would be helpful to me to be able to picture the area in my mind.

The day was perfect. It was only late May and we still had days that were cooler. This was one of those days. It was not cold. The sun was shining and warm but there was a breeze that made it pleasant. The sky was a beautiful blue and the trees were blooming with flowers of white, pink and even a few purples.

As we loaded into the golf cart to make our trip through the field, I noticed Nana had packed a picnic basket. She opened it to let me peek in. I saw a blanket, several bowls of food, a small lantern and the journal. The one we had started reading last night. We were going to read it at the willow tree.

I drove slowly through the field. The grass was not super high this early in the year, but it was high enough I wanted to take it slow. I could not really tell if there was anything in our path that might cause us to flip. Nana explained that there used to be a very distinct path from the house to the stream but it had been several months since she had traveled it so it had grown up. I listened to her directions and as we drove along, she would point out types of trees. She talked about her kids playing in this field.

"This was a perfect place to play baseball, or tag, and to chase after lightning bugs," she explained.

I remembered from what I had read so far in the journal that the stream was about a half mile from the house. About halfway the field started turning into forest. The trees started out thinly placed but soon it was impossible to drive the cart any further. We parked and I picked up the picnic basket.

"It's not much farther," she said. "Do you want me to help with the basket?"

"No ma'am, I've got it. Let's just get going."

I was anxious and that made her smile. I tried to walk slowly to allow Nana to walk just in front of me. Partly because I wanted to be sure she kept her footing and because I had no idea which way to go. Suddenly Nana stopped. She turned and looked at me with a sense of pride in her eyes. She was excited to share this with me. She stepped in between two trees into a clearing. I stepped in right behind her and it felt like Oz. It was beautiful. The stream with the sounds of water flowing through it. The green grass that was almost like carpet. She kept watching me to see my reaction. Then I saw it a few feet away. A tall majestic willow tree. The branches hung all the way to the ground like a beautiful flowing skirt.

The breeze made them sway and move in a type of dance and when I looked at her, I noticed her eyes were wet. She was not really crying but her emotions were definitely high. Looking at her made my chest ache. I knew then that this was a very special place. This was sacred to her. Almost religious to her. She walked over to the tree and so very gently stroked its skirt. Pulled its leaves to her nose to smell them and lovingly caressed them to her cheek. I just stood there giving her the moment. Once she had paid her respects, for lack of a better word, she turned to me and said.

"This is my willow tree."

I almost felt as if I should curtsy or introduce myself. I

smiled at my Nana and nodded. She was back to her usual self now. She started to point out things. She walked a few feet away where a massive tree stood on the bank at the edge of the stream. Some of the limbs hung out over the water and she pointed up for me to look at it. Again, she waited for me to see it.

"The planks you would sit on," I squealed!

"Yes," she confirmed "but the tree is much larger now than it was back then. After all that was 56 years ago."

She pointed across the stream to the path that led to Mr. Carlton's farm.

"It doesn't belong to Mr. Carlton anymore. He passed away many years ago and his farm was auctioned off to a construction company and now it is a subdivision of houses. Papa Sam purchased a few acres from him once he stopped farming because we did not want anyone to destroy the stream. We didn't want houses this close to our property line."

She explained that the little house that Mille and her grandmother had lived in was just a little way down stream.

"No one has lived in it for a very long time, but we always kept it in repair. Of course, It has probably been ten years now since anyone did anything much to it so it may be about to fall down."

She made no offer to go see the little house and I did not ask her if we could. One thing at a time, I thought. She started back toward the willow tree and asked me to bring the picnic basket. She parted the branches and motioned to me to go inside. She turned the lantern on and removed the blanket from the basket. She spread it near the edge so we could still see out but have the umbrella of branches over us. She used the basket to hold back the branches and began to unload the contents.

“I’m starving! How about you dear?”

“I’m hungry too Nana. What’s on the menu?”

Nana proceeded to remove the containers of pasta salad, deviled eggs, fruit salad, and small sandwiches. She also had a thermos of cold lemonade and two tumblers with lids to help prevent spilling. There were two plastic picnic plates and forks and a zip lock bag of wipes to clean our hands.

“This is awesome Nana. Everything looks yummy.”

“Thank you, Alex. I love pasta salad. And fruit salad, deviled eggs and…. she chuckled… I guess I just love food. Picnic food is the best.”

We ate until we were so full, we were miserable. We both leaned up against the tree trunk and just sat there daydreaming for a little while. I could have fallen to sleep easily except for the fact that there was one more item in the basket she had not yet pulled out. The journal was the dessert I was anxious to get to. I had made it my habit to wait for her to signal that she was ready to start reading again. I did not have to wait a long time. She reached in and pulled it out. She laid it on the blanket and proceeded to clean up from our feast.

I started helping her by putting the lids on the different containers and placing them in the basket in an order that would keep them from falling over. She told me to take the plates and forks to the stream and rinse them off.

“We can give them a proper cleaning once we get back home,” she said.

We used one more wipe to clean our mouth and hands and took one last long drink of the lemonade. She stood and stretched for a while before settling down and getting comfortable. Well comfortable for the ground at least. I sat beside her and waited. She picked the journal up. Ran her hand across the front of it as if she were dusting it off and handed it to me.

"I'm ready," she said.

JUNE 28, 1941

It is a Saturday. It has been an eventful week, so I am only now finding time to write in my journal. I did not try to go to the willow tree Monday because I was honestly exhausted from lack of sleep and fell asleep. When I woke up in the middle of the night it was because of a terrible storm. The rain was pounding, the thunder boomed, and the lightning flashed to show trees dancing in the wind. I did not dare take a chance. So, Tuesday night the 24th of June I was more determined than ever to see if Isaiah was waiting for me.

If he had forgiven me. I started to put on my old comfortable overalls but then decided I might as well look like a girl since he now knew I was one. I combed my hair and pulled it back away from my face with a ribbon. I put on my green swing party dress with a lace collar. It was one of the few dresses I owned that was not for church. It was meant for parties or dances. In other words, I had never had it on other than when it was purchased, and I needed to be sure it would fit correctly. I knew if my mother found out I had worn it to go through the woods she would skin me alive. I could not walk that far in my fancy dress shoes so I would use my flat saddle shoes.

I waited until I was positive no one in the house was awake. I did not want to climb down the tree in this dress and risk tearing it, so I held the shoes in my hands and made my way slowly down the steps. I had my overalls and shirt rolled up and tucked under my arm. I would place them in the barn just in case I was late getting back and needed to change my clothes. I knew after a certain hour my parents could possibly be awake and would hear me sneak in, so this way I could change clothes and climb the tree near my window. The tree is so large it keeps me well hidden while I make my way up the branches and enter through the open window.

I did not want the kitchen door to creak, so I took a small dab of lard and rubbed it on the door hinges. I had seen my father do this when he was leaving early in the morning to go hunting; so as not to wake mother or the girls. I always went hunting with him. Once I was out of the house I stood and listened for several minutes to make sure I didn't hear anyone coming down the steps and once I had my shoes on, I raced for the barn to hide my clothes before going down the familiar trail.

The moon was so big and bright it was almost like early morning when the sun comes up instead of late evening. I rushed to the spot that would answer my questions and once I arrived, I was out of breath. I leaned on my tree to try and catch my breath. I looked around and saw no sign of him. No campfire or outline of him in the stream. I did not hear his beautiful silky voice singing as he walked down the path from Mr. Carlton's farm. I was about to cry. I didn't want to, but my heart was aching at the possibility of never talking to him again. I was about to turn and leave when I heard him.

"Willie, is that you?"

He had been hiding under the branches of the willow tree almost afraid to show himself. It had taken a few minutes to be sure it was me and a few more minutes to work up his nerve.

"It's me," I said. "I didn't think you would come. I was afraid you wouldn't come," I confessed, and my voice gave away the subdued tears that had almost fallen. "Isaiah, I hope you have forgiven me. You are such a special friend and I would miss our talks so much."

He did not say anything but just stood there looking at me. He looked scared to death.

"Isaiah, are you going to say anything? Please say something.... anything."

"You sure can't pass for a boy now," he nervously responded. "You look very nice ma'am."

"MA'AM! Who are you calling ma'am? Isaiah it's me. The same person you have talked to almost all night, every night for the last 5 weeks.

"No, it isn't," he insisted. "I have been talking to some sissy boy who hid in that tree. You are for sure not a boy. I must get used to this. I will not lie.... I am scared. If someone sees you with me. The explanation that we are just talking will never reach their ears. They will hang me from that very tree you fell out of."

"How about I sit under the willow branches where no one can see me. You can sit outside of the branches and we can talk low. If anyone happens to walk up, they will only see you sitting by your campfire reading your Bible. They may think you are just reading out loud. I promise I will not do anything to put you in danger, Isaiah. Please can I stay for a while?"

"Okay, I guess that will work."

He still seemed a little guarded, but he pulled the branches open and reached into the space to lay out his blanket. He stepped aside to allow me to enter the willows skirt. I glanced at the blanket and looked up at him.

"I didn't want you to get that beautiful dress dirty," he said.

For a few minutes it was awkward and uncomfortable. Not like before when I was a boy in the tree, and he could talk freely about whatever came to mind. But once I started telling him about myself a little of the tension seemed to melt away and we were talking like before. It was odd to talk to his back, but he was obviously still nervous about my being there.

His speech was also more guarded than before. He was never crude in his speech but now he was polite in a way that reflected he considered me the more delicate of the genders. He was relaxed enough after a while to ask me questions about my family. He asks me about my drawings and wanted to know my age and school grade.

"I am 15 years old and will be in the 11th grade this year. I love to draw, and I have even made money selling my drawings. I love to paint too but not as many people want to pay for that because they also have to pay for the paints needed."

I took a chance here and admitted I had drawn several pictures of him. He looked shocked.

"What kind of picture", he asked? "Can I see them?"

"Oh, just pictures of you sitting under this tree. All the pictures I drew were of your back because I could not see your face well enough to make out detail. I also have drawn you while you were in the stream. Before you knew I was in the tree."

At this confession he looked almost sick.

"Miss. Willie, what kind of pictures did you draw when I was in the stream?"

He knew he only went into the stream to bathe and was usually naked, so I guess that pretty much told him what kind of pictures. I felt my face grow hot with embarrassment. Why had I told him about those drawings?

"Where are those drawings, Miss. Willie? Is there any chance

anyone will come across them?"

"Isaiah, calm down please. And for the love of Pete stop calling me Miss. Willie. It is just Willie. I have them well hidden but even if someone did find them.... which they will not.... they would not be able to tell it was you. I will never do anything to get you in trouble Isaiah. I promise."

He had not turned and looked at me all night but at this conversation he turned to face me. He was searching my eyes for answers and I also found myself looking deeply into his beautiful brown eyes. I noticed he had a deep scare that went through his brow above his left eye. I was curious about it but did not want to ask how he got it.

"Willie" He hesitated before asking. "Why did you draw me like that? In the stream like that."

I was not sure how to answer the question honestly without embarrassing myself. I did not want to tell him that the sight of him had stirred up feelings in me I had never had. That when he was standing there like that, I dreamed of touching him and wanted desperately to let him kiss me. I knew our friendship was a fragile one and I had to be careful.

"Because I thought you were beautiful," I said.

I heard his breath catch in his throat and he turned back around with his back to me.

"Willie, you are a very pretty girl. And I enjoy talking to you more than I like to admit. But you do realize that we can never, 'he hesitated,' be together."

I did not respond to his statement. All I could think about was that the way he worded it meant he liked me too. I guess I am a fool. I know that this can never be. Isaiah and I could never walk down the street holding hands or sit at the soda shop and order an ice cream. I absolutely could never take him home for Sunday dinner and introduce him to my parents. My mother would faint, and my father would throw him out and go for his gun. I knew all these things in my head but all I knew in my heart was that Isaiah Reed was the kindest man I had ever met.

He was interesting to talk to. He had plans for his future and was so smart. I knew that when he looked at me with those beautiful brown eyes, I stopped breathing because my heart swelled so big it filled my chest. I knew that when he sang it made my legs feel weak and I had to hold on to something to balance myself. I knew that I wanted him in a way that was new to me but overwhelmed me and consumed my thoughts.

I knew that all I thought about all day was when I could get away for a visit with him. I was falling in love with him and it was something that put us both in jeopardy. It could even cost him his life. I was not so naïve that I did not know how some felt about the blacks. Treated them as if God had not created them like he did us.

One important thing I had learned talking to Isaiah all those weeks when I did not know he was a black man was that we are all the same inside. The color of our skin is just like paint on a house. It is what we have inside that makes a house nice to live in. I had fallen in love with him before I knew and now that I know I cannot just turn the love off.

"Willie."

I realized he had been waiting for a response. I had been lost in my thoughts and he assumed I was thinking about his statement. I decided not to agree with him but took the conversation in another path.

"So, you think I'm pretty," I said in a sing-song kind of voice.

I almost giggled, which is not who I am. He just hung his head and shook it back and forth.

"Willie, it's getting late and I need to sleep so I can work in

the field tomorrow. Maybe you should head on home now."

"Can I come back tomorrow night?"

He was quiet for a while. Looking up toward the sky as if he were praying for an answer to my question. He cupped his face in his hands and wiped them down the sides of his face in a show of confusion or frustration. I was not sure which one it was. He stood up and held his hand out in order to help me up from the blanket I had been sitting on. I stood there looking up at him and waiting for his answer.

"Yes. Against my better judgment I would love for you to come back tomorrow. But can you please wear the overalls next time? I am not sure I can keep my wits about me if you keep wearing things like that dress."

I simply grinned and walked away swishing my dress in an exaggerated way simply to torment him because I had no doubt he was watching me walk away.

"See you tomorrow then," I said. And walked toward home.

I was floating down the path. I hurried home and went straight to the barn to change. Just in case someone was up and saw me I would look like I had got up early to do chores and not like I was sneaking in. I went behind several bales of hay to change and Millie walked in. She let out a quick scream, but I shushed her.

"Miss. Willamina, where have you been in that party dress? Why are you coming in so early in the morning?"

"You won't tell mother or father will you Millie? I was just visiting a friend and the time got away from me. Really it's nothing."

I knew she was Isaiah's cousin, but I did not think she would be happy about our visits. I knew she would not tell because it could get Isaiah in so much trouble. But she may tell him he needs to stop seeing me because it could get me in trouble, and he might leave to avoid it at his cousin's suggestion.

"I really need to go to Millie. I hope to get to my room before they all wake up. Maybe even catch a short nap."

I would have to make myself leave sooner tonight. I could not risk her seeing me come from the direction of her grandmothers' home on a nightly basis. She was not a stupid girl and she was already suspicious.

I closed the journal and placed it in the picnic basket. I noticed that Nana had been looking out longingly across the stream. Almost as if she expected that Isaiah would come down the path to greet her. I placed my hand on her shoulder and she reached up and placed her hand on mine.

"We had better head back," she said. "Mark will think we are lost and come looking for us."

I stood up and offered my hand to help her up. I folded the blanket and placed it in the basket. Then I picked up the basket with one hand and put the other arm around her shoulders. She put her arm around my waist, and we walked to where we had left the golf cart. The ride back to the house was quiet. I had a thousand questions. I wanted to talk about what I had just read but I could tell she needed the quiet right now. She was swimming in her memories, and I did not want her to drown in them so it could wait until she was ready for more. I had learned to wait for her ques. As we approached the garage beside the pool house Mark came over and helped Nana out of the cart and took the picnic basket.

"If you just leave it there, I will put it away in a little while," he said, nodding toward the cart.

"Okay thanks," I replied and followed behind them.

I did not think Mark had a clue what had Nana in such a

solemn mood, but he apparently knew her well enough to not ask right now. I watched him walk her to the kitchen door and open it for her. He was so sweet with her. I am starting to like this guy.

Chapter Six

The Weight of Unspoken Things

Once we had eaten an early dinner Nana excused herself and went to her room. I heard the water upstairs and assumed she was taking a hot bath to unwind. I waited about an hour and went to check on her. I tapped lightly on her door and opened her door just a little. Her room was dark, and I could tell she was in bed. I returned to the front room and placed the journal we had finished today in the box with the rest of them. The temptation to pick up the next one and start reading was strong and harder to resist than anything I had ever faced. I decided I needed to relax before bed. After all, it was only 8 o'clock and I was not sleepy in the least. I made myself a glass of soda and grabbed a bowl of chips. My go to snack to watch television.

Once I flipped through the channels I gave up on that plan and took my snack outside to sit at the pool side. The pool house was dark, so I figured Mark was either already in bed or had gone somewhere. I had just settled into a lounger by the pool when I noticed him sitting in the dark across on the other end of the pool. At first it scared me because I did not know it was him for a few seconds. My heart was pounding.

"Thanks for scaring me half to death," I said.

"Sorry. I did not mean to. Would you mind if I came over and joined you?"

I motioned for him to come over and he plopped down in the lounger next to mine. He looked a little upset or unsure. It was hard to pinpoint but I could tell he was not his usual self. He reached over and took a chip from my bowl, gave me a half-hearted grin and popped it into his mouth.

"Are you okay Mark?"

"Yeah. I'm just worried about Nana."

That took me off guard. I mean he did not know what was going on with her and she is an older woman so going to bed early should not be alarming.

"Why are you worried about Nana," I asked?

"I have known her since I was a baby. Spent more days here than my own house and after my dad passed away, I moved into the pool room and spent countless hours talking to her. I have never seen her like she was today. She is one of the most energetic, happy and positive people I know. Even when she had the flu last year or when she broke her arm a few years ago and could not paint…she was still so happy. Today she seemed sadder than when Papa Sam passed away and that is the only other time I have seen her sad. Something must be terribly wrong? Did you say something that upset her," he questioned?

"NO! I most certainly did not."

How dare he ask me that. Sure, I never knew she had the flu last year. And I vaguely remember my dad telling me she had broken her arm. Okay I have been a terrible granddaughter. But I love her, and I am enjoying my time with her more than I could have imagined...I would never say anything to hurt or upset her. I deliberately calmed myself before speaking again. After all, Mark had no idea about her past or the journals. I needed to play this cool.

"I think she is just really tired. We had a great visit today. Maybe seeing areas she had not seen in a long time made her a little sad. You're a man so you wouldn't understand that."

He blows out a little laugh at that comment and apologizes to me rather sarcastically for being so uncaring as to be a man.

"Apology accepted," I responded with just as much sarcasm.

I think he decided at this point to change the path of our conversation.

"So, would you like to go watch a movie in the pool house? I rented one but have not been in the mood to watch it by myself?"

He told me the name of the movie and it happened to be one I was wanting to see so I thought I might as well.

"Okay sure."

I gathered my snack and went into the pool room after he opened the door for me. I was surprised when I walked in to see a nicely furnished and very tidy apartment. I am not sure what I had expected. Maybe a blanket tossed over a lounge chair or a sleeping bag on the floor. I had pictured a small college size frig full of beers and pizza boxes laying around. I was wrong. This place was awesome. A small living room area with a love-seat sized couch and a recliner. A television hung on the wall and a nice floor lamp. One corner toward the back had a kitchenette set up. A hot plate, small microwave, small refrigerator and a sink with a small amount of counter space. Above the sink were three wall shelves. The bottom one had things like dish detergent sponges and dish towels. The other two had a few dishes, a skillet and a pot, and a few food items. I noticed bread and peanut butter on top of the refrigerator. He had a twin sized bed and nightstand in the other corner and one of those plastic rolling things with drawers that people used to store items such as clothes. I could see a bathroom through the door located between the two areas. He had a couple of posters on the wall of different football teams and a picture of his family on the wall near his bed. It appeared to be his mom and dad plus two young kids that had to be Mark and his sister Rhonda.

"Nice place," I said.

"Thanks, it's home. So have a seat and I'll make the popcorn. Do you need more soda?"

He made popcorn using one of those little pans that pop up big while you shake it back and forth on the stove. He used the hot plate. He made himself a glass of soda and refilled my glass after putting a couple of ice cubes in it. He put the movie in the player on the shelf below the TV, tossed me a throw to cover with on the love seat, fell into his recliner and covered with another throw and pushed the remote to begin the movie. It was like a male ballet. He did all this in a matter of seconds without hesitation or ceremony. I liked that. It made me feel very comfortable. The movie was a scary one. Full of gore and tension and I loved it. He laughed at me twice when I let out a scream. Then when there was an unexpected scare and he let out a scream we both laughed. Once the movie was over, I helped him clean up the mess. He did not have carpet anywhere except for a few well-placed rugs. One in front of the sink, one in front of the door and one in the bathroom.

"You want to sweep or do dishes," I asked him.

"I'll sweep," he offered.

As we worked to tidy up, we talked. Considering how tense things had been between us in the beginning our conversation was easy. No one would have guessed we hardly knew each other. He asked me questions about my growing up and I did the same toward him. We laughed and joked and teased each other like old friends would do. We had more in common than either of us expected but even our differences seemed to compliment rather than irritate. I tried not to make him feel like I was staring at him but I would find myself lost in his eyes when he was telling a story of his high school sports antics or his fear of medical school that was just around the corner. I had not noticed until tonight that he had dimples in both cheeks when he smiled. The sexiest dimples I had ever seen I thought as I found myself memorizing his face.

"Are you okay Alex," he asked and brought me out of my trance.

"Yes, I'm fine. Why do you ask?"

"I don't know you just had a goofy look on your face and you haven't answered my question."

Okay Alex, pull yourself together here.

"I'm sorry, what question did you ask me?"

"I just ask if you were ready to call it a night? It's pretty late and I have to be up early to work in the yard before it gets super-hot."

"Oh yes, absolutely. Obviously, I am really tired too and having trouble staying focused," I said and laughed a little too much.

We stood there feeling a little awkward for a minute.

"Well, I guess I'll go. I really enjoyed this. Thanks for the invitation."

He nodded and opened the door for me. I started to leave but the doorway was narrow with him standing there trying to hold it open. I had to turn sideways to exit and we found ourselves face to face staring into each other's eyes. I could feel my heart pounding and I noticed his breathing was faster than before. Okay, one of us needs to move, I thought.

"Well, good night then," I said and slid out walking away quickly.

I noticed he did not say goodbye. He did not say anything. I went in the French doors that led into the house from the back. When I turned to lock them and turned out the light, I noticed he was still standing in his doorway in the same position just staring at the house.

I got up early and showered. The only reason I was up so early was because I had not really slept. My mind was whirling. My sheet and blanket were in a knot and my pillow ended up across the room when I threw it out of frustration. When I was not thinking about Nana and how sad she seemed last night I was thinking about Willie, who is also Nana, and her night with Isaiah. I had to fight not to come to my own conclusions. I had to force myself not to finish with my own ending to their story. I knew if I let my imagination run free, I could ruin it for Nana or myself. I might even be disappointed if it ended differently than how I had imagined. The one time I drifted off to sleep, I dreamed I was at the willow tree with Mark. I woke up from my dream just as he was about to kiss me. As I recall that was about the same time, I tossed my pillow. I was a mess.

I entered the kitchen and for once it was empty. I had looked for Nana on the front porch, but she was not painting this morning. I stood staring out of the window toward the pool house while the coffee maker did its magic. I thought about last night and promised myself I would not let myself feel awkward around him. I was not stupid. I knew there was a tension between us. An attraction for sure. And it was not one sided. I knew that too. But my purpose here was to help Nana with her journals and to prepare for college in the fall. I did not want to make things uncomfortable for him or Nana so I would just act innocent. I would act as if I had not noticed the electricity between us. He will be working a lot around here and he will be back in his classes even sooner than I was scheduled to start so the key was to avoid any alone time. No more hanging around the pool at night and if I found myself alone with him, I would find an excuse to leave the room as quickly as possible. That is what I was telling myself at least but I knew I was probably fooling myself if I believed I could stay away from this man. I wanted to see him as much as possible. I found myself thinking of him all the time.

"Good morning sweetheart."

Nana walked in as fresh as a flower. She looked rested and beautiful as usual. I know I looked shocked and maybe a little confused. I guess I expected her to be a mess like I was. I assumed she had tossed all night, but then I realized …she knows how the story ends. She has no reason to toss and turn and let her imagination roam. She had no reason to wish she could skip ahead because she wrote the ending.

"Good morning Nana. How are you this morning?"

She walked up and placed her hands on my shoulders. She smiled and put her forehead against my forehead.

"I know I worried you last night and I apologize. I was a little overwhelmed by my memories and I think going to the willow tree made it a little too real. I was just so melancholy, but I am fine this morning. Once we get a few chores taken care of this morning we will start the next journal. Maybe after lunch. I am going to have Mark take me to town to pick up a few grocery items and my medications from the pharmacy. Unless you would like to go with him to get what I need. I can make you a list.

"No," I responded a little too quickly. "Maybe I can take you to town. I'm sure Mark has things to do around here. And I have seen so little of the town of Payne, Georgia. I need a tour of all the hot spots," I teased.

"Okay," she said "I'll be ready to leave in about an hour. Will that work for you?'

Just as she finished her sentence Mark walked into the kitchen. He was looking straight at me as if Nana were not standing right there beside him. I felt the heat in my cheeks and all but bolted out of the kitchen.

"I'll be ready in a few Nana," I yelled as I hurried up the stairs.

It was so nice to get out with Nana. She showed me all her favorite stores in the little town. We did the pharmacy first just to get it over with and we planned to do the grocery store last so no food would spoil. We made an appearance in her favorite dress shop where she insisted on buying me a blouse.

Next was the Little Old Lady's shoe shop. The owners were an older couple who thought a nursery rhyme theme was so cute. Mrs. Bowman was dressed like a nursery character. Which one I was not sure but maybe the little old lady that lived in a shoe. Mr. Bowman was a shoe repairman and dressed like an old-time shoe cobbler. It was hard not to laugh. Nana agreed once we left that the dear couple was a little nutty.

"They have a beautiful selection of shoes and Mr. Bowman can work miracles on older damaged shoes."

We also went in to meet her hairdresser. Both Nana and the beautician she used looked at my hair as if questioning my decisions.

"It's not a permanent color. It should be grown out completely in about two more weeks."

They both seemed relieved.

We had lunch at a diner that served mostly burgers, fries and shakes. They also had chicken strips and chili, but we had a cheeseburger and a chocolate shake. We opted to share an order of fries and put the ketchup in the middle of the plate so we could both dip our fries. We agreed we rather dip our fries than put ketchup all over them. One more thing we had in common.

Last was the grocery store. We had a list but somehow several items ended up in the cart that had not been written on the list. Once we got home and put everything away, I started the waiting game. I was trying to be busy but not so busy she would not want to interrupt me. I wipe the counters after putting the things away, folded the sacks and put them in the pantry, and swept the floor. She opened her mail and made sure she logged all she had purchased in her checkbook.

Nana had not mentioned the journal from yesterday at all. We had talked and talked about many things but not one word about what was constantly on my mind. Nana received a phone call and informed me that the woman who had commissioned her to paint the ocean scene was coming by to pick it up in a couple of hours. *Well, that takes care of that I thought. We will not start on the next journal before her client comes so I might as well find something else to do.* I killed time by cleaning my room. I even washed those sheets I had tortured last night. I cleaned my bathroom, put away my clean clothes, and I even called my mom to just say hi. She seemed surprised I was enjoying my stay so much.

Finally, I heard the doorbell ring. I listened as Nana had a short conversation with her client. The lady went on and on about the beautiful painting. She even talked about the possibility of Nana painting another one for her. I knew I was being selfish but all I could think about was how badly I wanted to scream down the stairs, *Would you just leave already!* I was very proud of my restraint. I heard the door close and made my way downstairs in record time. Nana looked at me and smiled.

"Are you alright, dear? You seem a little anxious?"

"I'm fine Nana," I said through my pretend smile. "Just checking to see if you needed me to do anything for you."

"No," she said while putting her finger to her chin as if thinking about it. "I can't think of anything I need… unless perhaps you would like to read to me."

She stood there smiling at me.

"I guess I could read to you for a little while," I smiled back trying not to be too obvious of how excited I was.

We decided to read in the den tonight. We made ourselves a glass of iced tea and made ourselves comfortable. She handed me the next journal and nodded. My signal to start.

JULY 5, 1941

I have not written in my journal for a while because of lack of opportunity, so this entry covers a time span from June 23rd through July 5th.

I had not been able to go see Isaiah since last Saturday the 28th of June. So yesterday when I finally made it to the stream it had been a week. I had seen him for short visits on Wednesday, Thursday, Friday and Saturday of that week but Mr. Carlton had been really working him hard and it was very late when he showed up. He would be hot and tired and hungry, so our visits were short. He would usually fall to sleep while I was talking and so I would sit there stroking his face while he slept. I knew by Friday what to expect so I had managed to save a biscuit and some bacon to bring to him. Once he was asleep, I took out my pad and began to draw. His eyes were closed but I knew them by memory. If I had been using colored pencils, I could have placed every speck of gold in those eyes but with charcoal I would have to depend on memory when I looked at them later. To finally capture that face on paper was my joy for now. I drew his scar then I traced it with my finger following its path through his eyebrow. I wondered how he had gotten it. He had never told me, and I had not wanted to ask him. Then I drew his mouth and the urge to kiss those full soft lips was overpowering. He is out cold I thought. He will not even know I kissed him. I leaned over him and placed my lips on his. I had never kissed anyone, so I was not sure how to do it, but I pressed softly against his mouth with mine and... HIS EYES OPENED. I stumbled with my words for a minute and then told him I needed to tell him something before I left. He sat up looking a little unsure if he had imagined what he thought just happened. I explained to him that I may not be back until after the fourth of July. I would come as soon as the holiday was over. He noticed the sketch pad and wanted to see what I had drawn. I hated to show him but could not refuse when he pleaded to see it. He looked at it for a long while and he touched the drawing of his scar with his finger.

"You want to know how I got this scar," he asked. I nodded and just waited.

"You know I told you my family moved to Washington so I would have a better chance at a good life."

"I remember," I said.

"Well that was only part of the reason."

He seemed so nervous about telling me, but I knew that whatever it was he needed me to know.

"When I was nine years old, we lived on the outskirts of Macon. I was helping work the crops on a farm down the road to help my family. On my way home I was walking past a field of wildflowers and I noticed a little girl sitting in the field making a headband from the flowers. She had very long golden blonde hair and the breeze that day made it dance. I was just watching her hair dance in the wind. That was all. I mean I was a young boy of nine and had no evil thoughts about her. She was probably only four or five years old. It was just so beautiful the way it looked among the flowers."

He kept emphasizing how innocent it was and then he sat

there for a while thinking back, I suppose to what happened next.

"I hadn't even heard her brother walk up. I knew who he was. I knew who his papa was too. They were well known in town and all the black families knew to not mess with them. They hated blacks and would cause trouble when given a chance. Without warning the boy flashed a knife at me and started cussing me. Telling me he would teach me to look at his sister like that. Before I could run away, he plunged the knife at my eye. He said he would fix it where I would never look at another white girl. He missed my eye, but it plunged into my eyebrow and the blood started to pour. He would have finished the job, but a car came by and stopped. It was the wife of the man I worked for and she offered me a ride. She could tell what happened, but she just acted like it was a kindness to give me a ride. Never mentioned my bleeding face. She nodded at the boy as if to say hello and as soon as I was in the car she took off before the door was shut all the way. She took me straight home and when my folks came out to see who was there, she told my papa we should leave town. She told him who did this and told my daddy that he knew this would not end here. My daddy thanked her, and he took her advice. We packed our old truck as fast as possible and we were on the road within an hour. What we could not get in the truck we left behind. Daddy told me if we stayed there that man would find a way to kill us all and no one would even try to find out what happened. This scar reminds me every single day of how much hate is out there. That people can hate you for no other reason than the skin God put on you."

He waited for a few minutes to allow me to absorb what he had told me.

"That's why I reacted the way I did when I realized you were

a girl. I could see it happening again. It's why I am so afraid someone will see us together."

I reached up and touched his scar. I ran my finger over it and a tear escaped his beautiful eyes.

"I understand now. I can see why you were reluctant to talk to me. What made you decide to take the chance?"

He touched my hair just for a second and looked into my eyes.

"If you were the last thing I could ever see... It would be worth it."

I could not speak. I was afraid if I tried to respond my heart would burst and I knew I would cry from the heart ache I felt knowing what he had been through.

He looked at the picture I had drawn of him again.

"I have a favor to ask," he said. "If I pay you the 25 cents you told me, you always earn for drawing pictures... would you draw a picture of yourself for me?"

He wanted a picture of me. He reminded me that he would be leaving soon to enlist in the Army, and he wanted something to remember me by.

"I will be glad to," I told him. I never want you to forget me.

I had to stay up late Monday helping my father prepare for a big party at our house for the 4th of July. I love my father so much. I helped him with all the things he would have expected a son to help with. I had always loved my one on one time with him but now all I could think about was how badly I wanted to go see Isaiah. I hoped he would not think I didn't want to see him.

I knew tomorrow was a holiday and there was no way I would be able to sneak off. My mother would be in control of me tomorrow. I would be busy from sunup till late in the night making and serving lemonade and tea, slicing watermelon, helping little kids cook hotdogs over the fire and running back and forth getting things from the house for both parents. If it was like past years, it would be the wee hours of the morning by the time the last guest was gone and the mess left behind was cleaned up. So, when the sun started to go down on July 5th, I was ready to go. I had been allowed to sleep later this morning and had even managed a short nap this afternoon.

My sisters both wanted to go to bed earlier than usual and my mother had been in bed for an hour. Everyone was exhausted which worked to my advantage. I made my bed look as if I were sleeping in it by placing a rolled blanket under my quilt. In the dark room it would look like me. It was not completely dark yet so I didn't want to take any chances that my father might decide to peek in on us.

When I arrived at the willow tree Isaiah was in the stream cooling off. He had not realized I was there. I sat down on the edge of the bank and just watched him for a few minutes. The water made his muscles shine in the low sunlight that was cast across the water. I had not seen him in light since that day at his grandmother's little house. All I could think was how beautiful he was. He turned around in the water and realized I was sitting there watching him and quickly dunked himself in the water till only his head was visible.

"Why didn't you tell me you were here?"

"I didn't want to disturb you while you were cooling off."

I grinned knowing I was telling a lie. I just wanted to look at him and I knew the second he realized I was there he would hide. I was right. He made me promise to go to my big tree and hide my face until he could get out and dress. I did as he asked. I was not trying to be naughty after all. I just wanted to appreciate him. Maybe it was the artist in me.

I had managed to save him a piece of pie from the party last night and a jar of cold lemonade. He was grateful. He had survived on cornbread and beans for the most part. He would go eat with his grandmother and Cousin Millie some but the reason he was working was to provide money for them to make it through the winter so he didn't want to take from what they had in previsions.

My father did not exactly pay her a big salary. My mother would share some of the canned fruits and vegetables with them that Millie had canned herself for my mother from our garden. They had given her a hen and a rooster one year for Christmas that provided eggs for them. The two chickens were now six chickens and on very special occasions they would have the meat from one they were willing to sacrifice. My sisters gave all the scraps of material from the things they had sown for people to Millie. Millie and her grandmother had made quilts from the scraps to keep warm and had made some clothes for themselves when the pieces were large enough.

He ate the pie in two big bites and drank the cold lemonade as if he were dying of thirst and had not had a drink in days. Mr. Carlton had finally eased up on him and he was beginning to recover from long hard days with little to eat.

"Thank you, Willie. That was so good. I appreciate you thinking of me."

"I think about you all the time Isaiah."

He got up off the bank of the stream and walked to his camp site. He would not look at me.

"Isaiah, I'm not trying to make you angry or embarrassed. I cannot help but say what is on my heart. I do think about you.... all the time. I worry about you and I dream about you every time I close my eyes."

He still did not say anything. He did not look at me. He pulled the tree skirt open to allow me to take my usual seat and once I had crawled in and sat on his blanket he turned and sat there with his back to me just like before. After several minutes of silence passed, he finally spoke.

"I dream of you too Willie."

He spoke in such a whispered voice I could barely hear him. When he spoke again it was not as low but still with obvious caution.

"I dream of you when I sleep, and I dream of you when I am awake. I sing about you when I work, and I pray for you every morning. I pray you will stop coming and then I pray you won't stop coming."

I started to go to him. I wanted to wrap my arms around him. But as soon as he heard me move, he jumped up and moved away.

"I'm sorry Isaiah. Please sit back down."

He sat back down, and we were both quiet for a long while. I noticed he was sitting with his arms all stiff at his sides with his hands flat on the ground. He was bracing himself and probably was not very comfortable. I knew I was taking a chance, but I turned around and moved to where my back was almost touching his.

"Lean on me for support," I suggested.

And he did. I slowly and cautiously placed my hands over the top of his and just let them settle there. I felt him relax after a while and my own heart stopped pounding.

"Willie"

He did not say anything right away.

"Yes Isaiah," I finally replied.

"I would gladly die just to know I can sit here with you like this for a while."

We continued to talk until the early morning. I knew I needed to leave but I did not want to go. We had changed our sitting position twice. Once we just sat side by side leaned up against the tree and eventually held hands. He rubbed his thumb across my hand and traced my fingers for a long time. The first time I hinted I needed to get home before it was discovered I was gone he turned slightly toward me and leaned his head on mine.

He stared into my eyes and I think he wanted to kiss me, but I could tell he was still very cautious about any move he made. Finally, he stood and helped me to my feet. And after a few awkward moments he wrapped his arms around me in a gentle hug. I put my arms around his waist and we just stood there like that for a while. When he dropped his arms and stepped back, I could see he hated to let me leave but we both knew I had to.

"Tomorrow?"

"Yes Isaiah, I will absolutely be back tomorrow."

Tomorrow is a Sunday, but I really did not care. I could not go another day without seeing him.

I am not sure if I was smiling or crying tears of joy on my way home, but I wanted to shout to the top of my lungs that I loved Isaiah Reed. Of course, I did not dare but, on the inside, I was rejoicing.

I closed the journal and lay it in my lap. I suddenly realized I had tears running down my cheeks. I was not crying but just felt so emotional after reading about the love between them. I glanced up toward Nana and she was just watching me.

"I guess you think I'm silly to be all emotional over this," I said.

"No dear, I was just sitting here thinking that I was right in thinking you were the one to share this with. Not once have you judged

me or Isaiah. But you have rejoiced in our joy and I know you will cry over tragedy."

"Wait, what do you mean cry over tragedy? What happens, Nana?"

"That's another journal for a later time. Right now, I am sleepy, and I think it is time for bed."

She got up from her chair and started to walk to the stairs.

"Be sure and put that journal away. It's for your eyes only... remember."

I put it away and stood there looking down at the box of journals. I picked up the next one and started to open it. I was going to go crazy waiting to see what happened. I struggled with my own emotions and finally reminded myself that I had promised to only read as she allowed. I didn't like it but I didn't want to hurt her by breaking my promise. I lay the journal back down and closed the box. As I turned to go upstairs, I saw Nana at the top of the stairs watching me. She smiled and silently mouthed, Thank you, Alex.'

Chapter Seven

A Wedding Without Witnesses

I had another restless night. This summer was supposed to be nothing but fun and freedom for me. I was an adult now and about to embark on a life on my own. College was going to be my new beginning, and no one would control me like I had been controlled in high school. But here I am a total mess only halfway into my summer break. These twelve weeks were my time to just relax and think about nothing before classes started and I would have to be back in the routine of study and schedules.

I thought staying with Nana would be the easiest job of my life. She did not really need me physically to care for her. She was a healthy and independent woman. She was not demanding on my time. I was free to explore the area and she was even willing to provide her own car for my use. But here I am at the sweet age of 18 wanting to spend every waking minute with my grandmother. My first thought each morning was the journal. What would I learn today about Willamina? I realized in my head that the girl in the journal was my dear Nana, but when I would read the journals it was as if it were a totally different person. I felt her pain, her excitement, her joy, maybe even her growing love for Isaiah as if I could put myself in her place. And of course, when I was not thinking about the journals my mind and heart were consumed with thoughts of Mark Armstrong. I was a mess. I looked in my bathroom mirror and cringed. My crazy hair was almost comical. The deep auburn that was my true hair color was mingling with what was left of the fading black color of my rebellion. Plus, the short choppy cut had grown out enough to just look like a joke. The dreaded in between stage when you decide to go from short back to long and it just looks like you do not care. I was also beginning to show signs of my lack of sleep. Dark circles were forming under my eyes and well… I did not exactly look like the hot little fireball I had planned on being when I started college.

"Yeah, girl," I said out loud to the mirror. *"I can see why Mark would be hot for you."* I started to laugh and that shortly turned into tears. I was crying uncontrollably. My Nana walked by my bedroom door in time to see this outburst and immediately came over to me and hugged me close.

"Oh, sweetie what is wrong? Are you ill?"

I could not help it. At her question I started to laugh again. Almost hysterically laughing. I looked at her very confused expression and then back into my mirror. "Well, I do look pretty sick," I said sarcastically and then hiccuped one last chuckle.

She hugged me close and under a little laughter of her own she said maybe we should pay another visit to the hair salon I took you to the other day. All I could do was shake my shaggy head yes as I hiccuped again and again.

By one o'clock that afternoon I was a new person. Nana

had gone all out with the makeover. We had both indulged in the works. Nana had only needed a trim as far as her hair, but she had joined me in facials, make up and getting our nails done. As for my hair. It was the color I had always had, and the cut was wonderful. Not short but more styled to allow my hair to grow long again without looking like a scarecrow. It was suggested I come back for a trim before leaving for college just to be sure the growing process was not too obvious.

"Thank you, Nana," I said for about the fifth time. "You are the best."

"I love you Alex. There is nothing I would not do for you. You look beautiful. Not that you weren't beautiful before… just more so now."

We had a nice lunch before heading home. We went to the nice restaurant she had told me about a few weeks ago. I had worn a sundress to go to the salon and now with the hair, nails and makeup I was getting noticed by a few of the patrons and certainly by our waiter. It was almost embarrassing the way he was falling all over himself to please me. Nana would laugh under her napkin every time he left our table.

When we arrived home, we went in through the kitchen door at the side of the house because we had a few packages and a small bag of leftovers from the restaurant. When we walked in the door Mark was foraging in the refrigerator and did not notice us at first.

"We have a doggie bag from our lunch if you would like dear," Nana offered.

"That sounds great," he replied.

As he turned to face us, he immediately dropped the bottle of soda he had in his hand. When it hit the floor, it sent a fountain of soda all over the kitchen. He was staring at me with wide eyes and his mouth was hanging open as if he were not sure who he was seeing. My Nana remained cool as a cucumber as usual, but I stood there turning beet red and feeling almost shy. I took a step behind her. Nana took my hand and pulled me back to the door and outside.

"Do clean up this mess dear," she instructed "Oh and here is the doggie bag."

She placed it on the counter nearest the door and we made our exit.

"Well that was a little weird. What was his problem, "I asked, trying to sound confused?

"You dear Alex," she proclaimed, "you are his problem." And she smiled with approval. "I guess the real question here is what are you going to do about it?"

"Nana, I'm not here for him, I am here for you. I don't have time for romance."

Nana suddenly got serious and led me to the library where she kept all her paintings. She motioned for me to sit in the window seat and she sat next to me. I could tell she was thinking hard about what she was about to say. I had noticed that she would always get a little quiet and thoughtful when she was serious about something, she needed to make it clear.

"Alex, you are such a special girl. I am so grateful that you have spent this time with me and allowed me to really get to know my youngest grandchild."

"Oh, me too Nana," I started to go on, but she held her hand up to stop me.

"I do not in any way want to force my opinion on you in matters of the heart. You are still so young, and I am guessing as naïve and innocent as I was when I met Isaiah.

But if my past has taught you nothing else, let it teach you not to pass up an opportunity for love. There is no guarantee you will find another like it. I do not know how you feel about Mark. You may be completely uninterested in him and that is fine. But don't use me as an excuse to hide from what is in your heart."

She stood and kissed the top of my head which had become her habit.

"I'm going to take a nap because we have another journal to read tonight and it will be mentally exhausting for me. When I wake, we will have a light dinner and settle in for a long reading session. If you are okay with that of course."

I shook my head yes.

"Thank you, Nana," I said again but not meaning the makeover this time.

Once she was up the stairs I sat there for a long while just thinking about what she had said. I looked at all the paintings in the room of that beautiful willow tree. I thought about Willie and Isaiah and the love that was growing between them. I knew I felt something for Mark, but I was not sure yet if it was love. I was absolutely attracted to him. But I did not want the emotions I had bottled up for the lovers in the journal to confuse my feelings for Mark. That would not be fair to him. I decided if he said anything to me about his feelings I would explain as much as I could about my uncertainty and suggest we go very slow. After all that would not be a rejection… just a hesitation on the side of caution.

I went upstairs myself and changed into my comfortable jeans and a tee shirt. I loved the makeover but decided to wash my face and take a nap as well. I slept the most wonderfully peaceful sleep I had in days. I didn't have a single bad dream or worrisome thought. I do not think I dreamed at all. I woke up a few hours later and realized Nana was already downstairs preparing dinner.

I made my way down to help and found Mark was helping her. I had a strange feeling that the two of them may have been in a conversation about me because when I opened the door to the kitchen, they both got quiet and looked very guilty. I wondered if Nana was trying to give Mark the same type of advice she had given me earlier. He joined us for dinner and the two of us were left to clean the kitchen.

"You want to wash or dry," he asked.

"I'll wash," I answered. Then because I can be a tiny bit sarcastic at times I added,

"I don't think we will need to sweep the floor tonight. It appears to have been thoroughly cleaned from corner to corner very recently."

I grinned and plunged my hands into the sink to clean up the few dishes. We had only had sandwiches and chips so there were only a few things to wash. No need to use the dishwasher for such a small load.

"Your hair looks really nice," he said.

"Thank you."

That was all it took to be back as the comfortable friends we had been while watching the movie. No mention of the awkward moment in the doorway or the response he had at seeing me after the makeover. We both seemed to have the understanding without words that we needed to go slow. We would just be the best of friends for now.

Once the kitchen was in order, he went in the front room to tell Nana goodnight. He then gave a slight wave and smiled at me as he left out the French doors at the end of the hall nearest the pool. I was surprised he had not hung around and talked for a while. He usually did but was quick to leave tonight.

"Nana, did you say something to Mark?"

"I didn't tell him what we were doing but I did explain we had a project you were helping me with this summer that required a great deal of your time and was of a very personal and private nature. Mark has known me a long time and he is not the type to pry into someone's business if asked not to. He trusts that when the time is right, I will tell him what he needs to know.

I explained to him that neither of us was trying to avoid or exclude him but there would be times when we needed to be left to work on the project alone and undisturbed. He promised he would always leave once we were finished with dinner or even before if I gave him notice. He is such a good person. He also said to let you know that you were always welcome at the pool house if you wanted to hang out or watch another movie."

She turned her head in my direction and gave the most devilish grin. I blushed as was my downfall as a red head. No hiding anything from her if I could not control my habit of turning crimson when she read me like a book.

"I'll keep that in mind," I said, trying but failing to appear unimpressed by the offer.

"Good," she replied. "So where should we read tonight?"

I gave it some thought.

"How about in the library? We can get comfortable on that couch in the corner and I'll get your afghan and a foot stool from the den. I think it would be nice to place the paintings of the willow tree pointing in our direction. It will almost be like they are witness to us."

"I like that idea," she whispered softly.

I went about making things ready. I got her afghan and a small ottoman that was in the den so she could put her feet up. I would be fine in the corner of the couch with my legs folded in a crisscross position or stretched out on the couch. I was only 5'3" so I did not take up a lot of space. I made sure I had a bottle of water and I made Nana a cup of tea. I put 4 cookies on a plate in case we needed a little snack. We got into our pajamas because we expected a long night. Then just in case we needed it, I had placed a box of tissues on the floor for easy access. She sat down and made herself comfortable. I did the same. She handed me the next journal and as I reached to take it, she placed her hand over top of mine.

"Thank you, Alex. For being so diligent to make this right for me. I see your love in your actions and it means the world to me."

I smiled and nodded. I was afraid if I said anything I would choke on tears. I took a long drink from the water bottle. Wiggled a little to get in just the right position and opened Journal 5.

July 6, 1941

I could hardly sit still during our church service and I inhaled my lunch like a starving work hand. I rushed through any chores my mother had planned for me and when my father wanted me to go for a ride with him on our horses I had to agree or draw suspicion. I used the time with him to talk about how I was really inspired to draw in the summer while everything was so lush and green and wondered if it would be okay if I went to a spot near our stream to draw early this evening.

He asked me if I had orders for drawings and I told him not exactly, but I was sure if I showed them around that I would find interested people. He had agreed to let me go right after dinner but made me promise to be careful and to get home in time to get enough rest before Monday morning chores came around. He said he would not have me working around the ranch in a daze half asleep. All I could think was... Oh, father, if you only knew how many times in the last few weeks, I have had to catch a nap in the loft of the barn just to make it through the day.

I had not even told Isaiah how many times I had leaned on the pitch fork and dozed off while mucking the stalls and had been so exhausted one day that I actually fell into the troth while slopping our hogs. Talk about your nasty awakening. I had to sneak off to the pond and clean up, but it took a hot bath at home to get rid of the smell.

I will father... and thank you.

As soon as dinner was over and the dishes were done, I gathered my pad and pencils and climbed up on my horse. This was one time I could chance taking her because father had given me permission. When I cleaned the kitchen, I managed to hide some cold fried chicken and a dinner roll in my pocket. One thing about overalls. Lots of hiding places. Isaiah would not be expecting me, and I hoped he would not be working. We would have several hours before it was too dark to really see each other. When I got close, I stopped and climbed down from my horse.

I led her through an area downstream that was not as overgrown and let her drink from the stream. I was not going to tie her to a tree. She was a good horse and had been with me a few years so she would stay close and could enjoy the lush grass near the stream. Just as I started to walk to my willow tree, I heard Isaiah singing. He was singing loud and it was beautiful. He was praising God in song and it made the singing from our meeting this morning sound very unworthy.

Our little congregation had several people with good voices and that was not the problem. But you could feel the joy and love Isaiah had for the Lord in every note. I felt more like I was at church right now than I had this morning. I made my way closer and noticed he was reading his Bible.

Once he saw me, he motioned for me to come over. He did not try to cover up what he was doing. He had no shame for his love of God's word. I sat beside him and he continued reading out loud for several more minutes. Then he took my hand and bowed his head to pray. This was his church service I had walked in on. He told me even if he had to work on Sunday once he was done, he had his time with God as was commanded. That began a habit of us reading together and studying the Bible every day and I looked forward to it.

July 20, 1941

The days have passed so quickly and suddenly days have become weeks. We had studied the Bible together many times and I had attended at least one more of his worship sessions on a Sunday. We talked and talked about absolutely everything. While we talked, I worked on drawings so if my father had asked, I would have drawings to show him to justify my leaving so early in the evenings to go to the stream.

I refused to work on the drawing of myself Isaiah had wanted. I only worked on it at home in my room. He has protested about it saying he had paid his good hard-earned money for it and should be allowed to see it. I told him not before it's fin-

ished, and he would pout for about a second and then smile and tell me it could never compare to the beauty he was looking at right now.

On Sunday July 20th I asked Isaiah if he would take me in the stream and baptize me. I had been baptized in our church when I was twelve. I think I only did it because my sisters had decided to during a gospel meeting and I got caught up in the emotion of it. But now after I studied with Isaiah, I had developed such a love for God and his son Jesus that I wanted to give my life to God completely.

When we came up out of the water, we embraced and cried together. Later I could not help but think how dangerous it had been to stand there in his embrace in broad daylight for anyone to see. But if we had both died that very minute, we would have been the happiest saints to enter Heaven's doors. We sat together under our willow tree and he wrapped his blanket around me until I was dry.

I wasn't really cold because the day had been hot but being wet had given me a chill and the fact that he wanted to cuddle me to warm me was so sweet that I didn't want it to end. Finally, the heat won out and I had to shed the blanket. I was glad when after I tossed the blanket aside, he put his arm back around me. I could have sat there forever with him. Together under our willow tree.

July 24, 1941

As I had done every day since the 5th of July, I made my way to the stream and to the man who I loved. I had not said the words, but I wanted to. I think he felt the same way about me, so I was trying to hold out until he said it first. He had not kissed me either. I think he is still so afraid someone will see us, and our world would end in tragedy. When I came near to our spot, I saw him sitting near the stream with his face buried in his hands. Something was wrong.

"Isaiah, what's wrong?" He got up as soon as he saw me and rushed over to me and swept me up in his arms. He buried his face in my neck and I could tell his face was wet with tears.

"Isaiah, you're scaring me. What has happened?"

We sat under our tree hidden by its skirt. He had not built a fire to give us light and he had not propped the tree skirt to one side to form a door. He sat against the trunk of the tree and motioned for me to come beside him.

"Willie, you remember I told you I was planning on enlisting in the Army at the end of the summer." I nodded yes without speaking. "What I had not mentioned was that I had arranged with my cousin and a friend to all join. I received a letter from them today. It arrived at my grandmother's house and Millie brought it to me. They are on their way to meet with me. I am supposed to join them in Tennessee, and we will make our way to Fort Knox in Kentucky. That base is forming a black battalion."

We sat in silence. I thought my heart would explode and I wanted to burst into tears, but I didn't want to make this harder on him. I could tell he was struggling.

"When will you have to leave?"

"In order to get there in time I will have to leave the morning of August 1st"

"A WEEK! WE ONLY HAVE ONE WEEK?" I could no longer contain it. I burst into tears and buried my head in his chest. "Isaiah, I love you. How can I let you go? How will I go on without seeing you every day?

I cried and pleaded and begged and cried some more and he just sat there holding me in his arms and looking lost.

"Willie, would you consider… would you do me the honor of

being my wife?" I pulled away and just stared at him. This was not a funny joke. I mean we cannot allow ourselves to be seen by anyone and he says he wants to marry me.

"Isaiah, who would marry us. We can't even let our families know we love each other for fear of death and you think they would just let us waltz up to a Justice of the Peace or a Judge and ask them to perform the ceremony of a black man and a white woman."

"Of course not. But I do not care if men are okay with it. I know God is okay with it. He brought us together, don't you see. He blessed this union when you accepted him into your life. I just know it is his will. We can have a ceremony of our own under the stars. Millie knows something is going on with us so I will talk to her about being our witness. Willie, I must know you will be here when I come back. That you will be my wife and you will wait for me. I just know that when this war is over, and the blacks and whites fight together for the greater good.... Well things will change and in a few years our love will be accepted."

I may have been the biggest fool on earth to believe he was right but my love for him won out over any common sense and I said yes.

"Yes, my love, I will be your wife." Our joy though short lived shone brighter than the stars. We made our plans. I spent as much time with him as possible and we talked about the future we dreamed of. That one day we could walk hand in hand down the street with no fear of those who would hate us. A world where the paint on the outside did not cover the treasures on the inside and a man or woman was measured by the heart like God measures us.

July 29, 1941

Our time was growing short. He had talked to Millie who now gave me harsh looks at home. I know she is just worried about her cousin. She knows what could happen to him if we are found out. We sat and held each other every minute we had. He had finally kissed me and so now if we were not talking, we were kissing. How would I ever be able to let him leave? I tried not to dwell on it because I wanted his memory of me to be happy and not me crumpled up in a mess of sobs and pleadings.

"Willie, what is your middle name?"

"Oh, it's no better than my first name. My middle name is Beulah." I waited for the burst of laughter I assumed would follow but it never came. He was smiling as if he liked the name.

"In the Bible the name Beulah means 'married'." I looked at him as if I thought he was making it up, but he continued.

"And do you know where that information is found," he asked while smiling even bigger?

"No. Where is it found?"

"Isaiah 62:4. And I know this because it was my mother's name and she taught me the verse. You see it was meant to be."

He asked me if when he wrote to me it would be alright if he addressed me as Beulah in his letters. I wanted to know why. He said if there were any jokester in his platoon, and there usually are, a letter he was writing expressing his love and devotion was addressed to Willie… Well, I have enough to deal with being a black man. I don't know if they would believe me if I assured them that Willie was a woman. I had to laugh. Sure, address me as Beulah or just maybe my dear wife.

He had one more request and it would be a hard one to keep but he did not want me to come for a visit the next day. He said he needed to spend one day with his elderly grandmother before he left.

"I want to tell her about you," he explained.

I know I looked at him with concern on that decision, but he promised me she would understand.

"She may not approve, he said, but she will love you because I do. If you ever need her, she will be there for you."

AUGUST 2, 1941

July 31st was my wedding day. I have been married two days now, but I have not been ready to write about it. I remember thinking as I prepared to go meet up with Isaiah how much I hate that I cannot share this day with my family. My father cannot walk me down the aisle, and my sisters will not be my bridesmaids. My mother will not help me prepare myself for the ceremony by putting little flowers in my hair or putting my great grandmothers' pearls around my neck. But I would not allow this to make this day any less than perfect.

It was a Thursday and normally I would be expected home and ready for chores early in the morning but I had already made up my mind that I would stay with my new husband until he had to leave and I would watch him until he was out of sight before I tried to come back to the ranch. I would try to make up a good excuse and if I got punished for staying out it would be nothing compared to the heart break I would be feeling once Isaiah had to go. I had spent a large part of the day finishing my drawing of myself to give him.

I had used my pastels to color the drawing. My hair would be auburn and my eyes blue. My dress was the green sundress he had liked so well, and I had a ribbon flowing down my hair. I was very proud of the job I had done. In my hand I had drawn a short branch from the willow tree and in the background was the stream. I rolled it up so as not to make creases in it and placed it in a metal cigar holder my father had in his desk. He would be furious if he knew I had taken it, but I wanted the picture safe from water but small enough to conceal.

I couldn't risk being seen in my prettiest Sunday dress heading to the field so I dressed in my overalls and carefully folded my dress small enough to fit in my hidden pocket on the inside of the bib on the overalls. I usually keep my sketch paper and pencils there but not today. I had taken time to wash my hair the night before. This was usually done on Saturdays, but I hoped no one would notice.

I kept it in my hat well-hidden until I was near the stream. When I saw Isaiah, my heart jumped. He had on a pair of clean slacks and a button-down shirt. He had put a lot of effort in cleaning his dirty work boots and he even had on a bow tie. He explained it had belonged to his grandfather and his grandmother had insisted he wear it.

"You look very handsome," I told him. He looked at me in my overalls and smiled.

"If you would please give me some privacy I need to change." I started to go under the willow tree skirt to change but he stopped me.

"Not there please… go behind that bush there and I will turn my back."

That is when Millie walked down from her house to our clearing. She did not look very happy. She walked up to me and held out her hand.

"Let me hold your dress for you while you get out of those

work clothes."

"Thank you, Millie. Please don't be angry at me Millie," I pleaded. "I truly love Isaiah with all my heart."

"I'm not exactly mad, Miss. Willamina. But I am very afraid for Isaiah. And for you cause if people find out they will kill you both. May even kill me for being witness to it."

I understood her fear but I loved him enough to take the risk. I hope and pray he is right about things changing by the time the war is over.

When I told Isaiah, he could turn around now he turned and looked at me for a long while without saying a word.

"Well, ain't you gonna tell her she's pretty," Millie scolded.

"No," Isaiah responded. "I'm going to tell her she is the most beautiful sight I have ever seen in my entire life."

"Thank you, sir," I sang back.

Millie was growing anxious, so we decided the time had come to start.

The sky was starting to grow dark and the stars were coming out. The moon was not as bright as I hoped but the stars were like a cathedral ceiling. There had to be thousands of them being witness to our union. We stood facing each other and holding hands. Millie asked what she was supposed to do. Isaiah told her nothing… you are our witness… so witness quietly. She folded her arms in a huff and stood there for a minute doing an exaggerated job of staring us down. Isaiah gave her a pleading look and she gave in to his silent plea and relaxed.

Isaiah began with a prayer. He asked God to bless our union and that we serve him all our days. He promised to be my husband till death should part us and he asked me if I would promise to be his wife till death should part us. I said I would. There were no rings because we had no money for them but also because we did not dare risk wearing one.

"Willamina Beulah Pettigrew and Isaiah Franklin Reed I now pronounce before God and this witness that you are husband and wife."

We smiled and he kissed me.

"Franklin is your middle name? That is so unfair. You get two good names."

He laughed a little and then cleared his throat.

"I have a gift for you," he announced.

He began to sing. He had written a song as my gift. It was the most beautiful song I had ever heard. Words expressing his great love for me and the true gift from God that I was to him. I clung to every word. To every note. I felt as if my heart would explode from the love I had for this man. His voice was as pure as I had ever heard and the words seem to drift straight up to Heaven's door. When he finished, he reached over and tenderly wiped a tear from my cheek.

"I will love you forever Mrs. Reed."

Poor Millie could no longer hold it in. She burst into tears and fell on us blubbering how happy she was for us and how much she loved that we had found each other. Isaiah had to walk her part of the way home to try and console her.

He had made me promise not to go under the tree until he returned. When he came back, he came over and kissed me again. We were both a little nervous.

"I have a gift for you too," I said and took out the cigar tube.

"You got me a cigar?"

"NO silly, look inside."

He pulled out the picture and unrolled it. His eyes grew wet and I could see he loved it.

"Thank you, Willie. I will treasure it always and it will keep you with me while I'm away."

Finally, he pulled the branches to the side and invited me into the tree shelter.

Under the skirt he had prepared a bed using straw from the field. It was not dry hay yet but still green and softer. He had obviously borrowed a quilt from his grandmother to cover it with and another one to cover us with.

"The quilts are wedding gifts from my grandmother and Millie," he said.

There was a Cole oil lamp turned down very dimly and a pitcher of water with two cups. Millie had made a tiny cake for us that sat on a plate in front of the water.

"This is perfect," I said. "I love it and I love you."

He motioned for me to sit down on the quilt and then he sat beside me. He started to kiss me softly. He was nervous but aware of how little time we had as husband and wife before he had to leave me. I was painfully aware of our time limit as well and decided I would just have to be brave. "Isaiah, it's okay. I love you and I am not afraid. I'm your wife and you are my husband."

He ran his fingers through my hair and rubbed it between his fingers.

"I have wanted to do that since you fell out of that tree."

We both laughed at the memory and relaxed a little. I reached over and untied his bow tie then started to unbutton his shirt. I had seen him without his shirt before. Had sketched him several times. But this was so different. My heart was pounding so hard in my chest I knew he could see it move. I was having trouble taking a breath. He reached over and placed his hand over my heart. He could feel me tremble.

"Please don't be afraid, my love, my sweet Willamina. I will be so very gentle with you and I will not do anything if you ask me not to."

My trembling was not fear as he had thought. It was desire and excitement.

"Isaiah, please love me," I whispered and lay down on the quilt. And he did.

We held each other all that night. He loved me as often as our physical bodies would allow. We observed each other and explored each other with gentle kisses and caresses as the dim light from the lantern glowed over us.

"You are like cream," he said as he ran his hand down my body memorizing every curve, I suspected so he could bring it to mind later when he needed to recall this night.

"And you my husband are the coffee dark and rich and warm waiting for the cream to be poured in and mingled."

That is how it looked to me as I wrapped around him, each time he made love to me. Like cream being poured into black coffee. I would probably blush at the breakfast table every time they poured their cream into their coffee and my parents would wonder what was wrong with me.

Neither of us wanted to bring it up but the sky was beginning to show signs of daybreak.

"Willie, I have a favor to ask of you. I want to make love to you one more time and I would like you to try and sleep afterward. In a couple of hours, I will have to leave, and I can't say goodbye. I want to remember you laying there on our bed. Your silky cream skin naked in the dim light. That image will sustain me through any battle I face. Knowing I can come home to you and love you again."

With tears in my eyes I agreed to his request. He made love to me one more time and when we were done, I felt the tears as they rolled down his face on my neck. He turned me over to my side and lay next to me stroking my hair.

"Sing my song again," I asked. "Oh, and what is the title of my song?"

"Beulah's Song," he answered and we both had to smile.

He sang it to me again very softly like a lullaby and as he sang, he continued to stroke my hair. I had not realized I had fallen to sleep until I heard Millie calling my name.

"Miss. Willamina. You best get up now and go home. It's almost time Mr. William be getting up and he best not find you still out."

I woke up with a jolt. I pulled the quilt up to my chin and realized I could still smell him on it.

"He's gone," I asked her. "Yes-um been gone at least an hour."

I began to cry, and I guess Millie took pity on me because she crawled on the quilt with me and rocked me back and forth like a baby. I washed my face in the stream and got dressed in my overalls and work shirt. "Millie, would you take these beautiful quilts to your house for today. I will come get them tonight so no one sees. And please do not wash them. She understood why and agreed to keep them safe for me.

I made my way home and managed to crawl into bed just as my father knocked on my door to see if I was awake.

"I'm not feeling well today, father. May I please stay in bed just a little while?"

One thing that all us girls knew about our father was his unwillingness to argue with his daughters if they did not feel well. Our mother had not only taught us this little secret but had used it herself on occasion. If we said we did not feel well and held our stomach he makes the assumption it had something to do with our monthly visitor and left without argument. I had never stooped to that low of trickery before, but I just could not leave this bed today. Not because I was tired but because of my broken heart. I wanted to just lay here today and remember his touch and his scent until they faded before

I even dared bathe.

Chapter Eight

You Were Warned

I closed the journal and just sat there looking at it. I knew I had tears in my eyes, but I wanted to get them under control before I looked at Nana. The pain she must have felt. Nana suddenly reached over and placed her hands on the top of mine and I took a deep cleansing breath before looking into her eyes.

"Oh Nana, I am so sorry. I don't know what to say. How did you ever stand it?"

When I looked at her the expression was one of pride instead of the sorrow I was expecting. I was confused and I knew she realized it.

"Alex, I was in more pain than I can possibly put in words. And would experience even more pain though I did not know it then. But your reaction has made me so proud that it almost overrides the pain."

"How? What do you mean?"

"You have read this story of young love. You have witnessed what the young lovers went through and how they handled all the challenges of that time… and not one time did you judge me. You never said anything or even showed in your actions any hatred for Isaiah because of the color of his skin. I know that compared to how things were in 1941 things are much better now. But I know that it is still a challenge for many to accept people for what is on the inside. Many still hate others simply because of the color of their skin. I just knew you would not care. You are such a lovely soul."

I blushed a little from her praise, but I was so happy that she was proud of me. I was proud of myself, too.

"Thank you, Nana. So, can we get started on the next journal? I mean if you are not too tired. It's not that late and I'm really anxious to see how Willie… I mean you… handle Isaiah's being gone. "

She sat there silently for several minutes. I thought maybe she was trying to decide if she felt like staying up later or maybe trying to think of what she needed to do before we continued. Finally, she looked up and I realized she had been trying to get her emotions under control. Her cheeks were wet from tears that had traveled down them and her eyes showed such deep sorrow.

"Alex, I realize that this is all new for you. I know that even though your heart knows this is all about me personally it is still hard to separate it from your curious mind. I understand and appreciate that. But these journals are my history. They are the memories of my heart from long ago. The pain and sorrow that I have when remembering these events has lay dormant for the most part for years but it has never completely left and reading these is like having a wound you thought you had scarred over suddenly burst open. I am dealing with my broken heart all over again. I need to deal with this a little while before I can go forward with the next journal. I hope you understand. I think I will go to bed now and I hope to return to them very soon."

She stood up and seemed to be a little unsteady on her feet. I jumped up to support her, but she smiled and assured me she was fine.

"I have just been sitting too long. I'll be fine."

She kissed the top of my head and then walked over to one of her paintings of her beloved willow tree. She reached out and lovingly touched it as if the newly married Isaiah and Willie were there just behind its branches.

"Goodnight Nana."

"Goodnight sweet Alex."

I cleaned up the library and just as she had done, I went over to the picture and just stared at it. I had looked at these pictures a few times now but they all seemed to be similar. This time I really looked closely. The one she had touched was a night scene. The sky had a thousand stars. I noticed something that I had not before. Through the willow branches was a dim light. It barely showed through the branches, but it was there, and almost unnoticeable was the corner of a quilt sticking out from under the tree.

Only in her heart could Nana see the young lovers who had one perfect night together. I started to examine the other portraits. One had a man in the stream, but he was hidden in shrubs and trees as if someone were looking from a distance. Another had a campfire that had almost burnt all the way down and it seemed like an early morning picture. Beside the old campfire was a Bible opened to Isaiah. Each portrait seemed to be a memory hidden for her heart only. No one else would know what any of it meant. I am sure my dad and aunts had seen them before. Probably Papa Sam had looked at his wife's work and been curious as to why she chose to paint that tree and stream over and over.

I suddenly thought about the unfinished painting on the front porch. The one she had been working on all summer. I turned out the light and closed the library door. The hallway upstairs was dark, and all seemed quiet so I assumed Nana was asleep. I eased the front door open and went out to the screened in front porch. I had a flashlight so as not to draw too much attention and carefully uncovered the painting. It took my breath.

She was painting a portrait of the young couple standing in the stream holding each other in an embrace so pure and sweet my heart ached and again my eyes teared. I wondered if it was her memory of the day Isaiah had baptized her. Or maybe just her interpretation of how things should have been. That she and the man she loved so completely could have stood there in the open without fear.

I covered the portrait back up and eased back into the house locking the door behind me. I needed to do something other than go to my room. My body was tired from all the emotions of the evening and I would have to try and deal with that before I could rest. I went out to the pool. It is usually dark because Nana never had lighting put around the pool. Only the back-porch light and the light outside of the pool house gave any illumination of the area. I sat down pulling the legs of my pajamas up to my knees and hung my feet over the side of the pool into the water. It was not as cold as I had expected. It was June and very hot during the day, so the water never cooled down that much at night. I was deep in my thoughts when I heard the pool house door open.

"Mind if I join you?"Mark asked.

"Sure," I answered "pull up a seat"

We both laughed at my feeble attempt to be funny and he sat down on the concrete beside me and put his feet in the water near mine. We sat there without talking for a while. He seemed to have something on his mind as well.

"Alex, I wanted to tell you something before I tell Nana. I did not want it to be a surprise to you. The Medical school I had planned to attend in August has a limited space for students during summer break which is why I had been able to come home for the summer instead of continuing without a break. That had always been my plan all along. To just keep on without stopping so I could finish sooner. You know the sooner I'm finished the sooner I can support myself and not be a burden on Nana financially."

I guess my brain was numb from the roller coaster I had been on because it did not register at first what he was trying to tell me.

"Anyway, they had a student drop out because of a personnel emergency and so they offered his spot to me. I will be leaving Sunday in order to start classes on Monday. I wanted to make sure you knew that I would still come home when possible to do work for Nana and if she needs me, I wanted to be sure you knew how to reach me. She can be a little stubborn and might not want to bother me with things so please be sure and call me anytime."

He sat there looking at me as I stared back at him like a zombie who had not understood his language. After a few seconds it became a little awkward for him and he shrugged his shoulders, raised his hands and said, *"Earth to Alex?"*

That was the final straw. I began to cry. Not just any little cry but the big ugly cry. The ugly red head cry that I usually avoided with all my might. My eyebrows, eyelids and nose suddenly became so flaming red that I looked as if I had a terrible sunburn that only reached those areas. My nose began to run like someone had turned the faucet on full stream. The tears were like small waterfalls that could have possibly filled the pool another foot deeper than it was. And while poor Mark looked on confused and mortified, I wailed out in my sobbing voice…

"WHY DOES EVERYONE HAVE TO LEAVE?"

It was dramatic, I know and though I had no doubt I would miss seeing Mark around the house I also knew I would be leaving for classes in a few short weeks myself. I was just still reeling from the heartache I had read about in the journal. But of course, I was sworn to secrecy and could not tell this to Mark who now looked so unsure of what to say. I know he thought I was more upset about his leaving than expected. Possibly thought, *This crazy girl has real issues.*

"I promise I will come home as much as I can. Please Alex, I didn't think you would care this much."

He continued to plead with me to understand and was putting his arm around me to console me. I continued to blubber out of control and could not form the words to tell him I was fine. I suppose out of desperation to shut me up he did something very unexpected… He kissed me.

Well, it worked. I stopped my hysterical crying and looked stunned at him… then I kissed him back. It was not exactly the first kiss I wanted it to be. I had to give him credit though. If he could kiss like that when my face was wet with tears and snot, he had real talent. Once we parted from the kiss I just gazed into those beautiful gray eyes. He truly was a handsome man. Nana had told me his dad was black which explained the wavy hair and his beautiful bronzed complexion. And those lips… those full, soft, warm and sexy lips that framed his smile so perfectly. I guess he thought the look on my face was anguish instead of the desire it was intended to be since he turned his head and looked toward the pool house.

I guess I will need to work on my skills, I thought.

I looked down so as not to embarrass myself any further. Again, he promised he would be back often, and he would miss me. I know the right thing would have been to explain that I had been upset about something unrelated to his leaving and he just came along at a bad time. I should have thanked him for the kiss but said it was not necessary. And I probably should not have kissed him back. I'm not sure why I did that. I probably should not have enjoyed it as much as I did either. What I did do was stand up and politely tell him goodnight as if he were dropping me at my door after a lovely night out and walking into the house and up to my room. Once I was in my room, I attempted to peek out of the window to see if he was still there. He was standing in front of the door to the pool house with one hand on the doorknob.

He was just staring at his hand as if unsure of how to work the thing. I felt so stupid and I knew I had messed up his thinking for the night. Possible for the week. I probably should apologize tomorrow. I couldn't tell him the entire story, but I needed to come up with an explanation for my bizarre behavior. I needed to do these things but what I really wanted to do was to kiss him again.

When I finally came downstairs the next morning, I checked first thing to see if Nana was out on the porch. She was not there, and she was not in the kitchen. I had checked her room before coming down, so I knew she was not there either. Her car was not gone so unless she had gone somewhere with someone she had to be here somewhere. I was not ready to face Mark but I needed to be sure she was okay, so I stepped out of the French doors to see if Nana or Mark were out there.

I noticed the garage door was open and the golf cart was gone. She must be at the stream, I thought. I started to walk down the path when I saw Mark walking back toward the house from that direction. When we got close enough to be heard he told me he had talked to Nana this morning and she said she was fine with my starting classes early.

"I'm not sure what's going on between you two, but she was acting almost as strangely as you were last night. Minus all the ugly crying that is."

I could not help but blush at that and he smiled.

"She asked me to take her to the stream and leave the golf cart. She said for me to tell you to meet her at the tree and that you would know what she meant."

I nodded and started to walk that direction. As I passed him, he reached out and grabbed my arm. It startled me and I jumped back.

"Alex, I don't know what's going on with Nana, but I do know the two of you are working on something together. She told me that much. And obviously whatever it is has both of you upset and emotional."

He grinned at me then and said as much as he would like to think I was that upset at his leaving he knew that was not what I reacted so strongly to last night.

"And after seeing Nana this morning I know that it has nothing to do with me," he added. Please let me know if either of you need anything. She is like my own grandmother and I love her dearly. I don't want her hurt."

"Neither do I," I replied almost in defense of his remark. I knew he wasn't implying I had done anything, but he did sound like he thought I could control it.

I again started to walk away but he stopped me again.

"What is it now," I snapped.

"I'm sorry you are upset, and I am sorry if you are mad about last night … but Alex, I am most certainly not sorry I kissed you. And I hope to do it again soon."

He dropped my arm and walked away. I could not talk. Just stood there like a crazy person. But I was thinking that I was not sorry I kissed him back either and I could promise I would do it again.

I made my way to the stream. I saw that the golf cart had been parked in the same spot as last time. I made my way through the trees and shrubs until I saw the clearing. After reading the story of Isaiah and his Beulah last night I felt like it was some sort of sacred place. Like I should remove my shoes before entering or something. I saw Nana standing near the stream looking out toward the path from Mr. Carlton's farm.

I think sometimes she expects to see Isaiah walking toward her all dirty and tired from his days labor singing her song. I bet in her dreams she sees him coming home to a little house next to the willow tree where they have lived happily. He would wash off in the stream while she made dinner. They would probably read a while from his Bible and have a prayer before turning in for the night. And Isaiah would make love to her until they drifted off to sleep in each other's arms.

"Alex! Alex… do you not hear me calling you?"

"I'm sorry Nana. I got a little lost in thought. Are you okay? Why did you want me to come back to the stream?"

I walked over and we both sat down on the bank. I began tossing little stones into the water and waited for her to explain. I had grown accustomed to giving her freedom to choose the pace of this journey. I tried never to rush her or push her into quick responses.

"I needed to feel close to Isaiah today," she finally said. "I used to come here quite often. When I was young. I would even bring my children here to play in the stream. A few times we would fish and build a fire to cook them on. I am a little ashamed to admit this but at times I would pretend the children belonged to Isaiah and I."

I had been right to think she dreamed of what could have been, but she seemed to be ashamed she had admitted it to me.

"Alex, I loved your Papa Sam with all my heart. If he had not come along when he did, I do not know what would have become of me. I tried to be a good wife to him. And we were very happy. I did not pretend the children belonged to Isaiah because I regretted that I married Samuel. I just was never able to mourn the loss of my first love. As much as I loved Samuel, I loved Isaiah too. I never stopped loving him even until this day. I always felt guilty for that. Like I was cheating on Samuel with Isaiah but also cheating on Isaiah with Samuel.

It is not easy to have two men hold every inch of your heart. The constant battle wears on a person. Once the children were older, I stopped coming here for the most part, but I still come occasionally. I have never once missed coming here on July 31st. I came here to celebrate our anniversary. Next month we will have been married 57 years."

She looked at me and smiled and walked over to the willow tree. She stood there playing with the long branches that danced in the breeze.

"I can still feel his touch. Still taste his kiss. I still see our bodies tangled together.... cream into coffee," she whispered. "Alex, the next journal will be the hardest one to read. I think I will wait a day or two before we start it but I wanted to come here tonight to visit my good memories. I hope you understand why I need to wait before starting."

"I do understand Nana. I will be ready when you are."

"I suppose Mark told you he will be headed to classes Sunday."

"Yes, he told me. I will miss having him around but I'm excited for him."

She gave a knowing grin. As if she knew more than we had told her.

We sat there for a long while talking about many things and nothing at all. Just being there in that place resting our spirits and watching the lightning bugs flash in the summer sky.

"Nana, I love you," I finally said.

"I love you too Alex."

She stood there looking under the tree as if she could see them perfectly. Isaiah and his Beulah loving each other under the patch work quilt.

"Let's go back to the house," she finally suggested. "It's been a long couple of days."

I drove us home and Mark was waiting by the pool house for our return. He helped Nana out of the golf cart and led her arm in arm to the house. She kissed his cheek and gave him a little hug. Then went in and headed toward the stairs.

"Thank you," I said.

He peeked to be sure Nana was out of sight then reached down and took my face in his hands.

"You were warned," he said.

And he kissed me a long lovely wonderful kiss.

Chapter Nine

The Ache of Arms That Cannot Hold

What is it that the song says? Rainy days and Mondays get you down. It had started raining late Saturday night and had rained off and on since then. Well add to that the fact that Mark left yesterday for medical school and Nana has stayed on her porch painting for most of the day and you will know my mood.

Mark will be attending The Medical College of Georgia in Athens which is only 97 miles from Payne Georgia so he could visit as often as his schoolwork load would allow. In three months, I would be attending classes in Macon Georgia and chances are we will not see each other very often if at all. I was working hard to convince myself it did not matter.

It was just a kiss or maybe twelve and well, not a big deal.

I was completely sure in my head that there was nothing to it and he would have to strain to even remember what I looked like by the time we were both finished with school. My head was sure of it, but my heart was still struggling with it.

I know Nana is dealing with a lot right now so I absolutely will not bug her about the journals but if she doesn't come around soon, I may jump in the pool with a large rock tied to me. I keep telling myself that it cannot possibly be as bad as my imagination makes it out to be. The crazy ideas of what could have happened. I knew she had married Papa Sam when she was very young. I think dad had told me she was only seventeen when they married, and Isaiah had left for the Army when she was fifteen so what could have happened in such a short time.

The possibilities were so hard for me to think about. I sat in the library for a while, listening to the rain, staring at the portraits and eating ice cream and cookies. If I did not get some answers soon, I would be as big as a house.

I heard the front door open and Nana called for me. I jumped up so quickly I almost dropped my bowl of ice cream. Then when I reached for the bowl, I bumped the portrait of two dogs someone had paid her to paint. Thank goodness I caught both the bowl and the painting before they hit the floor.

"Coming Nana!"

"Are you alright, dear? You seem flushed."

"I'm fine," I said in a less than convincing voice. "What's up?"

She said she was ready for a little lunch and then if I wanted to, we could get started on the next journal. I tried to play it cool…

Oh, no, I didn't. I screamed and fist pumped and hugged her.

"OH, YES!"

She looked at me as if I had lost my mind.

"Oh, Nana I am so sorry. I know this is hard for you. I have just been waiting all day hoping… I mean wondering if you were okay to go on. It is up to you if we start back of course."

She burst into laughter. She laughed and laughed for a long while and I wasn't sure if that was a good thing or if her cheese had slipped off her cracker.

"I'm sorry dear. I know I shouldn't laugh but believe me I needed that. I have been mopping around for four days and the release that laughter brought was just what I needed. Thank you, Alex, for your wonderful excitement and enthusiasm."

We went into the kitchen where I had left the mess I had made. A day of binge snacking was evident everywhere. An empty ice cream carton sat in a sticky mess on the counter. The cookie sheet from the slice and bake cookies I had made and the spoon and wrapper where I had eaten the cookie dough I had not baked. Chip bags and an empty soda bottle lay on top of an overflowing trash can that needed to be taken out and a half eaten bag of sour gummies was still open laying on the table. Suddenly I did not feel too well.

"OH dear," she said. "I'm going to assume you are fine with a really light lunch. Maybe some soup?"

Now it was my turn to laugh.

"I was a little stressed," I said, trying to look innocent. "I will clean this up and heat us up a bowl of tomato soup if that's okay. Then maybe I will go upstairs and clean up a little before we start."

"Sounds like a plan," she said.

It was amazing how she never seemed to get angry. Never made you feel like a horrible person when you were just having a bad day. I was so happy staying with her. I would not tell her yet but since my school would be so close. Only 3 miles away. Maybe I could just stay here and drive to my classes instead of staying on campus. I know she would not need me once Annie came back but I think I need her.

Once we finished eating our soup and cleaning up, we settled down in the den. It was the most comfortable of the options and she seemed to want to avoid the library and the paintings today. She handed me the next journal and we both just stared at each other for a few minutes with both of us still holding on but finally she let go.

"Nana," I started to say something like, *"Are you sure you are okay to start,* but she held her hand up to stop me.

"Alex, I'm fine. Just promise once you start you will not stop until the end of the journal. You know like they say. If you rip the band aid off fast without stopping it doesn't hurt as much."

She gave me a weak smile and tossed the afghan over her legs. I took a deep breath before beginning.

AUGUST 28, 1941

It is Thursday. Exactly four weeks since I married Isaiah. I have stayed busy in order not to lose my mind. Each day I work as hard as any of the hired hands around the ranch. When I am not working in the barn, I am working in the house helping my mother prepare for my sisters' debutante party. It should have taken place months ago when they first turned 16 but two of their friends had birthdays near the same time and mother wanted all the attention on Carolina and Georgia.

I was grateful for the distraction and the fact that it kept my mother too busy to notice my solemn mood.

I do not try to go to the stream every night because it hurts too much but I do try to go at least two or three times a week. I sit next to the stream and talk out loud as if Isaiah is there listening to me. I lay under the tree and dream of him. Millie had neatly folded the quilts and taken them home but once I retrieved them from her, I took one of them back to the tree.

I keep it in a box and cover it with a piece of plastic I found, to protect it from rain. The straw is still under there and the Cole oil lamp. Even the jug that contained the water. Mille had taken her plate home that had contained our tiny cake. I would spread the quilt over the straw and wrap myself in it. Georgia in August can be brutally hot even late in the evening. But I would strip my clothes and wrap up with our quilt pretending it was his arms around me. It still had his scent, but it was fading quickly. I would inhale him into my lungs and close my eyes. I would often dream he was there holding me and loving me as he had that night, but eventually I would wake up from my wonderful dreams and the reality would hit me again.

I slept all the time. I would sleep as late as my parents would allow and often hid to nap during the day once I had completed my chores. The nights I would go to the stream I would sleep in hopes of dreaming but often would not wake up until the morning light was shining in my face. I don't know why I am so exhausted all the time. I guess it is because my soul is so weary.

School would start back on September 2 the day after Labor Day and it would be harder to come here. I decided I needed to take my quilt home tonight and place it in my trunk with the other one. I wanted it to be ready when he came home. I was not sure how long he would be gone. How long did people stay in the Army after enlisting? I could not ask anyone because they would want to know why it mattered to me. He had promised he would write, and I questioned Millie daily to see if they had received any news.

September 2, 1941

Started back to school today. I do not fit in anymore. I am not the girl they remember. I am not the girl I remember. I do not draw anymore. I just cannot. Everything I draw reminds me of Isaiah. Carolina and Georgia had their party on Saturday before Labor Day and of course it was the party of the century if you ask them or mother. It was very festive, but I tried to hide most of the night. I tried to be helpful but the smell of the seafood salad my mother had prepared was making me nauseous. I would get hot and feel as if I might pass out.

Millie noticed and seems really concerned about me, but I assured her it was just the salad. I think maybe it was out in the sun too long. She asked me if anyone else had gotten sick from it.... I guess I have a stomach bug or something. When I got home from school Millie gave me a look of urgency. I told my mother enough about my day to satisfy her and rushed outside to find her. She pulled me to the back of the house where we would be out of sight and put something in my hand. A letter.

It was a letter from Isaiah. He had hidden it in the envelope with a letter to his grandmother and Mille. He knew he could not send it to me at my house. As much as I wanted to read it that instant I was going to wait until I could be alone at the willow tree. It took all my will power to sit and eat dinner with my family. My sisters chattered non stop about how wonderful the first day of their senior year had been. How everyone was still talking about their party.

Mother was clinging to every word and overjoyed that the party had been such a success. The clock must be broken, I remember thinking. Time cannot be going this slowly. As soon as I could possibly get away, I ran as fast as I could to the stream. I had taken a box of matches from the kitchen to light the lamp. I settled myself and took a few deep breaths because I knew my hands were shaking so hard, I would not be able to read his words to me.

I lit the wick on the lamp and turned it up to brighten the space. My hands were shaking as I opened the letter. I could only dream I was holding him again as I read his words.

My Dearest Beulah,

My wife, my love. I am in such pain without you. My first thought each day is you and when I can risk it, I take your picture out and look at it. Did I dream you? Are you really mine? Know I love you with all my heart and soul and I pray each day that God will watch over you until I return. I know you are probably at our willow tree when reading this. That is how I picture you.

I barely made it to Tennessee in time to meet with my cousin and his friend. I must confess I stopped more than once and considered turning around. I desperately wanted to be with you again laying on our quilt wrapped in each other's arms. The only thing that stopped me was the knowledge that we would never be safe together in this hate filled world and that my fighting side by side in this war might change things for people like us who love each other beyond appearance but with all our heart and soul.

But I have found that even in this situation where men depend on each other for protection and guidance and where trust of your fellow soldier is so important there is still a prejudice that forces separation from those who would be considered our brothers. I am limited on what I can tell you about our mission, but I am being trained to jump from an airplane. I am a little excited and a lot scared, but it is something to be proud of because we are some of the first black men to do this.

I know this letter is short but I have to write my grandmother and turn the envelope over to be mailed as quickly as possible or it will have to wait until the next time they give us permission to write. My address is on the outside of the envelope I mailed to Millie and grandmother. Get it from them and write me back. Put the letter in an envelope and give it to Millie. She knows to fold her own letter around yours for our protection. It will not always be like this. Remember the story of the apples. People will understand some day.

I love you forever my love. My arms will ache until they are once again around you.

Yours always,
Isaiah

Song of Solomon 1: 14-17

"Nana, what is the story of the apples? And what is Song of Solomon 1: 14-17? Why did he put that at the end of the letter?"

She would not look at me but stared out the window.

"Alex, you can look up the Bible verse for yourself. I will tell you about the apples later. Just keep reading please."

SEPTEMBER 29, 1941

It has been a while since I have written in my journal. My days are long and empty. The leaves are changing color and falling, and my beautiful weeping willow has turned yellow and its skirt has begun to grow thinner. I know that I will not come to this clearing until spring. I am still staying busy helping with the many things that prepare a ranch for winter. We have been storing hay in the barn for the animals to eat when winter takes away their green fields.

I still struggle with not feeling well. I can't seem to eat without getting sick to my stomach and have lost a little weight from lack of food, but I am sure it is probably because of my sadness. School is going well. I make good grades and they have added an art class this year. I am learning so much about oils and our instructor is extremely impressed with my paintings. He has encouraged me to paint a bigger variety. I seem to keep painting the same scene of a stream and a willow tree. I hope I receive another letter from Isaiah soon. I have sent two letters by way of Millie. She isn't angry at me anymore for putting Isaiah in danger. She said she can see our love for each other, and it shouldn't be wrong even if most people think it is. She seems to be really concerned about my sick stomach. She has asked me to visit with her grandmother. I plan to make a visit Sunday. I am glad they treat me like family now.

OCTOBER 5, 1941

I had lunch with Isaiah's grandmother and Millie today. I had to eat a light lunch at home in order not to cause suspicion but when I ran to the little house for a second lunch, I got sick and threw the first one up. Isaiah's grandmother had an answer for my mysterious stomachache.

"Girl," she asked, "When did you have your last womanly visit?"

At first, I was not sure what she meant but suddenly I knew she meant my monthly menstrual period… and I realized I had not had one since before Isaiah left and I told her so.

"You're with child, honey… you're going to have Isaiah's baby."

I looked back and forth at them and the tears started to flow.

"What will I do? I cannot have a baby. No one even knows I am married. Oh, Mrs. Reed, ma'am, tell me what to do."

"You keep it hidden as long as you can, child. Maybe Isaiah will be home soon. You been so sick you ain't

gained a pound, so you be alright for a spell, while we think on it."

We both knew Isaiah would not be home before the baby came. He was somewhere in Europe where the war was. She was right about one thing. I had to keep this hidden if possible or my parents would send me away. I could not leave because I needed to be near Millie in case a letter came. I counted the time and it put me having the baby in early May.

I do not guess I will finish the 11th grade. We do not get out until first of June and they probably would frown on me bringing any baby to class but especially one whose father is black. I had only known of my condition for a matter of hours and I was already being protective of my precious child. Isaiah and I had created this little one out of pure love for each other. I had to protect it at all cost.

DECEMBER 27, 1941

I had received a short letter from Isaiah in November. It was not long because he only had minutes to write it. He again told me of his love and devotion and how he counted the days till we were together again. As before he had ended his letter with a Bible verse. This time it was Romans 8:31. If God is for us who can be against us.

Oh, my love you have no idea how much I miss you right now. I have avoided sweets and tried to only eat enough to keep myself and this child I carry healthy. I still work hard around the house and the ranch, but I am growing. I have hidden my expanding waist and rounding belly easily in overalls but when I must wear a dress on Sundays or because mother just wants me to look like a girl for one day it is getting harder to mask my condition.

They had gotten me a new dress for Christmas and my mother was terrible upset when it did not fit me correctly. It was a new company she had never ordered from before and she said they must not be as true to size as the old one. She was going to give them a piece of her mind and return it. I feared that by the time the new one arrived in a larger size it would not fit either.

I have written Isaiah with the news. He has not responded yet but of course letters take a while to reach him and then a while for his return letter. Isaiah's grandmother had been a midwife in her younger years to many of the local negro girls and she was keeping an eye on me. She would mash around on my stomach and ask me a lot of questions every couple of weeks.

According to her I was doing fine. Since I could not exactly go to a doctor in town, I had to hope she was right. I loved this child already and had suggested a couple of names to Isaiah in my letter. He was big on biblical names but if it is a boy, he should be Isaiah Franklin the second. If it is a girl, the middle name should be Abigail which means joy of the father. But even if it is not exactly biblical, I want our daughter to be called Willow.

JANUARY 30, 1942

I finally received another letter from Isaiah. The post mark on Millie's envelope implied it had been mailed in late December, so it had taken a month to arrive. I could not go to the stream because it was so cold out. I waited until the ranch hands were eating their lunch and would not be working in the barn. Then I crawled up in the loft to read it. I hid in the loft deep in straw where no one could see me.

The sun that shown between the wood slats gave just enough light for me to see the words. Oh, Isaiah, if only I could hold you in my arms instead of this paper that was touched by you so long ago that the scent of you is long worn off. I notice a fingerprint left by you when you held the paper. It was not ink. I suppose it was the dirt of a foreign field that he was resting in while writing to me.

I placed my finger on top of it and imagined I was touching him, as I did the night we created this child.

Dearest Beulah,

My precious gift from God, my wife and now the mother of my child. The joy I feel at this news is only lessened by my fear for you. How will you keep this secret from your parents? I know they will send you away if they find out. If there were any way I could get to you I would be there and take care of you. We would find somewhere out of the sight of those who hate our love and raise our child to see only God's creation and not the color of skin.

I love the name Willow. I hope it is a girl and I hope she is as beautiful as her mother. I have put you in danger and I am so sorry you must deal with it alone. But I can never be sorry about the night we had that gave us this blessing. I think of you always and when I sleep, I dream that night over and over. I dream of the day I can love you again.

We are flying out in the morning and it may be a while before I can write again but know my prayers are with you and our child that God will keep you safe. I know that you need to leave your parents' home because of the circumstances. They will not understand our love and would never accept our child. Please know that my grandmother and Millie would take you in and love you as their own daughter and sister. And they will love my child without reservation. That I am sure of.

Stay safe my wife and feel my love surround you until I see you again.

Isaiah
Matthew 6:34

February 27, 1942

I have tried to hide my condition as long as possible. I avoided my family and tried to not draw attention to my rounding form. My mother is suspicious of something because she keeps looking me up and down and mumbling to herself as if talking it over before coming to any conclusion. Tonight, she sent my sisters and I to bed early for no reason and I can hear my parents in the study talking.

This child will not be still. At night it leaps and turns with zeal. I try to quietly sing to it when I lay in my bed. I want it to recognize my voice. I read to it from Isaiah's Bible which I keep hidden in my room. He had left it with his grandmother for safe keeping and I asked her if I could take it home with me. It makes me feel so close to him as I study all the underlined verses and notes made in the corners.

I noticed one night that he had underlined the verses in I Corinthians 13: 4-6 about love and had written Beulah out beside it. This of course made me cry and I drifted to sleep and dreamed of him as I did most every night.

MARCH 5, 1942

Again, I am in my room by order of my mother. This time it is to await their decision on what is to become of me. She watched me closely for a few days and when she could take it no more, she pulled me into my father's office, closed the door and locked it. She paced back and forth with one finger of each hand over her lips. I knew what was coming and my heart was pounding so hard it hurt my ears. Finally, she turned and glared at me.

"Willamina, is there anything you need to tell me?"

I could not speak. I knew I would have to admit it if she asked me, but I could not say the words. I simply looked at her with wide frightened eyes and waited.

"Willamina," she said again with more anger than the concern she had the first time. "Are you in a family way?

Tell me the truth! You are, aren't you?"

My child was due to be born in about 8 weeks so there was no point in lying to her.

"Yes mother."

She looked as if she might blow up. Her face was as red as a tomato from our garden and her fist were clinched so tight her knuckles were white.

"How could this have happened, she demanded? "You have had no callers, no boyfriend to hear of. You are always here on the ranch or with us at church or if you go to town for supplies, or at school with your sisters."

Suddenly her face went pale... "Were you attacked? Oh, darling, why didn't you tell us if someone had ... (she searched for a word) compromised you?

I just sat there. I was not sure what to say. She cupped her face in her hands in total distress and ran from the room to find my father. When they returned in only a few minutes my father was in a full steam ahead fury.

"WHO WAS IT," he demanded. "I will see to it that he is punished to the extent of the law.... That is if I allow him to live long enough to stand trial!"

He was so angry it frightened me. Finally, in a meek tiny voice that even I could hardly hear I said...

"I wasn't attacked. I wasn't raped."

They both stopped dead in their tracks and glared at me. I went through at least an hour and a half of interrogation. They named every young man they could think of. Every boy I attended school with, every boy or man that had attended our July 4th celebration. Every nearby neighbor who could have possibly talked me into such a thing. I simply sat there with tears streaming and shook my head no to each suggestion. They would not let up and demanded I give them a name.

I finally told them I had fallen in love with a man named Isaiah Reed. That we had married in secret and he was now in the Army. I had hoped they would not know the name. That Mr. Carlton had never mentioned his hired help by name to my father in passing. I hoped they would not ask too many questions as to where we met or where we had married.

I was sent to my room and told not to leave it until they gave me permission. I ran up to my room and tried to imagine what they might do. What will happen to me? I realized there were things in my room I needed to conceal. Isaiah's Bible was under my pillow and our quilt was under the bedspread my mother had bought me for my birthday last year. Surely, they would not look that closely in my room.

I double checked to make sure these items were not visible should they come into my room. I had placed Isaiah's letters in the Bible. I said a quick prayer asking God to not let them find his letters.

They never came up that night to continue our talk. I heard my father leave and my mother had gone to her room. Later in the early morning I heard my mother crying. I did not want to hurt her. I loved my mother and my father. But I knew once the truth was known they would no longer love me. I would be disowned by them without a doubt because my parents were the kind of people Isaiah and I had talked about.

The ones who hate for the sack of hate because of the color of a person's skin. They would hate me, and they would never love my child.

MARCH 8, 1942

After two days of only coming out of my room to use the bathroom the wait is over. My mother had brought my meals to my room. I had not been allowed to attend school and my sisters were told I was very ill, and they should not go near me. My father had hardly been home. He was on a mission to find out who this Isaiah Reed fellow was and deal with him.

On Friday, he finally found his way to Mr. Carlton's farm. He had been going to all the nearby homes just asking around about a fella he heard of that had passed this way.

"Oh, I know who Isaiah Reed is," offered Mr. Carlton. "He's that Negro boy I hired this past summer to help me on the farm. His grandmother had told me he needed work so he could give her some money before he left for the Army. He seemed like a good fella. Hard worker."

My father had not heard a word past Negro. He came home and came to my room with a hatred in his eyes I had never witnessed. I stood up from my bed and he slapped me back down. I think if my mother had not walked in at that exact moment, he might have beaten me to the point of death.

"How could you do this to me? You … You!"

He blew out a breath of frustration and sat on the end of my bed with his face in his hands. I wanted to explain how Isaiah and I loved each other. How wonderful he is. I knew nothing I said would matter. My fate was in their hands. I thought about running away to stay at Millie's, but I would be putting them in danger.

It did not appear that he had made any connection between them and Isaiah and I had to be sure it stayed that way. Once again, my parents left my room and I was waiting. Waiting to see how they would deal with me.

MARCH 12, 1942

Yesterday when I woke, I heard unfamiliar sounds coming from outside. My sisters were giggling with excitement as they loaded their suitcases in the trunk of our car. My father drove off with them and as soon as they were out of sight my mother came to me.

"Get everything you need together. Pack a suitcase with anything you think you will need for the next few months."

Then she just walked out of the room, closing the door behind her. My first thought was they were sending me away to some home for wayward girls. But why send my sisters away if that were the case. I pulled my trunk out from the wall under my window and placed my journals, my quilt and Isaiah's Bible in it. Then I put my clothes and toiletries on top of them. I made my bed neatly and looked to see if I had missed anything. My mother came back with Millie and instructed her to help me with the trunk.

"Take it upstairs to the attic," she instructed.

We did and she followed behind. I noticed a small area in the back end of the attic had been cleaned up and prepared for me. Four large pieces of plywood had been placed over the joist in the floor.

On top of them was a small twin sized bed with sheets folded on top of it and a pillow. Beside the bed was a nightstand with a pitcher of water and a bowl to wash in. And there was a small dresser and a standing mirror. This would be my home until after the baby came. I was told to keep completely quiet. No one was to know I was here other than Millie and my par-

ents.

"Millie will bring you food and clean linen. She has been so kind as to agree to take your soiled clothes home and wash them so no one would see them hanging on our clothesline. Everyone will think you joined your sisters in Atlanta to visit your aunt. They will be gone until after the baby comes. They must never know of your shame."

Once she had given her instructions she left without hesitation and closed the door and closed her heart to me I feared.

Millie gave me a hug and told me not to worry. She would check on me every day. I hugged her tightly and began to cry when my mother called for her from the bottom of the attic stairs.

"Millie, you have work to do."

APRIL 2, 1942

I have been in this attic for 20 days. It is hot and miserable, but I keep the two rose windows tilted open and it allows air to flow. At night it is almost cool with the breeze and I cuddle in my quilt and talk to Isaiah and our baby from my heart. Millie comes every day to bring food and check on me, but mother will not allow her to stay long. She has not received a letter from Isaiah since the one I got in January and I am afraid for him.

She has taken two letters from me to mail to him, but we are careful because if mother noticed, it would be bad for both of us. With so little activity I am getting as round as a pumpkin. My baby is very active and I long to meet this precious gift but at the same time I am so afraid. What will they do once the baby is born? My mother was adamant that my sisters would never know. How can they not notice I have a child?

I should have asked Millie to help me escape but now it is too late. I could never climb down a tree outside the window and others would do harm to me or the baby if they knew. I am at their mercy for now, but I pray for guidance and that Isaiah will come home soon.

APRIL 17, 1942

I will attempt to write of my heartache. It has been two weeks and my tears have not slowed. I only cry and sleep and beg God to take it back. Do not let this be true. Millie had eased into my room in the early morning on April 3 before anyone would possibly be awake. She woke me and sat down on my bed. She had tears in her eyes as she handed me a letter.

At first, I sat up in excitement thinking I had finally heard from Isaiah, but she shook her head to let me know it was not from him. It was an official looking letter. There was a seal in the upper left corner that said "Office of the President." It was addressed to Isaiah's grandmother.

We are sorry to inform you that the plane that was transporting the Black Battalion to Germany was fired upon and went down before reaching their destination. The plane was destroyed and consumed by flames and it is assumed that all those aboard have perished.

Please accept the condolences of a grateful Nation for the service of Pvt. Isaiah Franklin Reed, United States Army.

Then it had been signed at the bottom by some official.

I dropped the letter and was about to scream when Millie put her hand hard over my mouth and pulled my back against her chest. She rocked me while keeping my mouth covered and we both cried until we were weak. As soon as she felt I would not scream she removed her hand and turned me to face her. We embraced and continued to cry for an hour. He is not dead! I told her. It is assumed and I feel in my heart he is still with me. He will be found. Millie looked at me and as gently as she could she said "Miss. Willamina. I hope you are right. But the truth is they will never look for him."

The sun was coming up and we both knew she had to go before mother started looking for her. She said she would be up to check on me as soon as possible and left me curled up on my bed numb with pain.

Poor Millie. She had her own pain and grief to deal with. She loved her cousin Isaiah very much. Her grandmother was stricken with grief and Millie had to console her. Then when she was at my house, she had to try to console me. She would spoon feed me broth when I refused to eat, reminding me, I had to take care of Isaiah's child. I read the few letters I had received from him over and over.

I was glad my mother never came upstairs because I cried most of the time. I looked through my sketches at the many pictures of him I had drawn. I longed to go to our willow tree. To remember him alive and vibrant and loving. I tried to find comfort in Isaiah's Bible. I was angry with God and I did not know how to handle it. Isaiah would know what to say, I thought. But that is the problem. He is not here… and he never will be again.

APRIL 29, 1942

Two days ago, my mother came to my attic room for the first time since she placed me up here. For just a minute she looked as if she wanted to comfort me. She had to notice how weak and sickly I looked. I had dark circles under my eyes and my once beautiful auburn hair was brittle and dry. I was pasty white from lack of sunshine, and I looked like a prisoner who had been left in the cell. She started toward me looking concerned but then caught herself. She looked at my large stomach and then up at me.

"Are you alright?" She asked but there was no tenderness in her voice. No motherly concern in her eyes. She seemed to be following the plan to distance herself.

"I'm fine," I lied. She explained that she and father were taking a short trip to visit Carolina and Georgia and would be back on May 2nd. She just stood there looking at me for a while as if she expected some response like 'Oh how nice, tell them I send greetings.' Once she realized I was not going to say anything she left. I watched out of my window until they were out of sight. I tried the door at the bottom of the stairs, but it was locked.

Great, mom, I thought. Let's just hope the house doesn't catch on fire because no one knows I'm up here. Who knows, maybe that is their plan. No, they love this house too much to burn it down. But I knew there had to be a plan. They would not keep me up here hidden from everyone just to let me out after the baby is born hoping no one noticed. I was sitting on my bed after realizing the door was locked and just wondering when Millie might come.

Usually when we would go out of town, they would tell Millie she had the time off. Did that mean she would not be here to check on me until they returned. I had no food and little water. I started to panic and while I stood up to look out the window for signs of her, I had a sudden sharp pain and a gush of water came out of me. I did not expect to have this baby for another week. What did I know? I was only 16 and it is not like I have had a baby before. What if no one comes to help me?

I do not know what to do. I lay in my small bed for hours in pain. The pains got harder and harder to bear. I knew I was supposed to be quiet so no one would know I was here but the closer together the pains came the more severe the pain was and I began to scream to the top of my lungs with each pain. I felt as if I wanted to push the baby out, but I did not know what to do. I could not take it another second and began to push with each pain.

The burning pain from my body felt as if I were ripping open. Suddenly just as I felt my baby come out, the door of the attic swung open and Mille came flying up the stairs. Miss. Willamina, I heard you screaming from the other side of the field. She went to the end of the bed to check the baby. After a few minutes I heard the cry that told me my baby was okay.

"A girl," she said.

"Willow," I replied in a whispered voice.

She wiped her off with the washcloth that hung from my wash pan and wrapped her in the towel that was draped over a chair from when I would bathe myself and then she placed her in my arms. While Millie ran downstairs to get scissors and more water and towels, I lay there propped up with pillows and examined my new daughter. She was so perfect.

She looked at me as if she were just as impressed with meeting me as I was her. I touched her tiny hand and she wrapped her fingers around mine and held on. I opened the towel and looked to be sure she had everything that she was supposed to. That is when I realized she was still attached to me by her cord. Millie came back in and said not to worry.

"I know what to do. I've watched my grandmother before."

She tied some twine around the cord close to Willow's body and then tied another piece of twine a few inches away from that one. She then took the scissors and cut between the two. I began to cramp hard again and looked at her with wide eyes.

"Am I having another one? Was it twins?"

"No girl, it's just the afterbirth coming out."

It was gross but Millie gave me a fast lesson on how all this works. She put the afterbirth in a pan and said she would bury it later. "

It's bad luck if you don't bury it within a couple of hours."

I didn't know if that was true, but I wouldn't take any chances. She left me alone for a while so she could bury it and get some things I would need.

Oh, Isaiah I said out loud. Our daughter is so beautiful. She favors you. She has a small patch of tight curls on top of her head and I think her eyes are shaped like yours. She also has your full lips that almost look like a heart shape when she puckers them up.

While I held her near my breast she started to nuzzle and search. She obviously knew more about this than I did. I placed her near my nipple, and she latched on and began to nurse. I was so in love. Tears of pure joy ran down my face for the first time since the night she was conceived.

It was about two hours before Millie returned and she looked like Santa carrying his pack. She had diapers that she and grandmother had made and a couple of little baby gowns for Willow. She had made a blanket for her from the scraps of material my sisters always gave her. She also brought me some of the clean clothes and linen she had taken to wash last week.

Her grandmother had sent me some cold chicken sandwiches and cold lemonade in a jar. I sat in my one chair and ate like a starved animal while Millie cleaned up my sweet baby. Then I held her again while she cleaned up my bed. I do not know what I would have done without Millie and I told her so. I told her I loved her, and she was my family now. It made her cry, but she knew, as I did, that we would have to think of a way to get me and my baby out of the house soon.

"Could you hand me Isaiah's Bible Millie?"

She laid it on the bed side table near my chair. I took the pen I kept in it to mark verses and in the front of the Bible where I had put the date of Isaiah and my marriage, I wrote the information about our daughter.

Willow Abigale Reed born April 30, 1942 at 3:00 a.m. in the attic of her mother's house. Her father Isaiah Franklin Reed was unable to be there in body but was there in heart. Her mother Willamina Beulah Reed loves her so very much.

It was the first time I had dared to put my last name as Reed. I told Millie I wanted her to take his Bible back to her house. I wanted it to be kept safe. She told me she would keep it for me until we were able to join her and grandmother. I was their sister and their granddaughter now and they would love and care for me and Willow as best they could.

May 3, 1942

I had spent two glorious days alone with my daughter. When she slept, I slept. I was exhausted? Millie spent a lot of time with me since my parents were away. I was as weak as a kitten, but we made our plan to leave in a couple of weeks once I had the strength to walk to her house. Perhaps on a Sunday while my parents were at church.

On May 2, early in the afternoon I heard my parents return home. Thank goodness Millie had just left and they would not find her upstairs with me. My mother did not come up to check on me when they first arrived home.

It was around midnight when Willow cried to be fed and I rushed trying to get her to latch on. She probably reacted to my panic and would not stop crying. The door flung open and I heard her rush up the stairs. She stared at me and her mouth hung open.

"Her name is Willow. Your granddaughter is beautiful." She looked so shocked and I could tell the urge to come and see her was strong. She stood on tip toe and peered over at her and when Willow made one of those little babies squeaks my mother smiled. But then she caught herself and her face became stern again. I knew then that she would never hold her, never touch her because she did not want to risk loving her.

"When," she asked?

"Early in the morning on Thursday."

That was all she asked, and she turned and walked back down the stairs.

May 25, 1942

The last three weeks are a blur, a nightmare I cannot wake from. I woke up in my room last week and did not remember how I got there. The last thing I remembered was my mother coming to the attic when Willow was about a week old. She suddenly started acting like a mother. She told me my sisters who had attended school in Atlanta for the remainder of the school year would be graduating in a few weeks and then would be coming home.

She had brought my breakfast on a beautiful tray and even had a flower in a small vase on it. She sat there and talked about all the plans for the summer none of which included me or Willow. Never once had she asked about her or wanted to hold her. Never once had she even spoken her name. I ate my breakfast because I needed to regain my strength. I needed to get out of here. The last thing I remember after drinking my cup of tea was that the room was moving in waves around me and the next memory was of me waking up in my own bed a few days later. I had vague memories of mother holding my head up and instructing me to drink broth.

When I finally did wake up my head felt heavy and dull. I was confused and suddenly realized I did not see Willow anywhere. I tried to get up and fell on the floor. My legs were like rubber bands. I screamed for help and my parents came rushing in with our family doctor following behind them. It was the first time I had laid eyes on my father since he found out I was expecting. My father and the doctor helped me back into bed.

"Where is my baby, mother? What have you done with her?" I was screaming and the doctor started to give me a pill to calm me. I slapped it away and my father shook his head at the doctor as if to let him know they were done with him. He shook my fathers' hand and tipped his hat at my mother before he left.

I was not even acknowledged by the very man who had delivered me as a baby and had treated me for every childhood illness I had suffered. Once the doctor was out of the house my mother sat on my bed and took my hands in hers.

"Sweetheart, I'm so sorry I have to tell you this, but your little daughter has died."

"LIER," I screamed at her! "She was perfect, healthy and beautiful. What have you done with her? TELL ME!"

"It happens dear. You remember the Fosters two years ago. Their little boy just died in his crib during the night. Millie went up to check on you the Monday after we returned home

and found the little girl had passed."

"HER NAME IS WILLOW! SAY IT MOTHER ... WILLOW!"

"Yes, dear. Willow had passed away. I'm so sorry."

"Millie, I want to talk to Millie. She will tell me where you have put her."

For the first time my father looked at me and spoke.

"Millie and her grandmother had to leave," he said. "We hated to lose her as our help, but some of their relatives needed them. They left two weeks ago."

"Who, father? What family wanted them?"

"I don't know Willamina. I don't keep up with the comings and goings of my Negro help."

My father had never called me Willamina. Even when my mother pleaded with him. He always said I did not feel like a Willamina and he always called me Willie.

"Where is she? I want to see her. I want to hold my daughter one last time."

Again, my father spoke without sympathy or concern for me as he told what they had done with her.

"Don't be ridiculous, girl. She passed over two weeks ago, and you have been overcome with grief. We had to bury her. We placed her in the cemetery near the church."

He was done. He had said what he needed to say. He walked out of the room and held up in his office the remainder of the day.

My mother patted my hands and gave a slight smile.

"Your sisters will be home in June."

How will my soul survive this? I have lost my love; I have lost our child and my only friend in this world has gone. I could not believe it. She would not have left. I hoped my legs would be stronger tomorrow and I could go see the proof of their claims.

Before daybreak on the 22nd of May I made my way to the barn, saddled my horse and rode to the cemetery next to our church. In the corner of the cemetery where my grandparents were buried was a small grave. I could tell it was freshly dug but there was no head stone. No marker of any kind to tell people who this child was. Even in death my father was ashamed of his only grandchild. I lay on the grave sobbing until the break of day. I mounted my horse again and rode to the little house where Millie and grandmother lived.

I walked into the house without knocking because I could tell no one was there. I looked at the 4 bare walls of this tiny home. Most of their meager belongings were gone. The only things left behind was the pot belly stove they used for cooking and for heat, and the one cot-like bed in the corner.

It was not a large bed, but they had shared it because there was no room for another one. I could not help but remember how Millie had offered to share this humble place with me and my baby. It reminded me of the story Isaiah had told me from the Bible where the widow gave all she had.

I took my horse by the reign and led her to the clearing. The willow tree was green and plush again and the grass was a soft carpet. I sat in the comfort of my tree and cried until I was too weak to ride home. Sometime during the night my father found me. He picked me up like a small child and placed me on my horse. He led us home and carried me to my bed.

He never spoke but he did pat my cheek before walking out of the room and softly closing my door. God please let me die too was my last thought as I drifted off to sleep.

I was numb. I just sat there holding the journal to my chest. And my chest was aching with sorrow and pain like I had never experienced. I was not sure what to do or what to say. I remembered what she had said about living the pain all over again and she looked so fragile with her cover pulled up to her chin in her chair. Her head wasn't turned toward me, and I couldn't see her face.

"Nana."

I waited for her to respond. Finally, she turned to face me. I could see the tracks from tears she had shed as I read. I saw such weariness in her eyes. She moved her cover and turned in her chair toward me and without saying a word she held her arms out to me and I fell into them and fell apart.

We both cried for a long while. She had dealt with this for years and probably cried over it several times, but this was a fresh wound for me. My heart was broken. I wept for Isaiah.

I wept for Willow. I wept for Millie and I wept for poor Willamina who simply wanted to die from her grief, but I know she lived on and even found love again. What I did not know was how. How did she ever get out of that bed again let alone find love again?

It was getting very late. I looked at the clock and saw that it was almost midnight. Once we had stopped crying and pulled ourselves together, I stood up and helped her to her feet. I had so many questions. I knew most of my questions would have to wait until the next journal.

"Nana, tomorrow after we have rested, will you tell me about the apples?"

"Yes" was all she said.

We walked together up the stairs and I walked her to her door before going to my room. As I lay in bed wondering about the journal and about my sweet Nana all I could think was how I wish Mark were here.

Chapter Ten

Fireworks & First Confessions

It had been almost one o'clock in the morning before I had fallen to sleep and now at four o'clock, I am wide awake. Three hours and my brain refused to turn off. I sat on the side of my bed for a while thinking about the journal from yesterday. Sadness was hanging over this entire house like a blanket. As if some mysterious force had grabbed my head and pointed it where I needed to focus, I found myself staring at the typewriter on my desk.

I needed to get started on the novel… I mean there is no reason I must wait until we have read all the journals. I need to start while everything is fresh on my mind. While my emotions are raw and awakened… *and boy were they ever raw and awakened.*

I opened the desk drawer and found a pack of paper for the typewriter and plugged the machine into the socket nearest the desk. I was glad she had gotten me an electric typewriter because it would be so much quieter than a manual. I did not want to disturb Nana.

In my wildest dreams I had never imagined my first attempt at writing a book would be a true story about a family member. I had imagined it would be a great work of fiction. Some mysterious murder mystery or a romance of the ages. I may be right about the romance part. This was surely a romance for the ages, but I would have to be very careful with Nana's story. Unlike fiction where I did not have to consider someone's feelings, I would want to be truthful without being hurtful. I typed in my name and the date I started as a cover sheet. I wanted to remember that July 1, 1992 was the day I began the story of Willamina.

Oh, wow. Saturday is the fourth of July. I wonder if we will do anything special to celebrate.

"Okay focus Alex," I instructed out loud.

And I did focus. I was amazed at how easily the words came. I had absorbed this journey into my blood. As I began to type the beautiful love story the tears would flow freely. I would have to stop and wipe my eyes often, but it didn't slow me down. I knew that many people would read this with judgmental eyes. They would make assumptions about my Nana and some family members may even be outraged at her secret past.

I wanted my words to convince all who would read this that the pure love that existed between Isaiah and Beulah was real and lovely. I continued until seven o'clock when my ideas and my stomach became empty. I placed the pile of finished papers in the drawer of my desk and covered the typewriter back up. I would not tell Nana I had started. I would save it as a surprise until it was finished. I showered and dressed before making my way down to the kitchen. Nana was waiting for me.

I found her sitting at the small breakfast table near the window with her cup of coffee in hand and a pile of apples in the middle of the table.

"So, I guess we are going to hear the story of the apples," I said.

Nana smiled and told me to get my coffee first and please refill her cup as well. It was good to see her smile. She had not smiled a lot in the last few days, and I had missed that warm bit of sunshine she gave off when she was happy.

"Alex, do you know how many varieties of apple there are worldwide?"

I shook my head no and she proceeded to give me a lesson on apples.

"There are over 7,000 different types of apples. Some red, some green, some yellow and many others that range between. Some have all those colors on the same apple. Some are tart, some are sweet, some are juicy and others not so much. Some grow very large like a softball and some may be as tiny as a golf ball.

Some are grainy and mussy while others are firm and crisp. Some make a delicious pie while others may be better suited for cider or sauce. My obvious point is that there may be many differences in those 7,000 varieties but bottom line they are all apples and were created by God."

I know I looked at her dumbfounded by this analogy. What do apples have to do with anything? She was just smiling at me waiting for it to register. After a long pause she finally continued.

"Just like people."

I smiled because I knew what she was trying to point out.

"Some are white, some are black, some are brown or yellow or red. Some are a mixture of two or three of these.... like Mark," she added. "Regardless of what a person looks like or where they come from, they are all people created by God. That is what Isaiah taught me. I loved him before I knew he looked different from me. I love who he was on the inside, not how he looked on the outside.

I grew to love that as well," she said and had to blush as she recalled the things I had learned from the journal. "I tried to always teach my children this lesson. I told all of them the story of the apples when they were young. I even told your Papa Sam the story of the apples and he understood my point but never knew why I was so determined to make my point.

I could only push the idea on Samuel so much without him becoming suspicious of my motivation, but he was not as prejudiced as some. He would have never been okay with two races marrying but he tried to always be fair in his dealings and look on the person for their integrity not their ethnicity.

I know without a shadow of a doubt that if he had known of Isaiah before we married, he would have never gone through with the wedding. I also know if he found out after even years of marriage, he would have never forgiven me. I pray that when my children and grandchildren read this, they will forgive me and accept who I am. That they will still love me."

"I know one who will and does still love you," I smiled at her and placed my hand over her hand. "Thank you, Nana, for the lesson about the apples."

We made breakfast and cleaned up. We bagged up most of the apples to take to some of the neighborhood children. We could never eat them all before they rotted.

"If this was in my younger days, I would have fed them to my horse," Nana said.

"Oh, I meant to ask you. Are you planning anything for

Saturday? It's a holiday you know," I gave a hopeful grin.

"I think we should grill burgers and eat watermelon. Maybe shoot a few fireworks in the back field since it has been cut short and the ground isn't so dry after the rain. Fun around the pool, you know."

I gave a half-hearted smile. I had hoped we might go somewhere but I would not ruin her plans by complaining.

"Oh, and did I mention that Mark is coming home this weekend to do the grilling," she added with a devilish grin and raised her eyebrows up and down for effect.

Now it was my turn to blush. My Nana was such a sneaky rascal. I loved that about her.

Mark arrived late Thursday night and would have to head back early enough Monday morning to get to class. He sat around the table with Nana and I for a late-night snack and we got to hear about his workload.

"This is not going to be easy, but I'm determined."

Nana told him how proud she was of his dedication and assured him he needed to make his studies the main priority. They compared notes on what each of them had heard from his mom and all about the new baby. Mark even had a picture of his new nephew in his wallet. His sister had sent it to him along with the hospital issued announcement. Nana had a few chores she wanted him to do while he was there, but she tried not to overwhelm him.

While we sat around the table, he kept glancing over toward me. I was so happy to see him but did not want to take away from his time with Nana. Once unexpectedly he moved his leg over and bumped my knee with his. At first, I thought it was an accident, but he did not move it and he grinned without looking at me. I tried so very hard not to blush… I really did try… but my ruddy complexion failed me once again and my cheeks burned hot. I guess my Nana noticed what was happening.

Suddenly in the middle of the conversation she stood up, stretched and announced she was just exhausted and was going up to bed. We both looked at her a little shocked, but she kissed Mark and I both on the top of our heads and as she pulled away from kissing me, she gave me a little wink.

"Good night Nana," I called to her as she walked toward the stairs. "Love you."

She never turned around, just stuck her hand out and waved while she climbed the stairs.

Mark did not waste any time. He reached over and took my hand. Then as I had hoped he kissed me.

"I have wanted to kiss you since I walked in the door," he said. "I have missed you Alex. This has been the longest four weeks of my life. If I didn't have to study so much, I would come home every weekend."

"Your studies have to come first. And four weeks isn't that long."

He looked hurt. I had said it only to relieve his guilt for not coming home more often but I think he took it that I had not missed him.

"You don't want me to come home on the weekend?"

"No"

"NO, you mean you didn't miss me." He pulled his hand away from mine.

"You didn't let me finish… I was going to say… ***no,*** that isn't what I meant. I would love for you to come home every weekend, but I know that isn't going to be possible. I do miss you, very much. I reached and placed my hand back under his warm hand. Mark, I worry that once I start classes, we will not see each other very often and it actually scares me how much that bothers me."

We heard Nana moving around upstairs. I knew she wasn't trying to listen, but I didn't want us to keep her up. Mark suggested we go sit by the pool.

We talked for several hours about how we could make time to see each other while we were in school. I wasn't sure of my schedule yet and his would change after the summer courses, but we would make time. We both promised at least one weekend a month we would have a date. We had sat on a lounge chair in the darkest corner of the yard and before long we were laying in each other's arms just enjoying our time together. He would be super busy tomorrow doing Nana's list of chores and Saturday would be busy with the festivities of the fourth.

Nana had invited a few of her friends over and my aunts and uncles who lived nearest to Nana would be over as well. Aunt Kathy and Uncle Steve would be without their son Samuel this year because he had joined the Air Force in hopes of becoming a pilot. He had been named after Papa Sam. My other aunt, Susan and her husband Philip were on a vacation in Myrtle Beach along with their two daughters Isabell and MacKenzie who were grown but would rather go to the beach than come to Nana's.

Aunt Frances was single and had gone to a party at a friend's house with other singles. Guess hanging with us did not sound exciting enough, had been my Aunt Kathy's response to that. We had invited my parents of course but they said it was too far for a short weekend and the traffic would be horrible so they would come when it was not a holiday.

It was nice. Lots of food. Mark had grilled burgers, hotdogs and corn on the cob. Nana made her delicious potato salad and baked beans. I made cupcakes and decorated them with those candles that look like sparklers. We also had watermelon, chips and lots of soda in a big bucket of ice. First, we played around in the pool in the heat of the day. Even Nana sported her one piece and sat alongside with her feet in the water. Then came the eating part of our program. Once we had eaten to the point of being miserable, it was getting close to time for the fireworks. Nana had given Mark money to purchase some at the tent a few blocks away and Uncle Steve went with him and contributed to the cause.

They worked for almost an hour out in the field sitting it all up. Nana had told them to pull the garden hose close to them 'just in case'. They had to link four hoses together to reach far enough but it made Nana and I both feel a little safer. Before we let the men fire up the show, we brought my radio with the built in CD player pool side. I had purchased a CD of songs for Independence Day just for the occasion.

As soon as Mark and Steve heard the first few notes of the "The Star Spangled Banner" they started lighting fuses. It was spectacular. Some of the neighbors had wandered over to watch and several small children cheered and clapped. It only lasted twenty minutes tops but it was the most fun I have ever had for the fourth of July.

Once the fireworks ended and the neighbors paid their respects to Nana everyone started to make their way to their cars. Aunt Kathy hugged Nana several times and told her she would talk to her in a couple of days.

Mark and I began cleaning up. We insisted Nana go rest and leave it to us. At least most of the food had been in disposable pans and we had eaten off of paper plates, so we just loaded the dishwasher with the things that needed to be washed and pushed the button. We gathered trash up and put away the extra chairs. I sat my radio on the bottom step so I could return it to my room when I went up to bed. The last job was to roll up the hoses and hang them next to the garden shed. We then took flashlights and a trash bag to the field. We searched and searched until we had hopefully gathered all the garbage left from the fireworks.

"That was an awesome fireworks display," I said.

"Thanks," he grinned. "Steve helped a little, but it was mostly me being awesome."

We both laughed and then suddenly we were not laughing. He walked over and took me in his arms. The stars above us were more breathtaking than any number of fireworks.

"Let's lay here and look up at the stars," he suggested.

"Not here," I said, "follow me."

I took his hand and led him to the stream. I knew before we got there that I would not take him under the willow tree. That belonged to Isaiah and Beulah. It was sacred. But I would show him the stream and the clearing where the stars reflected off the water like diamonds. We sat there for a long while beside the stream. Mark had his arm around me and I laid my head on his strong shoulder. It was a muggy night and no breeze was blowing.

"Can we go for a swim in the stream," he asked"

"I don't see why not."

I had put shorts on over my bathing suit, and he had only put a tee shirt over his swim trunks. This was a good thing because I do not think skinny dipping would have been a good idea. My feelings for Mark were getting stronger and stronger the longer I knew him, and my desires could have easily gotten away from me. I think he felt much the same way as far as not pushing our chances at going further than we knew we should. We stepped out into the stream. In contrast to the hot air of the summer night the stream seemed cold and I gave a little squeal when the water splashed up on my back.

Mark wrapped his arms around me and just looked into my eyes for a minute. Then he kissed me tenderly at first and then with more of an urgency. I placed my hand on his chest to subtly remind him of our need to restrain. I knew the exact moment he got the message… because he stopped kissing me… picked me up and as I screamed for mercy, he tossed me up in the air and I landed butt first into the stream.

The next morning, after church service and lunch, Mark was busy. He had so much he wanted to do for Nana before leaving in the morning for class. He mowed the front lawn and cleaned up around the many flower beds. He vacuumed the pool and hosed off the area around the pool. In between those chores he was doing his laundry and cleaning up his tiny apartment.

I tried to help him some but there was just too much to do in a short time to do it. He was going to leave about five in the morning because his first class was at eight and he needed to get to his dorm and put things away before going to class. He also would need to grab his books and look over some notes to refresh his memory because this professor was famous for a test that he forgot to tell you he was going to give. He had dinner with us and we all sat in the front room and talked for a while.

"Oh Mark," Nana said. "I have one more job I really would like you to do dear. If you do not mind. It will not take you long."

"Okay Nana, what do you need me to do? You know I can never refuse you," he said with a wink and patted her hand.

"I have finally finished my painting. The one on the front porch. I have allowed it to dry for about a week now so it should be safe to hang it. I have a frame for it in the library and I would like it to be hung in my room."

"In your room Nana? Why not hang it for all to see. I'm sure it is as beautiful as all your other paintings."

"It's not meant for all to see dear," she replied "It is for my eyes to enjoy. My mind to reflect on," she seemed to drift off into deep thought for a few seconds. "At least for now," she whispered.

Mark had no idea what the picture was, but I did. I understood why she had to wait before others saw it. She would not take a chance on someone seeing it hanging in her den or front room just yet. The figures in the stream were of the young girl with long auburn hair and her dark-skinned lover as he held her close. I was not sure what Mark would think of it.

He did not know about Isaiah. Would he even make a connection to Nana or maybe he would just think she was afraid of how people would receive her art. He may just assume the lovers in the painting were made up in her mind and no one in particular.

He did as she asked. He carried it into the library to mount it in the frame. It was a beautiful antique frame she had saved for the occasion. He carried it upstairs with Nana and I following behind him.

"Which wall Nana," he asked

"The one above my dresser. I want to lay her and look at it before I fall asleep and I want it to be the first thing I see when I wake up."

Mark followed her instructions, but I could tell he was confused by Nana's request. He hung it just where she wanted it. Centered on the wall that faced her bed. It would be at eye level when she sat propped up in her bed. The three of us stood there looking at the portrait. Nana looking dreamily at it, Mark looking questionably at it and me looking a little uncomfortable.

I was not only worried Mark would realize that was the same stream we had visited last night but I was feeling a little embarrassed because I knew the memories that were flooding my Nana's mind as she watched the figures in her painting. Nana and I were the only two people who knew who those lovers were and what had happened to them.

"Hey," Mark said, and I knew recognition had occurred. "Isn't that the stream.... he saw my face and stopped mid question."

Nana was just smiling. She did not care that I had taken him there. It did not change anything as far as she was concerned.

"Goodnight children. Oh, and Mark please do not leave in the morning without letting me see you off. I promise to be up and downstairs with your coffee mug in hand by five o'clock."

"You got it," he said.

"Goodnight Nana," we both said.

He did not speak until we were down the hall in front of my door.

"Was that the same stream we went to last night?"

"Yes," I said without further explanation.

"You know if that had not just happened last night and if your hair was longer and my hair was shorter."

He made a flirty face and grinned at me. He was right. We did favor those lovers in the stream. I just smiled up at him and told him I would try to be in the kitchen in the morning when he left as well.

"Don't, really, it will be easier to leave if I say goodbye now. Plus, the whole morning breath and crazy hair thing… I'm not ready."

I playfully slapped his arm.

"I would shower and brush my teeth before coming down," I said defensively.

"I meant me," he said. "That's way too early for a lot of grooming on my part."

We both smiled and then he kissed me goodnight. It took a long time before he broke from the kiss and I could tell he did not want to stop.

"I'm going to miss you Alex. More than I thought I would. I think I am falling in love with you."

I wanted to melt. I could not breathe.

"I think I am falling in love with you too Mark. Actually, I know I am."

As soon as he left, I hurried to my window to watch as he walked to the pool house. I did not hide behind my curtains as I had before, but I wanted him to see me and know I could not get enough of seeing him.

He turned and stood in his doorway for several minutes and we just looked at each other. I knew neither of us wanted to be the one to turn away, but he needed to get some rest before he had to drive to class.

I decided to be the one to give in. I waved one more wave and let the curtain drop. The next few weeks would be long without him.

Chapter Eleven

Painted Memories

Nana and I both seemed to be a little blue on Monday after Mark had left and we were not much better on Tuesday but by Wednesday she was done with the pity party. Those were her exact words. "

We need to get back to work on the Journals Alex. You will start your classes in September, so we only have eight weeks to finish reading them. Annie will be coming home in August as well and we will have to be less open about reading them here at home.

I know Annie will be very understanding but I do not want to put her in a position to have to lie to my children or even Mark until I am ready to reveal it to all of them. How do you feel about a nice lunch in town and then we will ride to the lovely park and rest under a shade tree or something? Change of scenery might be nice."

"How about we skip the lunch in town and pack another picnic. That was a lot of fun before."

"Agreed."

We got busy packing for our outing. It was July hot in Georgia, so cold food, cold drinks and loose cool clothes. Nana wore a linen sundress of pale blue. She also had a sunhat and wore slip-on sandals of breathable material. I wore my pink shorts and a small white cotton tee and a pair of canvas tennis shoes. We put a blanket on the top of the basket that would not only insulate and help keep the food cool but would give us something to sit on. We found a lovely park and located the perfect area for our picnic. It was far from the area most used, where the playground was for kids. We found it by accident when we took time to stop and read the headstones at an old civil war error cemetery. Just beyond the cemetery was a path that led to a waterfall.

This was a beautiful secret and we spread our blanket and began to feast on what we had brought. A simple lunch of cold sandwiches and chips. We had packed several bottles of water to stay hydrated and of course we had to have dessert. Because I had been having too many of my late-night pity feast since visiting Nana and she had joined me more than once, we both decided a small bag of grapes was enough. We cleaned up and made ourselves comfortable. I wasn't sure if she had brought the next journal and I hadn't wanted to ask but when she told me to put the picnic basket in the trunk of the car she also told me to retrieve the journal which I would find in the back behind the driver's seat.

It was a dark cover and blended in with the floor mat, so I had not noticed it before. I handed it to her and once I had sat down and made myself as comfortable as you can on the ground, she handed it back to me. She leaned back against a tree and tilted her hat to where it covered most of her face. It gave the impression that she was going to nap but I knew that was not the case. She would most definitely listen to every word. When I first opened the journal, the first thing I noticed was the date. It was her and Isaiah's first anniversary. I made a mental note to remember that there would be another anniversary of that day at the end of this month.

July 31, 1942

I have brought my journal and my sketch pad to the stream. I will spend this day with my dear husband if only in memory. To think that one year ago this was the happiest day I had ever experienced. I had loved Isaiah for the first and last time and we had conceived our precious daughter. I still cannot accept that either of them is gone. Shouldn't I feel he is gone?

But instead my mind will not hold the thought. My heart causes me to feel he is still alive and waiting for me somehow. And I visit the tiny grave that my sweet little Willow is supposed to rest in everyday, but I cannot accept it. I can only pray that if it is true that they are together, and Isaiah is taking care of our daughter. I will sit here until it is too dark to see and draw what I have in my memory of them.

When I sketch Isaiah now, he is holding our baby in his strong arms. He would have been the most wonderful father. I start to hum as I draw and realize I am humming my song. Beulah's song which he had composed as a wedding gift to me. Words that caused my heart to sore on our wedding day but now squeeze my heart to the point of pain. I close my eyes and lay my head down on the soft grass and listen to him singing in my memory. I can almost hear him, almost feel him.

Happy Anniversary, my love.

August 15, 1942

My sisters are growing restless. They came home from Atlanta in June once they had completed their high school obligations, but both wanted nothing more than to return to Atlanta. Georgia had found opportunity to design clothing for a shop owner who was impressed with not only her sewing skills but her sense of fashion. Carolina had found a gentleman who was most interested in her, however my aunt would not allow them to court without father's permission and he would not give it.

Now that they had been home a while and driving father mad with their complaining he was ready to consider letting them go back to Atlanta. They had tried to talk to me on several occasions but my deep sorry was more than they could understand. They had no knowledge of my loss. No empathy for my grief because they did not know what had happened to me. They seemed oblivious to the fact that father and mother were so distant to me.

Finally, last night while mother sat and cried bitterly my father announced that all three of us would be leaving in about a week to stay in Atlanta. Our aunt, his sister Eula, had agreed to allow all of us to stay for a while on the condition that each of us tried to find work and support ourselves within a year. It was probably the first time I had smiled in weeks. I was afraid and the idea of leaving my Willow was hard to conceive but I had to get away from this sorrow before it completely consumed me.

SEPTEMBER 11, 1942

We have been in Atlanta a little over a week now. My sisters know the area quite well and are showing me around. It is the closest I have felt to them in a long while, but I cannot tell them anything of why I have been so sad in the past weeks. They have asked me if I plan on completing my education, but I do not think I will. For one thing I must find work as I promised Aunt Eula I would. But I am no longer a young schoolgirl. I have lived a very long life in only a years' time.

People often compare things to 'dog' years. Well I guess in grown up years I am much older than most 16-year-old girls. Carolina had contacted her gentleman friend within days of our arrival and because she is going to be 18 years old soon father gave her his blessing. His name is Arnold Stevenson and he seems very nice. He is devoted to her, so I am expecting an announcement very soon. Mother will be thrilled to have such an event to plan.

Since I am no longer the son father never had, perhaps Arnold will fill that void.

Georgia had started working for the department store within days of our arrival. She was to design and make clothing for the well to do of Atlanta. She loved meeting those people who could help her make a name for herself in the fashion world. Me? I was still looking for a job. Jobs were not easy to come by and I had nothing to offer. I was only 16 and had not finished high school. I had no formal training. What could I do other than clean toilets in the hotels or wash dishes somewhere? I didn't think myself beneath it, but I just couldn't help but think there was more to my pitiful life than that.

A verse came to mind that Isaiah had read to me when I would fear what could happen to us. Jeremiah 29:11 'For I know the thoughts that I think toward you, says the Lord. Thoughts of peace and not of evil, to give you a future and a hope.' I had spent so much of the last few months angry toward God. I had screamed at him for taking everything from me. I felt abandoned and forsaken. But Isaiah had always trusted in God to see him through anything. He told me many times that God had a plan and even when things seemed as if he had forgotten us and was letting terrible things happen… if we would just hold on to our faith that down the road his plan would show itself. I was sure hoping that was true.

I had looked in the newspaper for possible jobs and the newspaper had a job listing for someone to draw pictures for advertisements in the newspaper. It told the address to apply in person. Ask for Samuel Stone, owner and editor of the Evening Post. The next day I made myself presentable and tried to look as professional as a 16-year-old girl could look. I had put together a portfolio of sorts. Basically, it was a lot of my drawings in a folder.

My best dress was the one mother had purchased when I was first expecting and so now it was too large for me. I had forgotten my dress shoes when we packed so quickly for this trip and had not had the funds yet to replace them, so I borrowed a pair of Georgia's. They were a little loose, but I pushed some tissue in the toe to make them fit more snugly. I had twisted my long hair up in a bun on top of my head to make me appear older and used a little of Aunt Eula's lip stick. This would have to do. I looked in the mirror and thought to myself... I hope this Mr. Stone is old and half blind. I might have a chance if he does not look too closely.

SEPTEMBER 14, 1942

God truly does work in mysterious ways. I found my way to the office of the newspaper and managed to get by the receptionist without an appointment. I sat waiting for Mr. Stone to invite me in and when I am extremely nervous my feet tend to perspire a little. Which, when that happened, the tissue paper in the shoe became wet and mashed down which meant the shoes were too loose. I was nervously flipping through my drawings trying to be sure the best one was on top. A little box on the receptionist's desk buzzed and a voice told her to send in the next applicant and do it quickly because he was facing a deadline. She jumped at his bark of command which caused her to give me a frantic look and tell me to hurry up... he was ready to see me but had very little time. It was like a ballet of clowns. I jumped up from my seat just as Mr. Stone opened his office door. My momentum along with my loose shoes and my papers began to fall from my folder and boom...I fell on Mr. Stone knocking him to the floor and tossing papers everywhere. I lay on top of him for a second completely shocked and unsure of what to do.

"I am so very sorry sir. I do not know what happened. Please accept my apology."

I said all this and more while attempting to gracefully crawl off the man and pick up my papers that were scattered about. And my shoes had come off leaving tissue paper on his floor. My hair had fallen from its neat bun and .... Mr. Stone began to laugh. He laughed and laughed and laughed while I just stood there looking like a red headed scarecrow. I reached out and offered my hand to help him up. Once he was on his feet, I realized he was not old at all. Possible 25 but no older. And he was very handsome.

"Again, sir I do apologize. Just let me gather my things and I will get out of your way."

"Are those your drawings," he asked pointing to the pile of crumpled paper I held to my chest. "Miss," and he paused waiting for an answer.

Oh yes sir these are mine. I am Willamina Pettigrew."

My heart ached a little when I said my name. Was I betraying Isaiah by not saying Reed? I could not chance it getting back to my sisters or my Aunt Eula.

"Well may I see them please," he asked, holding out his hand.

I just piled the entire stack in his open hand. "Yes sir."

He looked through them two or three times.

"These are superior. You are a very talented artist Miss. Pettigrew."

"You're hired. Be here in the morning at seven o'clock sharp. I cannot abide tardiness. And please for the love of Pete find some shoes that fit."

He left the room in a big hurry but did stop long enough to tell his receptionist to allow me to fill out my employment paperwork.

"I have a job!" I wanted to yell it to the rooftops. When

I told my aunt and sisters, they were all thrilled. I left out much of the details of my interview. I knew well enough that my sisters would never let me live it down if they knew. One of the first thoughts in my head when I left the newspaper office was how excited Isaiah would be for me. Would I ever stop thinking of him? It has been close to a year since I received the horrible news of his plan going down and yet it is still unreal. I wanted to tell him he helped me get the job. Every picture I had taken was either of our willow tree or the stream and one was of him holding Willow. I knew I would never forget him and that I would love him until the day I took my last breath, but this felt so good. I had a new beginning for my life. I was feeling joy for the first time in a long time. I placed the picture of Isaiah holding Willow back in the frame I kept it in. I could not display it out in the open as I would have liked to but it stayed in the drawer of my nightstand so I could tell them goodnight before I fell to sleep each night.

DECEMBER 20, 1942

Life is speeding by. Georgia has been promoted and is going to have the chance to travel around America to different fashion shows. Possible other parts of the world. She is so happy and for the first time in their life she and her twin sister are taking much different paths. Carolina has married Arnold and they are living happily across town in a cute apartment building. Mother and Father come to visit her often and they are so very happy to find out they are going to be grandparents. I try hard not to show how bitter I am about the difference in their reaction about her baby compared to the way they treated me. I have spent a lot of time in prayer trying to forgive their ignorance. They do, at least attempt to talk to me now. Of course, the subject of the past year never comes up and my father still calls me Willamina. I will never be Willie to him again.

I am so busy I cannot find time to eat most days. With Christmas so close I have had to draw ads for the many stores that would advertise in the newspaper. The paper is only once a week thank goodness because If I had to do this daily my hands would cramp up and my fingers would curl up in knots. I am glad I am so busy because it helps me not to think. My sadness seems to be mostly in the early morning hours when I think about the willow tree and lying next to Isaiah.

My daughter left me almost eight months ago and though there is no milk in them my breast aches to nurse her when I dream of her sweet little face. God please heal my heart and give me peace is my constant prayer.

My only happiness is my work. Mr. Stone is a dear man and a kind boss. He has invited me to dine with him at his country club on Christmas Eve. I know I heard him talking to his receptionist about her Christmas bonus and he gave a special envelope to several others on staff so I am thinking I will get a bonus as well. I have not worked for him for a long time so the dinner may be my bonus this year. He is funny and charming, and I always look forward to talking to him. I have taken his advice and purchased new, better fitting shoes and several new outfits for work. Georgia helped me find the most flattering for my size and coloring and thankfully used her employee discount to help with the purchases. As an early Christmas gift, she personally made me a lovely gown to wear to the country club. She said I looked like a princess going to the ball.

December 27, 1942

Well I guess if I were a painting it would be called Naïve. The dinner at the country club was not my bonus. It was a date. Mr. Stone who now insists I call him Samuel when we are not in the office appears to be taken with me. I had no clue. Perhaps my heart was just not open to see it. He is a perfect gentleman. He is kind and considerate and very handsome. But it is too soon. I don't want to hurt him or push him away, but I am not open to love another yet. Maybe never. I reminded him I was only 16 and this was too sudden. I tried to really play the innocent naïve young girl to help explain my distance. How could I possibly tell him I had lived what felt like a hundred years in one. How I had married, conceived a child, been a prisoner in my parents' attic, lost my husband, given birth by myself, and lost my child in a years' time. OH, and did I mention my husband was a black man. He seemed to be an understanding man, but I am sure he has his limits and I needed this job. He did not seem discouraged by my dismissal of his confession of interest. He asked me to be so kind as to attend the New Year's Eve Party with him at this same club. I am not sure why, but I said yes…this time knowing it was a date. OH, and I still did not get a Christmas bonus.

January 1, 1943

I borrowed a dress from Georgia. She is slightly taller than I am but the dress was meant to be a little shorter than I was willing to wear so with the height difference it was perfect. I knew she would not have time or the inclination to make me another dress so soon after the first one. I left my hair down but pulled back from my face with clips. It was a wonderfully festive party. Dancing and food and campaign which I carried around most of the night but did not drink. I had never had alcohol and was not sure this was the best time to try it. After all, I had already fallen on this man just because my shoes were loose... If I were to get tipsy, who knows what might happen. Samuel had led me around introducing me to everyone. He seemed very proud to have me on his arm and I had to admit it felt nice. We ate lobster and steak which was so good. I have had a steak many times. I mean I grew up on a cattle ranch so ...yeah, I have had steak. But I had never had lobster. It came with a little bowl of butter to dip it in and a bib you were supposed to wear to keep your clothes clean. I felt like a baby wearing the bib but after I dripped butter on it a few times I could see the need for it. When the band started to play a very slow song, he asked me if I would dance with him.

"I'm not sure I know how."

"I'll lead you," he said and pulled me into his arms.

My cheeks burned red as they always seemed to do at the worst times and my heart was pounding. I could hardly breathe. He held me so close and his eyes seemed to hold me as strongly and his arms did. As we danced slowly swaying back and forth to the music people around us started to stop where they were and started counting down. It was ten seconds until the new year, and I knew what that meant. I had no time to really react. No time to decide if I was ready or not to have another man put his mouth on mine. But everyone said Happy New Year and the confetti went flying into the air and the noise makers whirled and Samuel Stone kissed me. It was a soft, easy kiss. Not forceful or demanding but as gentle as a whisper. When he pulled away from the kiss, he looked in my eyes and waited for a reaction. I smiled.

FEBRUARY 3, 1943

It is my birthday. I am now 17 years old. The past month has been amazing. I have gone somewhere with Samuel at least twice a week. Usually Friday and Saturday we will go out to a play or have dinner. We have seen a few movies which I had never been allowed to do before now. We attend worship together on Sunday and he comes to Aunt Eula's for lunch. My parents have met him and seem to think he is a wonderful young man. I know now that my heart can love again. I have not pushed Isaiah out of my heart, but I have let two men occupy it. At times I struggle with the feeling that I am being unfair to Samuel because my heart still loves another. Then when I feel love for Samuel, I feel like I am being unfaithful to Isaiah. I have finally accepted that he is lost to me forever. If he had not died in that plan, he would have found his way back to me. I know he would want me to be happy again. Samuel has told me this would be a special birthday. He said he had something he needed to ask me, and I saw him talking to father alone the other day, so I am thinking... I am hoping he will ask me to marry him.

Oh, Isaiah please forgive me. I will love you forever my sweet angel, but I need to move on. Take good care of our little girl.

March 26, 1943

I will marry Samuel Stone tomorrow. He wanted to give me a large wedding. I told him I did not want a large wedding. I only wanted a small church wedding with his family and mine. He did not understand why.

"Don't all women want big elaborate weddings? I can afford it and I want you to have everything you want."

He looked a little panicked at the tears that sprang to my eyes. He had no way of knowing my inward struggle. I loved him so much. I knew I would be happy with him. But I also knew if Isaiah Reed were to walk in that door at this exact moment, I would leave with him and never look back. That was so unfair to Samuel and I hated that I had this ghost that lived in my mind that would never let me completely give all of me to this lovely man. I had to give him some type of reasoning for not wanting the big wedding.

"Samuel, you know my history on entrances. I can't risk falling on the minister when I walk down the aisle."

He chuckled at that and said... "You have a point my love."

I know that this will be my last entry for a while in a journal. I will take it back up soon enough, but I can't risk Samuel finding them. I purchased a trunk as part of my luggage for our honeymoon. I found it in a specialty shop, and it has a false bottom meant to conceal valuables. For now, it will conceal the missing pieces of my heart. Tomorrow I will give the remaining pieces to Samuel Stone.

Nana sat under the tree with the hat still covering her eyes for a few more minutes once I closed the journal. I just sat quietly and waited.

"I want you to know Alex, I truly loved your grandfather. I loved him more and more as the years went by. We made a good life together and I never wanted for anything. Truth be known he spoiled me.

"I know Nana. I was not around you and Papa a lot growing up but when I was, I could tell. It was almost embarrassing sometimes the way you two kissed and held hands. That stuff is kind of gross when you're a little kid. Old people making out can give you nightmares."

We both had a good laugh at that and started to make our way to the car. I did not ask her about the journals. I knew this was not the last one she wrote. There were a few more left in the box I brought down from the attic. I knew she would get to them in her own good time. I would be very curious to find out where in her life she started writing in them again.

That night I stayed up very late typing what I remembered from the journals. I may re-write them a thousand times before I have a finished novel, but I did not want to forget the details. I could not be sure, but I imagined that Nana was laying in her bed looking at her painting and possibly glancing at Papa's picture on her nightstand. Even now after all these years, her heart still belonged to two men.

Chapter Twelve

A Ghost in the Marriage Bed

It has been two weeks, three days and 14 hours since we last opened a journal. Not that I am anxious or anything… but I am about ready to just grab the next one and start without Nana. I know she needs time after each one to process her emotions and I am really trying to be patient, but Nana was the one who pointed out our limited time frame after all. She has spent a lot of time going over old picture albums with me and emphasizing how happy she and Papa Sam were. The beautiful family they had created. How much he had spoiled her and how wonderful their lives had been for the forty years they were married.

I am getting the idea that she is preparing me for something in the next journal or at least in one of them. Annie is due to come home next week and Mark will be coming as well to see his mom. We have talked several times on the phone, and we met halfway one Saturday to have lunch. Nana asked to come with me because she also missed Mark. I wanted to tell her three's a crowd, but I could not refuse her.

We held hands and enjoyed our visit but all I could think about was how desperately I wanted to be in his arms. How hungry I was for his lips to be on mine. In a phone call after the date he told me he felt the same way.

"Maybe Nana realized we needed to keep our desires under control," he had laughingly said. "She is a very wise ole bird after all."

I knew he was right. I would have to keep my desires in control because as much as I liked Mark, I was not completely sure that I loved him. I think I do. I had even told him I thought I was falling in love with him, but we have not really known each other that long. I realized after the portrait Nana hung in her room reminded Mark of us that I had allowed the journals to romanticize everything. I wanted to have what Isaiah and Beulah had. It would not be fair to Mark if I was reacting to emotions brought on by the journals and not my true feelings. I would have to keep my emotional reins pulled tight and in control. For Marks sack and for my own. That way no one would be hurt.

Finally, on the Wednesday before Annie was to return Nana allowed me to read another journal. She warned me before I started that it would be fairly mundane.

"It was the first year of our marriage and I only journaled a few times."

After the last few journals, I was relieved to hear that this one would be uneventful. I was not sure how much more I could handle. I also felt Nana needed time to recover.

April 26, 1943

I am alone in my new home for the first time in weeks. Our honeymoon was wonderful. Samuel had offered to take me anywhere I wanted to go. I had always wanted to spend time at an ocean beach front. To sketch and paint the beautiful ocean and the different plant life and wildlife that I would see there. We chose to spend our time on the South Carolina coast. Almost two full weeks in Myrtle Beach in a lovely house he had rented with its own private beach access.

I would sit for hours on the balcony outside of the bedroom either drawing or painting the most wonderful scenery. It was so different than anything I had seen up to this point of my life. Samuel was so good to me. He of course would have wanted nothing more than for us to stay in our honeymoon bed most of the time. He lavished me with flowers and little gifts almost daily. We attended the theater and went on a fishing boat expedition.

We ate out in nice restaurants and strolled along the beach at sunset gathering shells and memories. I do truly love him, and I am so happy to be here with him but it is hard to completely love this man while a ghost shares our marriage bed. Our first night as husband and wife as Samuel so tenderly made love to me for the first time, tears began to flow from my eyes and he assumed it was because I was a virgin and he had caused me pain.

"I'm so sorry my love. I was trying to be very gentle so I wouldn't hurt you," he had said.

I felt guilty for letting him continue to think it but what could I have said?

'Oh, it's not that dear. I had sexual relations with my first

husband several times the one night we were together and conceived a child. Now all I can think about is that night and as you touch me... as your mouth finds my breast and my secret pleasures, I am remembering him instead of thinking of you.'

I am pretty sure that would have made it the shortest marriage on record. Plus, I truly did not want to hurt Samuel. He is such a good man.

I kept reminding myself that Isaiah was gone, and I needed to focus on my future with Samuel and not cause myself this pain brought on by grief of what can no longer be.

On our way home we drove down the coast as far as Savannah, Georgia before heading home to Atlanta. Once we were home, he took me to his home. Our home. A small house not too far from downtown and the newspaper.

He had checked on the paper daily while we were gone. Even our first couple of days back he would go in for only about an hour then rush home. He says he did not want to leave me alone in a new house. He told me to make any changes to the house that would make it feel more like home. I will make it more feminine with lace dollies and pretty curtains. I also must get different pillows for the couch in the living room and a lighter colored bedspread for our bed. I will try to make it home, but it just does not feel like home.

I wanted to go back to work and he was fine with that. It helped to be back at the newspaper, but the other employees started to treat me differently. I was now the boss's wife and not a co-worker. After only two weeks I decided to stay home and paint.

May 10, 1943

I am so happy. God has given me another chance to be a mother. I probably conceived on my wedding night because the doctor puts me at six weeks. This baby will be our Christmas gift. Samuel is thrilled. He is already planning schools up through college and wants to pick names. I cannot wait to hold my baby. But no matter how much I love this child or any other children we might have they will never replace my sweet Willow. She was my first born even if no one knows except me. Oh, and my parents, but I am sure they have forgotten all about her.

August 7, 1943

I have returned from a short visit with my parents. I had no real desire to see them but I had to have a reason to be there on July 31st. Samuel wanted to go with me because he was so protective, but he was glad to stay home once my sister Georgia agreed to come with me. She had traveled a great deal in the past year and had missed every one of their visits to Atlanta, so she was thrilled for the chance to visit our parents. On the 31st which was a Saturday they had wanted to take their girls out for a nice dinner. At the last minute I told them I was just too exhausted and would love to just rest and keep my feet up. Being pregnant helps when you are trying to get out of something you don't want to do. The minute they were out of sight I walked to the stream. I knew I couldn't stay all night as I would have liked to, but I figured I had a few hours at least. I sat under the willow tree for a while and simply cried.

"Happy Anniversary Isaiah," I sobbed.

I began to talk out loud telling him everything that had taken place since our anniversary last year. We would have been married two years and our daughter would have turned one in April.

I moved to the stream for a while and put my feet in the cool water. As I looked out over to the path on the other side, I could almost imagine Isaiah walking toward me. Hot and tired from a day's hard labor but smiling and waving at me. I leaned my head back and closed my eyes. Beulah's song played in my head as if he were holding me and whispering it to me as he did the last time I heard it.

I returned to the house just in time to retreat to my room before mother, father and Georgia came in laughing and talking about the wonderful food. I lay in my bed and pretended to be sleeping when Georgia peeked in to check on me. I felt guilty for the deception. I hated that I had lied to Georgia and to Samuel. I was not feeling guilty that I lied to my parents. I still had nightmares where I would wake up thinking I was locked in the attic and the house would catch on fire or I would be injured, and no one could hear me. I was still working hard to forgive them. I prayed about it daily. But I had to be honest, I was not there yet. I begged God to take away my deep sorrow. It is so hard to love two men so completely. To want to give complete devotion to Samuel who was so good to me and obviously loved me very much, while at the same time clinging to the memory of a man who I can never let go of. To the man I had given my whole heart to and who still lives there in my crowded heart keeping me from being truly happy.

October 31, 1943

It is Halloween. My stomach is as round as any pumpkin on display. Samuel and I had so much fun handing out candy to all the little children in our neighborhood. It made me so anxious for this baby to get here. My arms have ached to hold a baby for such a long time now. Our nursery is ready. We have decorated it in pale yellow so it will work for either boy or girl. The newspaper employees insisted on giving us a baby shower. So many little gowns and booties. I looked at the great treasure of gifts and items purchased by my parents, sisters, Samuels family and by Samuel and myself. If I changed this little one hourly I could not possibly use all the nice things, yet all I can think about are those few diapers and shirts that Millie and Grandmother had made for Willow. And the lovely blanket made from the pieces of material Georgia had donated to them. How precious those meager gifts had been and how perfect my little angel had looked in them.

December 26, 1943

My baby daughter Susan Marie Stone arrived on December 21st 1943 at four o'clock in the afternoon. She is beautiful and has Samuels eyes and nose. She has very little hair, but the tiny bit of fuzz appears to be reddish. The doctor was amazed at how easy it had been for me to have my first baby.

"Most women do not stay so calm and well you were a real trooper Mrs. Stone."

What could I possibly say? I just smiled and said I come from sturdy stock.

I continued to read the remainder of that journal. It was all about my Aunt Susan as an infant. Then there was a great deal about her turning from a baby to a toddler. The next journal took up basically in the middle of the year. I guess with a baby you do not have as much time to make entries on a daily or even weekly basis.

June 8, 1944

The terrible war is all over the news. On June 6, our soldiers landed on the beach at Normandy, France. The news tells of so many killed and injured. Samuel is busy at the newspaper almost all-night preparing articles to keep our city informed. I am frightened and as ridiculous as it is, I wonder if Isaiah is in France. Perhaps they will find him and bring him back home for a proper burial. Or could he still be alive and has been a prisoner. Maybe he will come back to me. The minute the thought passed through my mind I felt such disgrace and shame. I am sitting here holding my precious little girl as she drifts off to sleep.

September 20, 1944

My daughter is crawling and pulling up on everything. She keeps me so busy and I just found out I will be twice as busy in a few months. Samuel and I are expecting a second child. We are hoping for a boy this time. When I called my mother to tell her, she told me that father was not well. He has taken to his bed and refuses to listen to the doctor.

The ranch is in disrepair because father is no longer able to work and has only a few hired hands to care for a few animals and tend to the grounds. Mother is very worried. I probably should go see how I can help but with a little one and one on the way I don't feel I would be very useful.

I can remember the days when I was one of the hardest workers on the ranch. As good as any of the other workers. My father's almost son… Willie.

December 22, 1944

Yesterday Susan turned one. It was a wonderful celebration with a lovely cake and lots of gifts from her Aunt Georgia, Aunt Carolina and uncle Arnold and her cousin John. Carolina and Arnold's son. Mother was unable to attend because Father was still very ill. The doctors seem to think he has congestive heart failure and could never make the trip.

January 4, 1945

Father passed away quietly in his sleep on December 27th. I am sad to say no one except mother was there for him. We all came for the funeral of course. Mother was adamant that she would not spend another night on that ranch. It was too lonely and she wanted to live near her children. Carolina was thrilled at the idea of mother staying with them. She had the extra room and mother would be a lot of help to her.

"Father left the ranch to you Willamina," she announced very matter of fact.

She looked at me as if to imply I would understand. I did not really but I was thrilled.

APRIL 6, 1945

Poor Samuel. I have talked of nothing except my desire to move to the ranch. I told him how wonderful it would be for our children to run and play in the fields and to enjoy the animals. He investigated every possibility and finally agreed he would sell his newspaper in Atlanta and start a new one in Macon which was only about 3 miles from Payne Georgia where our ranch was. It would be later in the year before we can move.

I am due to have my second child any day now and there would be a lot of loose ends to wrap up. I was determined to be there before July 31 in hopes to celebrate my and Isaiah's 4th anniversary. I know it is crazy that I still do that, but I have not missed a single year so far. I am so busy and so happy that I do not miss him as much as I once did, but I just can't help but feel I need to acknowledge our special day.

MAY 12, 1945

This is my first opportunity to write in my journal since the birth of my second daughter. Kathy Elizabeth Stone was born on April 30, 1945 at 7:40 a.m. on the day that would have been Willow's third birthday.

That was the last entry in the journal. Nana was very quiet for a while and finally looked at me with little emotion in her eyes.

"My girls were so close they should have been twins."

She was talking about Susan and Kathy who were only 16 months apart. She had no comment about Kathy having been born on Willow's birthday. I had noticed that Nana seemed to be partial to Kathy out of her three girls. Perhaps it was because she compared her to what Willow would have been doing at any certain age.

September 1, 1945

We moved into the ranch house on July 28th. Samuel was a little put off at my rush to get it finished so quickly.

"It's not as if the house is going anywhere," he protested.

But Samuel wanted nothing more than to make me happy and I am ashamed to admit that there were times when I used that knowledge to get my way.

The house will need a lot of work. Mother has not tried to keep the place up as she had when we were young. It could take me a year or more to get it in the proper shape, but I was home and that's what mattered. I packed all my journals in the trunk I had purchased for my honeymoon and have simply added one to the collection whenever I finished writing in it. I have placed old clothing in the trunk to conceal the bottom and we placed it in the attic. Once we sat it down under the rose window Samuel noticed the bed and dresser at the other end of the attic.

"Seems like an odd place to put a guest. Why did they have a makeshift guest room in this dusty, hot attic," he asked?

"I guess they thought it would come in handy if they had an unexpected visitor."

It was not a complete lie. Willow was an unexpected visitor.

"Should we get rid of it," he asked?

"No, please let's keep it."

My dear Samuel did not ask me why. He saw how important it was to me and that was enough. I hated keeping this secret from him. But he would never understand, and I think it would be hard for him to forgive such deception. I needed to see that bed where I had spent my short time with my first child just as much as I needed to visit the stream and the willow tree on the 31st of July every year. I loved my new life. I loved Samuel and my precious daughters, but I did not want Isaiah and Willow to be forgotten. I was the only one who would care enough to mourn their passing and as long as I live, I will remember.

Chapter Thirteen

Don't Tell Me... Show Me

Annie arrived about noon on Friday. She seemed thrilled to be back. She is not what I remember. I guess the truth is I don't remember her. She is a petite lady with dark hair and beautiful gray eyes. Marks eyes I thought. She looks to be in her forties and is bubbling over with excitement at meeting me.

"Oh, Alex, I am so thrilled to meet you. Your Nana has told me all about you and the fun you two have had this summer. Have you seen our little town? I hear you have met my son Mark. Isn't he a sweetie? Are you excited about starting classes soon?"

"Annie, would you breathe please and maybe let her answer one of those questions?"

We looked at Nana and all of us began to laugh.

"I'm sorry dear," Annie said. "I guess I do tend to get carried away."

"It's okay Annie. I am thrilled to meet you also and yes; I have been having fun with Nana. OH, and yes I have met Mark and I guess he is a sweetie," I jokingly shrugged my shoulders.

We sat around the kitchen table while Annie told us all about her new grandson. We saw what must have been a thousand pictures of little Robert Allen Sayre. "They named him after his grandpop," she said, choking up with emotion.

Nana patted her hand and of course told her how beautiful her grandson was and how good it was to have her back. Nana made tea and Annie jumped up to get cookies from the pantry. Back on the job without hesitation it seemed. She decided to go to her room and unpack before starting dinner. Nana insisted we would order Chinese to be delivered.

"You are still off the clock until tomorrow," Nana insisted.

Later that evening Mark finally made it home. He had to wait for the end of his last class and would only be home until Sunday afternoon because of his study load. I knew his mother was so happy to see him and I selfishly wondered If I would get any time with him at all.

We all sat around the pool eating out of our little cartons. Nana and Mark were pros with the chop sticks but Annie and I finally caved and retrieved a fork from the kitchen. The conversation was constant. Several times while Annie or Nana would be talking my eyes would travel to Mark who was almost always looking at me. He had gotten up to toss his carton in the trash and instead of returning to his seat next to Annie he sat on the end of the lounge I was in. He placed his hand over my ankle and did the eyebrow thing he liked to do if he was trying to be flirty. Yep you guessed it. My face flushed eight different shades of red. Annie and Nana both beamed and were suddenly exhausted and thought they would go to bed.

"I'll see you in the morning son," Annie said

Nana kissed both Mark and I on top of our heads and grinned at us knowingly.

We watched as they entered through the French door and the light in the hallway went off. A few minutes later I noticed the light come on in Nana's room. Mark grinned and crawled up the lounge to sit beside me. I started to open my mouth to tell him how much I had missed him but he placed his finger over my lips to stop me.

"Don't tell me you missed me… show me."

We kissed for a long while. At first very gently and almost teasing. The longer we kissed the more passionate the kisses became and soon we were both kissing with such a hunger for the other. I wasn't sure if I would be able to stop if this went on any longer. I was pulsing with desire for this beautiful man and those gray eyes were making me forget where I was. What if Nana were looking out of her window?

"Nana," I yipped.

"Where," he asked and jumped up from the lounge.

"No, she isn't here. I just got to thinking she could be looking out of her window."

He glanced up toward the window which was dark and then at me. You guessed it. My face was flushed. Not just from the embarrassment of my reaction but from the passion of our kisses. I was out of breath and obviously he had caused a reaction in me.

"I think she is asleep," he said with a sexy grin.

He began to climb back on the lounge this time more on top of me than beside me like before. He lowered his month to kiss me again….

"Ah Mark," I said and placed my hand on his chest in

order to keep a distance.

He lowered his head and said nothing for a while then flipped over and sat on the edge of our seat.

"I'm sorry," I said

"No, don't be sorry Alex. I should have never got that carried away. It's my fault."

"Are you mad," I asked in almost a whisper.

"No," I am not mad. I promise I am not mad. But would you excuse me for just a moment while I take care of a little problem… well not little, he grinned, but a problem."

At that he turned and jumped in the pool. He swam back and forth several times and I remembered seeing him do this after our first meeting. After a while he got out and shook the water off like a dog would. His hair was going in every direction. His wet shorts and tee shirt were clinging to his skin. Okay, I thought, stop thinking this way or you will have to jump in next.

We took a walk and without really planning it we ended up at the stream. We sat down and placed our feet in the water. The stars were so bright and numerous that it made me feel tiny.

"Mark, you understand why I stopped you, don't you?"

"I know why I should have never let it go that far. I know what God's will is when it comes to sex before marriage. I do not know where our relationship is heading Alex. But I do know how I feel about you. I know that you are always on my mind and so deeply embedded in my heart that I feel consumed by you. You are like my oxygen and without you I cannot breathe. I also know you just graduated high school and are barely 18. I know that it will take time for you to decide where you want this to go. Don't be afraid to stop me when I take things too far. And I will

'TRY' to keep myself under control. But your stopping me will not make me leave. I will only leave if you tell me you want me to. It may be after we have both finished school before you are sure. I may think I am going to die if I must wait that long... but I won't. I wasn't kidding when I told you I thought I was falling in love with you."

Mark took my hand in his and kissed it softly.

"Nana used to read her Bible to us when we were kids. One day she read to us from 1st Corinthians 13. It talked about the things that love is. Love suffers long. It is kind and does not envy. Does not behave rudely. I don't remember the whole thing right now, but she told me when I grew up and started looking for someone to love that these are the things I should look for in a woman. And these are the things I needed to be for her. I think I have found that with you and I will do nothing to drive you away."

He kissed me several times very softly and cautiously. We sat there for a long while with me leaning on his strong chest and his arm around my waist. It was enough for both of us for now to just be together... surrounded by the stars.

The next day Mark tried to spend most of his free time with Annie. He also had a few chores to do for Nana. He was going to mow, and I asked him to show me how to operate the mower.

"I'll do the mowing and you can trim with the weed eater. We're a team," I said.

Saturday had flown by and I dreaded his leaving the next day right after church. The four of us sat in the den and watched a movie that night. Annie had been sitting on the couch beside Mark when I came in with a big bowl of popcorn. She jumped up and insisted I sit next to Mark. She sat on the other end of the couch giving us a little space and Nana was in her chair with her feet on the ottoman and her afghan over her legs. I had to assume since the three of them kept looking at each other and giving knowing grins that I had been a topic of conversation at some point. I would be asking Nana as soon as the opportunity presented itself. Mark held my hand during most of the movie, so I assumed he had for sure told Annie about us. This was certainly turning out to be a better summer than hanging at the mall back home or working fast food to make extra money before starting school. I was where I wanted to be, and I don't think I can ever make myself leave. Unless I am leaving with Mark of course.

After Mark left Sunday afternoon Annie decided she would go to the market to get the groceries for the week. Once she was gone Nana told me Annie was giving us some privacy. Nana had pretty much given her the same talk she had given Mark. That she and I had a project we had to complete before I started classes and needed some time where we would be undisturbed. I think she also needed something to focus on because she hated to see Mark leave. Nana told me to go to the library and she would go get the next journal.

"We will have privacy there with the door closed. Annie will not bother us if she returns before we are finished."

"Nana, before we start, can I ask you something? Have you and Annie been talking about Mark and me?"

She looked down and grinned, then looked at me with pride in her eyes.

"Sweet girl, Mark told his mother how he felt about you.

He is very close to his mother and he wanted her to know how wonderful he thinks you are. I merely agreed with him. He is very taken with you."

"Thank you for telling her I was okay," I said "I am very fond of Mark. I may even love him, Nana. We are trying to go slow and not let ourselves get carried away."

"I think that is very mature of both of you," Nana praised.

"I just know that the story of you and Isaiah is just so romantic and I don't want to get my emotions mixed up with the journals and make a wrong decision. I would never want to hurt Mark."

"You are very wise Alexandria. I am so proud of you. I love Mark and I love you. I don't want to see either of you hurt."

"I know what mother would say. She would say you are only 18 years old and you are too young. Do you think I am too young, Nana?"

"I was 15," she said and handed me the journal.

MARCH 26, 1946

We have worked so hard over the last five months getting the house in perfect shape. I have had no time to write in my journal or paint or hardly eat with all the work plus taking care of two very young and very active little girls. Last month I had my birthday and until Samuel came home with a lovely necklace and a bouquet of flowers I had forgotten. I am 20 years old. That is so very young but suddenly I feel very old. Tomorrow will be Samuel and my anniversary. We would have been married for 3 years. So, in the past five years I have married twice, and given birth 3 times.

I look at the words as I write them and start to cry. Not because I am sorry about any of these things but because I found out today that I am pregnant again. I think this baby may be the result of celebrating my birthday until the wee hours of the night so I guess it is only fitting that I break the news to Samuel on our anniversary tomorrow. The baby is due the first part of November so 3 children in less than 4 years. My body does not look like that of a twenty-year-old. I have trouble looking in the mirror in our bathroom without being sad. I stay busy and eat very little, so I am not overweight.

But I remember the firm breast and flat stomach of my first night with Isaiah. He was mesmerized by my body that night under the willow tree. He told me over and over how perfect I was, how beautiful every inch of me was. And when I married Samuel. Even though I had given birth to Willow my body did not disappoint. I looked at the line of stretch marks and the fact that my stomach was not firm and flat anymore. Would it ever be again? Samuel tells me all the time that I am still so very beautiful, but I don't believe it. All I know is that I am exhausted all the time.

I know with all the money we have spent on the house I cannot ask for help now but maybe by the time this baby gets here I can hint to Samuel for a nanny or a housekeeper. When this baby arrives, I will already be dealing with a two-year-old and a one-year-old. With Samuel at work most of the day and mother busy helping Carolina with her second baby there is no one for me. I surprised myself today when Millie came to mind. She had been my only friend at one of the worst times of my life. I wish she were close by and could help me now.

June 3, 1946

Samuel came home with a copy of today's newspaper. He does that often but especially when there is something unusual to report. His reason today was an article telling that AT&T had developed the first car phone. Samuel was always interested in improved communication. I guess since he reported news for a living that made sense. He was talking to me about how he wanted to be one of the first to get a phone in his car.

As he explained all the advantages of getting the scoop on breaking news, I noticed another article. It explained that the U.S. Supreme Court ruled that segregation on interstate bus travel is unconstitutional in the case of Morgan vs. Virginia. All I could think about was that Isaiah would be so happy. He had enlisted in the war in hopes it would make a difference for the black people of our Nation. He dreamed of a day when he could walk down any street with me on his arm without persecution. I smiled and a tear started to fall down my cheek. I stopped it before Samuel noticed.

I will tell Isaiah when I go to the stream next month. It will be our 5th anniversary. I only go to the stream once a year on that day. I sit under the willow tree and tell him everything that has happened over the past year. There will be a lot of news this year.

November 30, 1946

I am only now physically and emotionally able to write in my journal. The last two months are impossible to explain. Let me first tell the wonderful news of my third daughter with Samuel. Frances Emma Stone was born on November 9, 1946 at

2:14 in the morning. She is beautiful and healthy. After what happened at the USO club at the Halloween dance I now have a housekeeper who also helps with the children. Her name is Carla and she is a Godsend. She will only be with us for about a year before she will leave for college, but I will deal with that later.

I am shaking as I try to write of the events of October 31st. Samuel had asked me to accompany him to a Halloween dance at the USO club in Macon. I tried to explain that I was only days away from giving birth and really did not want to go. Samuel had never served in the military, but he had provided coverage in his newspaper and had interviewed many of the local veterans once the war ended in 1945. They had invited him as an honored guest and hoped he would put something in his newspaper about the event which was a big fund raiser. It was a nice party. Plus, he had hired a sitter for the night, and I did not have to carry a single child except the one inside me.

They had a live band and lots of refreshments. The music was wonderful, and they had a gentleman who sang several of the famous ballads of that year. I had managed not to dance any so far because Samuel was so busy interviewing people but near the end of the evening, he talked me into a slow dance. Once the song was over, we stood clapping and the band announced that their last song was an original composition and a special request.

Samuel put his arms around me as he had for the previous song and I laid my head on his shoulder. Then the music started, and the gentleman began to sing the words on the paper given him. My knees started to buckle beneath me. I knew I was dropping to the floor and there was no way of stopping me. I was shaking violently from the shock. I knew I was passing out. The room was growing dark all around the edges and before I completely passed out, I whispered ... 'that's my song'.

I opened my eyes to find the ambulance attendant listening to my heart and taking my pulse. As I blinked to bring the room into focus, I was looking at all the faces trying to find Isaiah. The USO club was still segregated in most areas. A sad truth that the men who had fought beside them and, in many cases, saved their lives were not allowed in the club provided for Veterans. I wasn't sure how I had missed seeing him come in, but he had to have brought the song to the band. No one else would have that song. I asked Samuel to have the singer come over. He thought I was probably not thinking clearly.

"You need to lie still, Willie. They are bringing the stretcher now."

"I need to talk to him." I began to raise my voice and realized everyone including Samuel was looking at me as if I had lost my mind. I lowered my voice and calmly said, "Samuel please I want to thank him."

It was one of those things where people did something because you were pregnant, and everyone knows pregnant women can be a little crazy this close to their due date. I had to be crazy if I thought that was my song. Once the singer came over, I motioned to him to come closer so I could ask him something... he politely did as I asked.

"Where did that song come from? The last one you sang. Didn't you say it was a special request? Who requested it?"

He explained that a boy who had been out with friends for Halloween had brought it to him.

"A man had offered him fifty dollars to bring it to me and sent fifty dollars for me as a tip. I figured if he were so desperate to have it played that he would fork over that much cash I would have to do him this favor."

"Where is the man?"

"He didn't hang around according to the kid. I never saw him."

"Can I see the music sheet please?"

He held it out to me and said,

"Lady you can have it."

In bold letters across the top it said 'BEULAH'S SONG'

I apparently passed out again and the next thing I knew I was in the hospital under observation. At first, I was hysterical. I cried for hours until the doctor feared I would cause dehydration. Samuel was at a loss as to what to do. When he would ask me what was wrong I would say I did not know. I could not tell him the truth.

Could this mean that Isaiah was alive? Had he found his way back to me after five years. Where could he be now? Maybe he is waiting for me to be alone and he will come to me. But if he did... what would I do? I could not just walk out on Samuel and our children. I just needed to know he was alive and well. The hospital sent me home the next day and I returned on November 8th in labor and ready to give birth. I managed after two weeks of recovering to make my way to the stream. I frantically looked for any sign he had been there. I moved every leaf from under the willow tree to see if he might have left a note. Despite my exhaustion I even managed to walk to Millie and grandmother's little house to see if he might possibly be living there.

Again, there was no sign of him having been there. I had managed to hold on to the paper the singer had given me. When I realized I still held it in my hand, I placed it in my small clutch purse. Once I was home, I put it in one of my journals for safe keeping. I looked at it again this morning. I will put the song and this journal in my trunk upstairs so no one will find it. My heart is broken all over again because I have lost him. But at the same time my heart is filled to overflowing with joy. My Isaiah is alive. He did not die in that plan. I may never learn the truth of what happened to him. I may never set eyes on him again. But to know he is alive is a blessing in itself.

Oh, Isaiah my love. Thank you for giving me back my song.

I sat there staring at the journal in total disbelief of what I had just read. Then I looked at Nana. She would not make eye contact with me at first. When she finally did, she just stood as if we were done for the night and business as usual.

"Wait just one minute! Are you telling me that Isaiah is still alive? That you knew he was not killed in that plan and you have let me grieve all this time for your lost love? Nana, why didn't you look for him? I do not understand your paintings and your sorrow. Your yearly visits to the stream on your anniversary. Why?"

"I'm sorry if I hurt you Alex. I did not mean to deceive you at all. I do still grieve the loss of Isaiah and I do still love him, but I had a husband and three little girls all under the age of 4. I had no idea where he had gone or where to find him and if I had found him, then what? Was I to abandon my children for my selfish desires? Besides, he must not have wanted me, or he would have stayed or at least contacted me later. I have stayed in this same house all these years because I thought he might come to me. He made the choice for me and I have to accept that."

"NO, you do not have to accept it. Yes, when Papa Sam was alive and when your children were young, I understand you had to let him go. But he may not know that Papa Sam is no longer with you and that you still love him. You have got to let me help you find him."

"Alex, I hate to tell you this since you already seem angry but there is something else. It is in one of the other journals but now that I see your reaction to this news, I don't think it is wise for me to wait and let you discover it."

My heart was pounding. What else could there be? I am in such shock over Isaiah I'm not sure how much I can handle without saying something hurtful. I know she had her reasons but what could they possibly be that would make her think it was okay to put me through this.

"I'm listening."

"You asked me why I chose you to write my story. Well the truth is I only decided to do this last year when my mother passed away. She was 85 when she died in May of 1991. Shortly after her death her lawyer contacted me. I was to come to his office alone and to please not tell my sisters about the meeting. I could not imagine what was so secretive. He gave me a letter that he had been keeping since before my father died. He was instructed to give it to me in private after they were both dead. The letter was a confession. And an apology I suppose."

Nana reached in the box and pulled out the journal that was at the bottom. It was not filled with words but had her sketches and the letters Isaiah had written to her. It had the song given to her at the USO club and an envelope from her parent's lawyer. She handed it to me and nodded in signal for me to read it.

July 10, 1942

To: Willamina Pettigrew
From: William and Francine Pettigrew
Our dearest daughter:

If you are reading this your parents are both gone. This is not only a confession but an apology for the horrible thing we did to you. We feel our actions were the best option under the circumstances but we both hope you will forgive us the pain we caused you. We were uncertain what to do about your child. We had actually considered suffocating her and letting you find her so you would think she had died in her sleep. We drugged you, Willamina. We are both ashamed but equal in guilt. When we went up to the attic to carry out our plan, we could not go through with it.

Little Willow was such a beautiful child and she looked at us and smiled and we could not harm her. Our dilemma then was to keep anyone from knowing our young daughter had not only delivered an illegitimate child but the child of a negro. It would be too much shame to bare. We took the child to Millie and her grandmother. We told them if they would take the child with them and move away somewhere that you would never have a chance to see them, that we would pay them a yearly amount of $5000.00 to be used to raise the child.

We agreed that once a year father would travel to see them to check on her and give them the money. If anything happens to father then the law office is prepared to send them a lump sum provided by an insurance policy made out to Millie.

Our hope is that by the time you see this letter the child will be grown with a life of her own and you would have moved on with your life. We hope you see that this was for the best. Please continue to keep this situation a secret as we have.

All our love,

Father and mother.

When I looked at Nana this time the tears were streaming down her face.

"Oh Nana, how could they do this to you? How could they keep this from you for almost 50 years?"

"Alex, When I first read this letter last year, I was so angry. I was angry to the point of making myself ill. Angry that I had been deceived, that I had been cheated out of my child. I was angry that my father had witnessed Willow grow up. The very man who took her from me because of his hate and prejudice was getting to see her grow up while all the while watching me cry on her grave. I was angry at my mother who saw me grieve for years over the child I had lost knowing all the time that she was very much alive. I was even angry at Millie.

She was my friend and betrayed me. But later I concluded that Millie did this for me because she knew how deep their hate ran and it was a chance to save Willow. At one point I realized that Isaiah must have found out about Willow when he came back because he would have found his family and he may have been raising our daughter all this time. Maybe that is why he chose to not stay after leaving the song. He did not want me to have to choose between Willow and my other children.

He still loved me and did not want to put me through that pain. It is also possible that he has married and has another family. Maybe he just felt I had a right to know but he was not free to be mine. Maybe he found someone who could love him freely and openly and be proud of the wonderful man he is. Giving me the song was his way of saying goodbye."

She sat in silence for a while, probably running it all through her mind again.

"I spent several weeks in prayer, in tears, with my soul ripping apart over this. That is when I came up with the idea to have you write a novel about my life. I thought perhaps Willow would see it. That Isaiah might see it and come back to me if he is now free to do so.

I guess I should have just told you everything from the beginning, but I knew the journals could tell it so much better."

"No Nana you were right. I needed to see it like this to really understand it. To see it all through your eyes."

We both sat quietly for several minutes just taking it all in. She took a ragged breath and smiled at me through her tears. It was one of those breaths people take when relief suddenly sweeps over them. She had the story out now. No need to read any more journals. Now I would need to work diligently on the novel.

But first I would have to think of a way to find Isaiah and Willow. Somehow, I would bring them back to her. I wasn't sure if I could talk her into it, but I needed Mark's help. If she agreed I would tell him. I wanted to explain the story behind the portrait in her room.

Chapter Fourteen

The Scenic Route to Trouble

Mark was so surprised when I showed up in Athens Friday morning. It is only 97 miles from Payne, so it only took me two hours to get here. It would have been even faster except for rush hour traffic in Athens and I traveled the scenic route rather than interstate most of the way. I needed to clear my head and prepare for this. It had taken me four days of reasoning with Nana to convince her not only that we needed to look for Isaiah and Willow but that I needed Mark's help in doing so.

"What's wrong? Are you alright? Is it my mom? OH, is it Nana," he rattled off?

"Mark, everyone is fine. I just needed to see you about something. I have something I need to tell you. I am hoping you will help me with… ahhh… a little project once you hear what I have to tell you."

He looked very confused. He was still in his boxers with his hair all crazy and needing a shave. I don't think he had shaved since I saw him Sunday. He stood there rubbing his eyes when he realized why I was grinning at him and looking him over from head to toe.

"OH, sorry. Please come in and excuse me for just a second. I will make coffee as soon as I shower."

"I'll make it," I yelled back, and he just tossed his hand up to acknowledge.

I had to admit I was enjoying myself. Making coffee in his kitchen. Looking around for cups and sugar. I looked in the refrigerator for creamer or even some milk, but he didn't have any. There was a jar of peanut butter, a partial loaf of bread, one can of soda and a jar of pickles. I am going on the assumption that he either eats out or has a peanut butter sandwich. He was out of the shower before the coffee finished making. He walked over and pulled me into a kiss so quickly it took my breath away.

"Good morning Alex," he said as he finished the kiss.

"Now that is the way to say good morning," I replied and kissed him back "good morning to you."

"I hate to break this up because I am really glad to see you, but I have a class in an hour. Can you hang out until I get back? It's the only class I have on Fridays but it lasts 3 hours," he was pleading with his eyes.

"Actually, I am here until Sunday afternoon. That is if that is okay with you."

"I guess that's okay."

He said it while trying to look unfazed and cool. Then grabbed me up in a hug and twirled me around.

"Let me take you to the cafeteria for breakfast before I abandon you for the morning."

Once we had eaten, he gave me the key to his apartment so I could get back in. He had to rush off to class. It was only two blocks from where we had eaten breakfast. The minute I walked in and locked the door I headed straight for his bed to get a nap while he was in class. I could smell him on the pillow. His distinct bodywash, which was heavenly. I hugged the pillow up to me and dreamed the most wonderful dream. I imagined being with him. Being his wife and making love to him. Waking up with my arms around him instead of this pillow. I thought I had just drifted off when I heard him knocking on the door. When I opened the door, he burst out laughing.

"I guess the roles are reversed. You have been sleeping, haven't you?"

"NO," I defended myself. "I have been dreaming."

I knew I had plenty of time to tell him my purpose for being there so first I allowed him to give me a tour. He showed me all the places on campus that he thought I might find interesting. He saw a few of his classmates and introduced me… as his girlfriend. The first time he did it I giggled which made me look like a silly child. And you guessed it. When he and the classmate looked at me a little surprised by my reaction, my face could have fried an egg, it was so hot. Later I apologized for my silly outburst and told him I was a little nervous meeting his friends.

"I found it to be very sexy," he said and kissed my forehead.

"Yeah right," I said. "I guess I wasn't sure if that was what you considered me to be. I have never been a girlfriend before. It sounded nice."

He only smiled and wrapped his strong arms around me. He was probably tempted to tease me about turning so red but decided to give me a break.

We stopped at a little market to purchase a carton of milk and more soda. I told him I would be glad to make breakfast for him in the morning if he wanted to buy eggs and sausage.

"No can do," he said. "No skillet and no spatula. Oh and no plates."

We opted to order a pizza and some wings to be delivered. I was enjoying my time alone with him. We sat on his small couch watching a movie and just cuddling.

"So, are you ever going to tell me what you came to tell me?"

I sat up and turned to face him. I took a deep breath and released it to ready myself.

"Okay, here goes," I said at last.

I proceeded to tell him in as much detail as I could remember the story of Isaiah and Willamina {aka} Beulah {aka} Nana. It took me well over an hour and he sat patiently listening without saying a word. I knew how much he cared for Nana and that there were parts of the story that moved him. I would notice his fist clinch when the subject of her father would come up. I noticed a tear run down his cheek when Willie woke up to find Isaiah gone. And he full-out cried when Willow was supposed to have died. Then came the song at the USO club followed by the letter from her mothers' lawyer.

Once I finished, we just sat there for several minutes. I was emotionally drained, and I think he was a mixture of emotion and anger. I realized that because his father was black, and he was also considered mixed in his ethnicity that he was seeing this in ways I could not understand. He had observed firsthand the hatred some people have if you do not fit into the category, they think everyone should fit in. Nana had told me once that as a young boy in school he had trouble fitting in.

He was not white, and he wasn't black. And even though

people are becoming more accepting in the 90's we still have a long way to go before people will see others only as people and not rank their importance according to their color or gender. I remembered the apple lesson Nana had told me and wondered if she had ever shared it with Mark.

He got up and went to the kitchen. He needed to do something. He was cleaning up our mess from dinner. Tossed the boxes from our pizza and wings. He even ran a little soapy water in the sink to wipe down the counter-top and wash our glasses. I said nothing and did not offer to help. He was not doing it because he was a neat freak or trying to impress me. He just needed to do … SOME-THING.

"I am glad you told me. I am glad Nana trusted me enough to let you share it with me. But why? Why tell me this now. You did not come here just to spring this on me and leave. Did you?"

I studied him for a minute and then walked over to him. I wrapped my arms around him and lay my head on his chest. I could hear his heart pounding. He was really up-set by this. He probably had more emotionally invested in this than I did. He had lived with Nana since he was young. He had dealt with race issues his whole life. He had also known Papa Sam and loved him like a grandfather.

As much as I had grown closer to Nana in the few weeks, I had stayed with her and as much as I am affected by her story it is so much more personal to Mark. I held him for a long while and he seemed to slowly relax. His heart rate slowed, and I could feel the tension lesson in his arms. I slowly pulled away and investigated his sweet face.

"Mark, I want you to help me find Isaiah and Willow for her. We have to find them."

"Absolutely," he said and wiped a tear from his cheek.

It was getting late and we were both so tired we could not think. I insisted I sleep on his couch. He argued that he would give me his bed and he would take the couch. Mark is probably at least 6'1" tall and I am 5'3". We are talking more of a love seat than a couch. I did not say anything. I just looked at him then at the couch then back at him and back to the couch.

"Really?"

"Okay you're probably right," he confessed. "We could share the bed. I promise I will behave."

He could not even say it with a straight face. We both just shook our heads and said our good nights. The truth is it isn't him behaving that I am doubting. I am doubting that I could behave. I was still remembering him from this morning when he opened the door. Yep, I better take the couch.

We both had a restless night. Both of us had way too much on our minds. Nana and her situation. How could we go about finding those she loved so dearly? I was trying to compose the novel in my head. I was feeling the pressure to complete it before my classes started. And to be honest I could not stop thinking about that gorgeous man just a few feet away from me who claims to love me and would welcome me into his bed and into his arms.

Did women take cold showers? I know we both had the same problem sleeping because when I told him about my horrible night and that I had considered a cold shower he told me if he had heard me, he would have joined me. I know he meant he also needed a cold shower, but it still came out a little funny.

"I'm pretty sure that if you had joined me it would have

defeated the purpose of the cold shower."

We made coffee and had cereal for breakfast. He had purchased a box of the cheap generic Honey Nut O's at the market. He only had one bowl and one spoon, so we shared. It was kind of fun and sweet that he would feed me a bite each time before he took a bite.

We had planned on spending our day at the campus library. We need to make notes and decide who will follow up on which trail. We sat at a small table in the corner as far away from the larger study groups as possible. This was going to take concentration.

We realized we would need to get more information from Nana. I had no idea what Millie's last name was or grandmother's name. I had only heard her referred to as grandmother. I could not remember if the journal had mentioned where Isaiah had lived before coming to Georgia to work.

I needed to ask Nana if she had any ideas as to where Millie and grandmother might have gone with Willow. And we needed to see if we could find any military records on Isaiah. When did he find his way back to the United States and where had he been? Why had he not written Beulah any more letters? It did not take us long to realize how very little we knew and how hard this project was going to be.

We agreed that until we could talk to Nana there was very little we could do. I had taken a lot of notes and listed all the specific questions we wanted to ask. I also told him that I felt Nana would be okay with me putting the journals in my room while I was writing the novel and that would also give me a chance to look harder for answers to our questions.

The library closed at 3:00 on Saturday. We decided it was time that we had a real date.

"Would you join me for dinner and a movie Miss. Stone?"

"I would be delighted Mr. Armstrong," I said and giggled again.

I have got to work on the giggling thing. I sound like I am 5 years old. He noticed my embarrassment and assured me again that the giggling was sexy. I knew he did not really think so, but it was sweet of him to try and make me feel better.

We had dinner at a lovely affordable little restaurant with golden arches. It featured beef and chicken specialties and potatoes prepared in a long crispy manner with a red sauce. At least that is how Mark described our fast food cuisine.

"Man, on a serious budget," he said. "And I'm afraid the movie is the free one in the park. Probably something you have already seen."

Now he seemed embarrassed.

"I am having a great time. As long as I'm with you it is a 5-star date."

When we finally got back to his apartment, we flopped down on the couch to just talk a little while. He started to kiss me and as happens often with us it got a little intense.

"I'm sorry," he said. "I know we need to take it slow and we are not married yet, so certain things need to be kept for when we are, but I just love you so much. I think about you all the time, and sometimes I want you so desperately I cannot control myself. I guess I need to go in my room while I still have a functioning brain."

He started to get up and was about to walk away when

he noticed I hadn't said anything. I was just sitting there looking a little shocked.

"Alex, are you okay?"

"You said yet."

"What," he repeated. "What do you mean I said *yet?*"

"You said we are not married… YET."

"Oh, I did say that, didn't I?"

He smiled and kissed me a quick good night kiss. Then he walked to his room in a comical strut and closed his door.

Well, here goes a second night with absolutely no sleep, I thought. But I was wrong. I slept like a rock.

Sunday morning Mark took me to worship service at a little church close to the campus. He explained that a lot of the students attended this service. It was lovely and I enjoyed the service. I also enjoyed sitting there next to Mark and fantasizing about being Mrs. Dr. Mark Armstrong. It was going to be difficult to concentrate on anything else now.

Get your head out of the clouds, I told myself. *You have a novel to write, two long lost people to find and four years of college to achieve before the Mrs. thing can happen. It is going to be a long four years.*

Once we finished lunch I started to prepare to go back home to Nana's. I could tell he hated to see me leave. He kept thinking of things he wanted to tell me or show me. He even started explaining some of the medical lessons he was working on.

"Mark, I'm going to miss you too," I said and put my arms around him. But I really need to get home and check on Nana. I know she will be on pins and needles waiting to see what you have to say."

"I'll call her after you leave. Not only can I relieve her mind about me but I can make sure she watches to make sure you get home safely."

He kissed me several more times before finally helping me into Nana's car.

"I love you Alex," he said as he shut the car door and stepped away. "More than I can put into words."

"I love you too Mark. Please come visit as soon as possible."

I had to pull away. It was hard for either of us to say goodbye. If I had not made a move, we might both still be sitting right there for hours.

Is this how it felt for Isaiah and Beulah? If the love Nana felt for him was half as strong as what I feel now for Mark, I do not know how she stood it. To wake up after making love all night to find him gone. To think he had died for all those years. To lose the child conceived in your love and be left so empty.

My heart could not stand thinking of such pain. It felt as if someone were squeezing it and stopping it from beating. I could barely breathe from the emotion welling up in me. I began to cry so much that I could hardly see how to drive. I pulled over and wept bitterly for about thirty minutes before gaining control of myself. I had shed many tears when Nana and I read the journals. It had made me sad and broken hearted for Nana.

But until I had to leave Mark just now, I do not think I had even a tiny realistic idea of the pain that Nana and Isaiah had experienced. My sorrow for the young couple had overpowered me and I had to grieve. I would have no problem writing my novel, I thought. It was coming to me now. Overwhelming me with words. I wiped my face and blew my running nose. I got to get home. I have work to do.

Chapter Fifteen

Roots & Branches

When I walked in the kitchen, I found Nana and Annie sitting at the little table. Annie was frantically trying to comfort Nana and looked up at me pleading with her eyes for my help.

"Mrs. Stone got a phone call and she has been crying since she hung up. She will not tell me what upset her. She just keeps telling me she is fine."

I looked at Nana and through her tears she smiled at me and nodded. I knew she was letting me know Mark had called and assured her he thought no less of her. He probably loved her more knowing what she had endured.

"I'll sit with her now, Annie. I'm sure she will be fine if you give her a few minutes."

Annie looked at her and Nana managed to squeak out a 'yes please Annie dear' so she left us alone. I gave her a few minutes to gather herself. She took a few ragged breaths and wiped her eyes and nose with tissues from the box on the counter.

"Mark is such a sweetheart," she said. "He said I was so brave and strong and an inspiration. Can you believe it? He thinks I am an inspiration."

And she cried some more. I just sat there waiting for a while. Then I made a cup of tea for her and got a bottle of water from the refrigerator for myself. About halfway through the tea she seemed to level out. She moved the cup away and placed her hands over mine.

"Thank you, Alex, for telling him for me. I have been terrified to tell anyone. It took me a long time to work up the courage to tell you and even then, I made you read it in the journals."

"Nana, we all love you. I know you don't feel ready, but I think you need to start telling others. It is too much to expect everyone to read the story along with strangers who might read my book. They could get blindsided if someone asked about it before they have had the chance to read it for themselves. You can start with poor Annie. She has been by your side for so many years. Who better to understand loving a man because of who he is even when others judge? Maybe invite your sisters over and tell them together. Then your children. Give them a chance to process it before it is made public.

"Let me think about it. You are probably right. Mark's reaction has given me new courage," she said and smiled.

"Nana, Mark is going to help me find Isaiah and Willow. At least we are going to try. We will need to ask you a few questions to help us with our search. The next time Mark comes home we want to sit down with you and brainstorm. I feel confident we will find them. It just feels right. That is another reason to tell others. You can't exactly introduce him to the rest of the family as your first husband and your oldest daughter without a little preparation," I teased.

"You are right of course. I'll start with Annie tomorrow. If I manage to survive that I will call Carolina and Georgia and see if the three of us can get together."

She took another deep breath. When she exhaled, she laughed nervously and wrapped her arms around herself. She stood up then and stretched out her arms to hug me.

"Thank you, Alex, from the bottom of my heart."

"Nana, is it okay if I take the journals to my room? I need to refer to them while working on the novel. I promise to take good care of them."

"Of course, you can," she said. "And be sure you read the couple of journals we didn't. The one from 1948 will include the birth of my only son who just happened to grow up and father a most wonderful daughter."

"Yes, ma'am I will be sure and read that one."

The journals left that we had not yet read were just stories of bringing up her four children. She would occasionally bring up the subject of Isaiah or Willow but just remembering and comparing them to her life now. She stopped writing in 1950 and started expressing all her thoughts and ideas in her paintings. Her reputation for being an artist with so much life and emotion in her paintings made her very famous in the art world and she was making a great deal of money from her art.

Often, she would think about the pictures hidden in her trunk of a beautiful black man who owned her heart and a sweet-faced baby with lips that seemed to form a heart when she pouted them. She also thought of the picture of a red headed girl that she had placed in an old cigar tube and given to her new husband as a gift. He had given her 25cents for her labor and said it would keep him safe. She wondered if he had kept it. In the same way he had kept her heart. Those were the last words of her last journal. I could not help but wonder if she would start to journal again after this all came out.

I was up late night after night working on the novel. The story was so embedded in me I seldom had to review the journals. It was not always easy for me to express her emotions in words because this was not a made-up story of a fabricated couple where I could simply let the story go where I wanted it to. This was my flesh and blood grandmother. I had not met Isaiah, but I felt I knew him. I would sometimes go to the library with my note pad and look at the paintings for inspiration. I had even stood in front of the painting in Nana's bedroom a few times. This one always made me miss Mark so much I would have trouble concentrating on the book. I had even gotten permission from Nana to go to the willow tree one night and camp out under the skirt.

"You go right ahead," she said. "I have spent many nights there myself."

The novel was coming along so fast I could not believe it. I would not be able to complete it until we found Isaiah and Willow and brought them back to Nana.

Mark had not been home for over two weeks. Not since my surprise visit. He apologized when I talked to him for not coming home but had several exams that were stressing him, and he had to get through them first. He is finally coming home this weekend and I hope we can get busy with the search. Nana told Annie and she was so wonderful about it. She had started working for Nana and Papa Sam in 1968 long after the children were grown. She came to help with the house because Nana was painting so much, she could not keep up with things like cleaning and cooking. That meant Annie had been with her for twenty-four years.

"I can't believe you kept this a secret from me so long," Annie said. I pray they find them for you. My Mark is a good boy and very smart. I'm sure he and Alex will find them."

She cried and hugged Nana so tight. I could see how much these two ladies loved each other. This was not an employee and her boss. These were two good friends that helped each other as best they could.

Next came her sisters, Carolina and Georgia. Both lived in Atlanta. The twins were now 68 years old and because Carolina's husband Arnold had died last year and Georgia had never married, they lived together in a very nice condominium where all the outdoor chores were handled by landscapers and someone came weekly to clean for them. Georgia was rich in her own right and Arnold had left Carolina well taken care of so the two sisters loved to travel. They had only just returned from New York where they enjoyed several Broadway plays.

"We would love to come for a visit," they agreed. It's been too long Willamina."

They came on a Monday and Nana spent the day entertaining them with a lovely luncheon and lots of catching up. On Tuesday she sat them down in the library among her many paintings and began to tell them her story. Both sat there with eyes wide and mouths open. They still looked so much alike it was like a trick mirror when you had them side by side. They had even started styling their hair the same again. Sometimes when they would speak if you were not looking at them you might not be sure which one had spoken. But their reaction to Nana's story was not the same. Not the same at all. Georgia laughed a little sarcastically and said, "Well that just beats all. You have had two great loves in your life and I never found one I even liked all that much. Good for you. I hope you find them."

She had never been the serious one and from some of the conversations she and Nana have had over the years she probably had a few secrets of her own. She had traveled the world and dated a lot of men not really looking for the right one… just having a good time. She did not judge but did make a comment that the rag magazines would have a field day when it came out.

"After all dear you are famous for your art and your husband owned one of the biggest newspapers in the state. Well your second husband that is."

Carolina was a different story. She was appalled. She had taken after her mother a great deal as far as personality. She was very hard-nosed when it came to her opinion on people and what place they had in society.

"How can you even consider letting this out? What will people think? This will be an embarrassment to all of us."

She even made a comment about understanding why their parents had done what they did. They could not let this scandal get out and now after all they did to conceal the shame, she was going to flaunt it.

I was listening but had promised Nana I would not speak up. I would let her handle it and just observe quietly for the sake of my book. But when Carolina stood up and because of her anger knocked one of Nana's paintings of her willow tree off the easel I had to react.

"Don't you touch those," I ordered! Then I picked it up and carefully put it back where it belonged.

"It's alright Alex," Nana said.

"No, it's not," said Georgia! "Willamina… Willie," she

corrected herself. "You have suffered more pain in your life than anyone I know. You deserve to find this man you loved and find joy that you were cheated out of. And to Hell with anyone who thinks otherwise," she spat out and glared at her twin.

We could hear the twins arguing later in their suite upstairs. Both had promised not to tell anyone before she had the chance to tell her children. I do not think we had to worry about Carolina telling. She probably would not talk about it even after everyone else knew.

They left early the next morning with a quick hug and a rush to the taxi that would take them to the airport. Nana stood in the doorway waving to them as the taxi pulled away from the curb.

"Well that went well," she said with a hint of sarcasm. We let out a laugh of relief that it was over.

Mark would be home in two days, so she decided to wait to tell her children after he went back.

I knew she dreaded telling them. She wanted Annie and Mark to accept what had happened to her and was thrilled when they handled it so lovingly.

She had hoped her sisters would be gracious about it but even with the negative response from Carolina she was still feeling hopeful.

But if her children reacted negatively or were angry with her, she just did not know what she would do. She loved her children so much. She not only worried about how they might react to her having married another man that their father was never told about, but would they be upset that it was a black man. She had taught them as they grew up to love everyone the same. As members of the human race. They had all had friends from different races and they never were exposed to the ugly titles given by people like my father. No labels, no distinctions and no prejudices. Even Samuel had never pushed his negative thinking on them. He realized that his wife was trying to teach them to be accepting of all and he honored her by never giving a conflicting attitude. That is how they were raised. I guess she would soon find out if her teachings had taken root. She also worried that they would feel cheated by never knowing about their oldest sister. She was part of their blood and they had never been given an opportunity to know her. Of course, until last year Nana had thought she had died when only a few days old.

I was in my room Friday night working on the novel. It was really coming together well, or at least I thought so. I guess I would know for sure once I sent it to a few publishers to see if any of them would be willing to publish it. I got up to stretch and noticed the light come on in the pool house. ***Mark must be home.*** It was almost midnight and everyone else was asleep so I'm sure he didn't want to wake anyone. I eased out of my room and down the stairs. I opened the French doors and was about to go out when Mark was in front of me. He was going to try and ease up to my room to say hello. We both jumped back, and I gasped loudly. I closed the doors and we had to laugh.

"Shhhh," he said. Do not wake Mom or Nana.

He pulled me into his arms and kissed me long and lovely.

"I have missed you so much Alex. I couldn't wait until in the morning to hold you."

We sat in the shadows in a lounge and held each other while I told him about the sisters' reactions. I knew he had talked to his mom several times since Nana told her, so he knew she was just fine.

"I hate that Carolina was so upset. I know the few times she has come to visit she acted uncomfortable around me. I remember the day she realized my dad was black. She looked at Nana like she was insulted or something. I heard them talking later and she told Nana she had assumed I was adopted since my mom was white. Up until that day she thought my mom was great and a genius in the kitchen. Then suddenly mom could not do anything right. It made Nana so mad, but mom told her to please not make a big deal out of it. She said since Carolina seldom comes to visit, please just let it slide."

"That is so wrong. One thing that I have learned from this. You see people for what they are. I have heard people say they do not see color. That everyone is the same. But that is not true. Everyone is an individual and different from everyone else. Willie saw Isaiah and she saw he was black, and she told him he was beautiful. He was not beautiful to her despite the fact he was black… and he was not beautiful because he was black. He was beautiful to her because he just was… beautiful. She loved Isaiah who happened to be black and he loved her, and she happened to be white. They loved each other, not their color."

Mark raised up and looked so lovingly into her eyes. He almost seemed to be struggling to speak. His eyes looked wet like he may have wanted to cry.

"If I had not already fallen in love with you Alexandria Stone, I would have fallen in love with you in this exact minute. You really do get it."

We lay there in each other's arms and before we realized it the sun was peaking over the trees and into our faces. We had drifted off to sleep.

"If you will make me coffee, I won't tell Nana we slept together," he teased.

"I'm going to shower, but if you make coffee, I won't tell your mom we slept together."

We both headed for showers and decided Annie would start the coffee by the time we were done. He rushed over to his pool house and I bolted upstairs. It was early so no one else was up.

When I came down to the kitchen not only was the coffee ready, but Annie had gone all out for her baby boy. Waffles, bacon, eggs and fruit.

"Did you two sleep well," Annie asked.

We looked at each other and both of us said 'yes ma'am' at the same time. She looked at us as if trying to decide if there was something strange about our response before turning back to the waffle iron and once her back was to us Mark made a crazy face at me and made me giggle. She whirled her head around as if she were trying to catch us at something and we all laughed.

"That giggle is going to get you in trouble someday," he said and winked at me.

Nana walked in and she looked worried. She told Annie she just wanted some tea.

"Nana are you okay," I asked.

"Yes sweetie, I'm okay. Just a little nervous. Your parents, Kathy and Steve, and Susan and Philip will all be here Monday. None of my other grandchildren could make it and Frances will have to get back to me. It is just so hard to get everyone together at the same time. I can rarely get everyone here for a holiday so to get them here on a random Monday is really a challenge. I may have to tell Frances separately. I had just hoped to get it over with all at once."

"It's going to be fine Nana," Mark assured her. "They all love you and nothing will change that."

"Absolutely," I added. "You raised them to be kind and understanding people."

She thanked us both for our encouragement.

"Nana, we need some information. We need to know where Isaiah lived before coming to Payne Georgia. We need to know Millie's last name if you know it and maybe grandmother's name."

She took a tablet and pen from the drawer nearest to the door and started writing things down for us as she told us out loud.

"Isaiah grew up in Washington D.C. and apparently graduated high school there. After the cruelty of the boy that cut Isaiah had forced them to flee, they went where they knew they would have more opportunity. He was more educated than poor Millie. She had only attended school through the 4th grade. I think her last name was Waters. She was not a lot older than me so she could have married after they left so her last name would have changed. Grandmother was the mother of Isaiah's father so her last name was Reed. I think her first name was Mabel. I do not think my father ever realized they were related to Isaiah. Everyone called her grandmother or Ms. Mabel. No one ever addressed her as Mrs. Reed. Isaiah said she had lived there her whole life. The little house they lived in had at one time been a slave house and she had been born in that house. Of course, Ms. Mabel was very old back then so I'm sure she passed on years ago."

"This is great Nana," Mark said. "This gives us a start at least. I need you to check a few things for me when you can get the chance. I need you to try to find your fathers bank records to see if there is anything that might lead to the money he paid to them. Also, maybe if your parents' lawyer is willing to talk to you, he may have information. I am sure he won't talk to me or Alex, but he might talk to you. I am trying to find some of the army records for soldiers missing in action or assumed dead but not found. I have a few teachers who are helping me with that. They are veterans and know how to ask."

"OH, DEAR you didn't tell them Mark," Nana asked. "I just wouldn't want strangers to know before I have a chance to tell my children."

"I just told them I was helping a friend find out about someone from their family. I was very vague about detail. Do you know what Isaiah's date of birth was?"

Nana looked like she might cry. She started to get up and was looking unsure of what to do.

"I can't believe I never asked him what his birthday was. I know he was older than me and I think he was 18 which meant he was born in 1923 or 24. I'm just not sure."

"It's okay Nana. You have given us a lot to go on. You can ask him his birthday when you see him," I said.

Nana decided she would go out on her porch and paint for a while. She had been working on something new, but she never likes people to look at her paintings before she is finished. I knew painting always calmed her and as nervous as she was about Monday, she might just finish it.

Mark spent most of the time he had left doing the yard work that had been neglected. I had tried to mow some but did not know how to handle the trimmer. He also vacuumed the pool. He mentioned that next month he would close it up for the winter. It was hard to believe summer was coming to an end. We tried to find a little time together but because he came so seldom, he hated to neglect his mom and Nana. We all played cards Saturday evening. We ate pizza and drank soda. It was good to see Nana laugh and enjoy herself, but I knew her mind was pre-occupied. Once Annie and Nana went to bed Mark and I took a walk to the stream. We placed a blanket on the grass and just lay there holding hands and looking at the stars.

"It's strange, but now that I know the story of Isaiah and Nana, I feel like I'm intruding when we come here," Mark confessed. "I expect to see them sitting over there in front of that tree. I have even found myself checking up in the large tree to see if young Willie is sitting up there sketching."

"I know what you mean," I agreed. It is as if their ghost lives here. I know that sounds stupid. They are not dead. But the ghost of their lost love or something."

"EXACTLY," he said.

We talked for a few hours about Nana and Isaiah. We wondered about Willow. If she knew about her mother at all. And we talked about us. Our hopes for our future and how we could never lose what we had.

"I know it isn't fair of me to say this. I know we are young, and you are still unsure. But Alex, I promise to love you until I take my last breath."

A tear ran down my cheek and he reached over and took it.

"I promise to let you," I said.

Chapter Sixteen

No Time Like the Present

On Monday morning Nana and I were both up at the break of day. This would be an eventful day regardless of the outcome. My Aunt Francis had finally accepted Nana's invitation once she realized her siblings would all be there. She had asked Nana if she could bring someone with her. Aunt Francis at age 46 had never married. However, she had finally found her Mr. Wright and wanted everyone to meet him at the same time. Nana told Francis that she would love to meet her friend and to bring him with her. I could not help but wonder how Nana would feel telling her story in front of a total stranger. It was going to be hard enough telling it in front of her children.

"I was made to believe this gentleman may become a part of our family in the near future so I decided he might as well hear the skeletons now rather than later," Nana explained.

"Good point," I said.

My parents had called last night to assure us they would start heading our way very early. Nana had to assure them numerous times that I was okay and this had nothing to do with me. Dad was concerned I might be ill but mom was almost sure I had caused problems and I would be sent back home when they left. ***Thanks for the vote of confidence mom***, I thought.

Aunt Kathy and Uncle Steve lived closest of all of them and told Nana to call when the others started to arrive. Aunt Susan and Uncle Philip had come as far as Aunt Kathy's and spent the night. The four of them would come together once my parents arrived.

"Heaven forbid they come visit their mom for a while," Nana said with a hint of hurt in her voice.

I had never noticed how little time they spent with her or even how seldom they called until this happened. Maybe now I understood why she was so nervous about telling them. When I commented on it to Nana, she assured me they loved her very much and she did not doubt it for a second.

"Children grow up, become adults and have families of their own. I know how it is. They are not thinking about calling me anymore. They are thinking about their children calling them. The sad reality is that until I am gone, they will not realize how much they miss me. They have all made comments to me about how much they miss their father. How they wish they could run this or that by Papa Sam to see what he thought. I know when I have moved on it will hit them that they missed a lot of opportunities with me too but it is just human nature. You appreciate things and people more when you no longer have them. I feel good about today. Nervous but good."

My parents arrived at noon sharp and Nana called Kathy's house while we watched my parents unload a small suitcase from the trunk of their car. It would only take about 40 minutes for the others to arrive so Nana would have lunch for all of them.

Annie had been busy in the kitchen for several hours preparing a lovely buffet type lunch with cold cuts and cheeses. Several types of bread and of course all the fixings for sandwiches. She made her potato salad which is to die for and a beautiful bundt cake with fresh strawberries and whipped topping to go over it. A fancy version of strawberry short cake. And of course, pickles. We had to have pickles. Annie was so nervous you would think the guests were royalty of some sort. She knew all of them. Had even babysat their children on a few occasions. She was just so worried for Nana. She knew how important this was to her.

My parents came in and greeted us with hugs and kisses on the cheek. My father placed a hand on each of Nana's shoulders and looked at her as if to say… are you okay mom?

My mother placed a hand on each of my shoulders and looked at me as if to say… What have you done?

Nana and I looked at each other, rolled our eyes and said nothing. Well nothing out loud.

I took their suitcase up to the guest room across the hall from my room. My mother wanted to see my room and of course the first thing she noticed was the stack of paper beside the typewriter.

"Oh sweetie, what are you working on? Can I see?"

I practically knocked her down getting to the papers before she could.

"NO," I screamed. "I'm sorry mom. I did not mean to scream at you. It is just that I am working on my first novel and I would rather no one see it until I am finished. You understand don't you mom?"

"I suppose so dear," she replied, looking more than a little hurt. "That is wonderful. I am glad to see you are making good use of your short time here."

I wanted to tell her I had no intention of leaving here unless Nana asked me to. I loved staying with her. I loved this house and my room, and I loved that Mark would come here often to see me. I loved the stream and the willow tree too. I loved Annie and the pool. I honestly cannot think of anything that would make me want to leave. I had not asked Nana if I could just stay with her instead of in a dorm room and commute the small distance to classes, but I felt she would be thrilled when I did ask.

We heard the doorbell and knew someone else had arrived. Either Kathy and Susan with their husbands or Frances with her friend. As we made our way down the stairs, I saw my father shaking hands with a very distinguished looking ***black*** man. My Nana was hugging Francis and I could see from their faces that there was a great deal of relief being felt from both sides. Nana smiled up at me and gave a tiny shrug of her shoulders. I interpreted it to mean. *Who would have guessed?*

I felt like letting out a laugh until I felt my mother grab my arm tight. The look on her face told me one thing. She would not be accepting of Nana's secret at all. We made our way down the stairs and I hugged my Aunt Frances first and then introduced myself to her friend. I would have normally shaken his hand but for my mother's sake I gave him a small hug.

"Well hello Alexandria. I have heard good things about you," he said.

"This is my fiancé Adam Richards," announced Aunt

Frances and I heard an audible gasp behind me.

My father shook his hand again and congratulated them. Nana hugged him and said how thrilled she was to have him in our family. I agreed with Nana.

My mother stood behind my father as if she were afraid he might speak to her. Until this minute I had never realized how deeply prejudiced my mother was. She had not voiced it as I was growing up. At least I could not remember her saying anything. Never had she encouraged me to think I was on a different level than anyone because of race. But her feelings were showing through loud and clear.

As we stood there in the doorway another car pulled up and my Aunts and Uncles started pouring out. No suitcases because they lived close and would return home later today. All the introductions were made and from what I could tell my mother was the only one with an issue. If the others were concerned it was not obvious. We all made our way to the kitchen where Frances happily introduced Adam to Annie.

"Is that the potato salad that Frances has bragged about I see on the table," Adam asked.

"Yes, sir it sure is. I hope you all enjoy."

Nana asked my dad to give the blessing and we were lined up like starved animals the minute we heard the amen.

Annie made sure everyone had whatever they needed. She had glasses of ice ready for tea or lemonade. Whichever we wanted. Once we had eaten our fill, we left the kitchen for the living room and Annie started cleaning up. She took my arm before I followed everyone out of the kitchen.

"Don't let them upset Ms. Willie. I'm so worried about her."

"We got this Annie. It's going to be just fine."

I said it like I knew it was truth, but I also was saying a little prayer under my breath that I was right.

We all chatted for about a half hour about what was going on in our world. Everyone wanted to know how Frances and Adam had met and when they were planning to marry. She told the story of going to Paris for a vacation last year. Adam had been a passenger on the same flight, and they sat across the aisle from each other. They talked the entire flight and ended up making plans to do some sightseeing together in Paris. He was on a business trip alone and thrilled for the company. They discovered they lived within an hour of each other and began meeting for lunch and then dinners and just fell in love. They were planning a small wedding with only immediate family.

"We hoped you might consider letting us have it here mother," she said to Nana.

"Oh yes, that would be wonderful," Nana replied.

I guess the situation was starting to wear on my mother because she bluntly spoke out.

"So, wasn't there something you wanted to talk to us about Nana?"

Everyone turned and looked at my mother and then turned to Nana as if they had suddenly been reminded. She looked them all in the face for some sign I suppose and then cleared her throat.

"Yes, Martha you are exactly right. I guess there is no time like the present."

Nana got up from the chair she had been sitting in and moved to a spot in the front of the window where she was equally visible to all her family. I brought her a chair from the kitchen so she would not have to stand. I was a little afraid her legs would not support her for the length of time this might take. I also brought her a glass of water. Just in case nerves made her throat dry.

"It's okay Nana," I told her and gave her a little hug. "Everyone here loves you."

She nodded and gave me a small smile of appreciation. She looked in the eyes of her children. Her wonderful blessings from God and she began to speak.

"I'm not sure how you will feel about what I am about to tell you but before I start, I want you all to know how very much I love you. And I want you to believe that I loved your father with all my heart. He was such a good man and a wonderful husband and father."

They all started looking at each other a little confused by her proclamation.

"We know, mother. We all love you too," said Kathy and all the rest mouthed or nodded their agreement.

She looked at me as if to gain a little courage.

"Well, Samuel Stone was not my first husband."

The gasp in the room almost seemed to suck out all the air, and they all began to mumble toward each other as if to confirm they all heard the same thing.

"I am about to go into a lot of detail to explain myself and I have but one request. This is going to be very hard for me and I am pleading with all of you to not interrupt me. Let me get through this and please just listen to me. Then after I have finished, I will listen to anything you have to say. I will answer any questions you want to ask of me. Do you all give me your word?

They all nodded in agreement and promised to let her

talk without interruption.

Nana began at the beginning. She poured out her heart and spilled her very soul in front of those who would judge her. She expressed openly the way she felt about Isaiah Franklin Reed. I was trying to get a feel of their reaction, but no one seemed to move a muscle. They were all entranced by her tale. When she got to the part about the marriage and the night of passion it was a little uncomfortable for them and for Nana. After all no one really wants to think of their mother as a sexual being. And no one wants to hear their mother describe the erotic feelings she experienced on her wedding night. I mean that is the kind of thing that you stick your fingers in your ears to drown out. But she wanted them to understand that her love for Isaiah was not fleeting. It was real and still existed even today.

Later when she told how she had been forced to stay in the attic and gave birth all alone every one of them seemed to look toward the stairs. Growing up they had all played in that very attic. They had all seen the bed under the rose window and had probably played on it.

And when she told of her husband missing in action and presumed dead followed by the death of her baby… her only connection to him… they all seemed to have wet eyes and some even shed tears.

She told them the story of how she met their father. They had heard it before, but it took on a different tone now. She had always started the story where she and her sisters moved to Atlanta. She had never explained why they ended up there. She told them that though Samuel Stone never knew about her past he saved her life. He had given her joy again which she thought was lost to her at such a young age. She felt again that she needed to assure them of the love she felt for their father and for them.

"This past life takes nothing from my love for your father or the family we had together," she repeated.

They were all still listening, but most were no longer looking into Nana's eyes. It was getting more uncomfortable now that they were part of the story. They all seemed to be examining their childhoods for clues. For some sign that their mother had such a hidden past that none of them knew about. Not even their father who loved their mother so deeply. They were stealing glances at each other. Looking to see how the others were reacting.

Frances had both her hands firmly around Adam's hand. Philip and Steve who had been sitting toward the back of the room behind the couch were both squirming in their seats and looking a little concerned for their wives. My dad was sitting calmly listening to her, but I knew from the way his brows were twisted downward that he was in deep thought. Maybe upset or maybe just worried.

I knew the brows meant he was reacting. I had been on the other end of those crazy brows a few times myself. My mom looked furious. She was the only face in the room that gave no doubt. She looked as if it were all she could do to sit still and not grab her purse and my hand and storm out.

Nana told of the night at the USO club when she knew that somehow Isaiah was still alive. She never saw him and never tried to find him, but she knew he had seen her and had chosen to leave her alone and not try to talk to her.

She fast forwarded to the death of her mother… their grandmother… and the letter from the lawyer. She had tucked it in her pocket and allowed them to pass it around if any wanted to read it for themselves. Susan was sitting in the middle, so she read it out loud and the rest of them leaned in to see it.

Then came the kicker. She told them about the journals she had kept all these years and how she had brought me here so I could help her by writing a novel about her life. The minute she said it my mother's eyes shot to me and to the stairs. She had immediately made the connection. She told them that originally, she had just hoped that Isaiah or Willow might see the book and come to her.

"Alex and Mark are working tirelessly to help me find them. I am not so foolish as to think that a good man like Isaiah did not marry again and have other children but just to be able to talk to him again would be such a gift. And to see my daughter that I believed dead all this time," Nana started to tear up.

There was really nothing else she needed to say. I jumped up and went to her.

"You did great Nana," I whispered.

I gave her a tissue and handed her the glass of water from the coffee table.

For several minutes, the room was dead silent. No one seemed to want to be the first to speak. All three of my Aunts had tears streaming down their faces but I could not tell if it was because they were hurt, angry or just touched by this heart-breaking story.

My dad seemed to be about to speak. He stood up and took one step toward Nana when my mother could take it no more.

"Alex, go pack your things. You are coming with us. We are going home right this minute. And there will be no book, young lady. You just get that idea out of your head. We will not have this scandal out there for the world to see!!!"

"I'm not going anywhere mother." I replied and was about to continue when my father spoke.

"MARTHA, SHUT UP!"

"William," she began to argue with him, but he was having none of it;

"You heard me. Sit down and shut up."

Now do not get me wrong. I do love my mother. I would never want to see her mistreated in any way. But I had never loved my dad more than at that exact minute. I looked around the room at each face. My mother started out with her mouth open wide a little in shock I think, but it quickly turned to anger as she folded her arms tightly at her chest and turned a glorious shade of purple.

All three of my Aunts who loved their baby brother to pieces, had their heads bowed to conceal a huge grin. I think secretly they had all thought my dad needed to… well as they say… grow a pair when it came to my mother.

I noticed Philip and Steve do a little hidden high five. They had also enjoyed the show. Poor Adam looked as if he was wondering what he had gotten himself into. Should he stay or run for the hills? Frances had a death grip on his arm now, so I guess she was noticing the same thing.

Once the dust settled my sweet daddy knelt in front of my Nana and said the one and only thing she needed to hear at that moment.

"Mom, I love you."

Okay we all lost it. Not a dry eye except for my mother. I noticed Annie had the kitchen door cracked open just a little and she was also crying. When she saw that I had noticed her she started to close the door, but I motioned for her to come in.

"You're family too Annie."

She took a chair from the dining room and sat next to Philip and Steve in the back.

"You don't hate me," she asked.

Frances got up first. She hugged Nana so tightly there was no space between them. I honestly think she was feeling as if she and her mother had a special bond now. And she knew that her mother was not being at all deceptive when she welcomed Adam to the family.

Kathy and Susan came to her next.

"Mom, we are not angry about what happened to you. I mean of course we aren't angry, but I am a little hurt that we never knew about Willow," said Susan.

"We used to see you go to the cemetery and cry over what we thought were your grandparents' graves. We never knew you thought you had a child buried there," said Kathy.

"Yeah we thought you must have really loved your grandparents," added Susan.

All of them seemed to have questions. Nana had kept her promise and answered them all with total honesty. I think the hardest thing for her children to understand was how she could love both Isaiah and Samuel so deeply at the same time. My father asked the hardest question out of all of them.

"Mom, If Isaiah had come to you after the dance. Once you realized he was alive. Would you have gone with him?"

The room fell silent at that. I think it had occurred to

my dad that if she had chosen Isaiah at that point then he would have never been born. I guess for that matter neither would I.

"I have asked myself that same question a thousand times, William. I have played the scenario from every angle and I must be honest with you. I do not know what I would have done. I loved Samuel very much. Loved my babies. But if Isaiah had come to me and especially if he had Willow, I do not know what I would have done. For a long time now, I have thought that he knew how hard the choice would be. He knew that no matter which I chose someone would be heartbroken. And he knew I would suffer over my decision regardless of what it was. I think he made it for me.

He saw me dancing with your father and saw that I was expecting a baby. I have no idea if he knew it was my third child with Samuel, but he knew I had moved on and he only wanted me to be happy. I don't know if he decided that after he gave the song to the little boy or if the song was just so I would know he wasn't killed, and I could stop grieving for him. But I know he was a caring man and he knew it would be hard for me to survive if I had to tear my heart in two. It was his last act of love toward me.

That helped me through it and I was content to leave it alone until I received the letter from my mothers' lawyer. Having lost my love was one thing but to steal my child out of my arms and let me think she had died. That was more than I could stand.

Nana continued to explain to them how the last year she had so much anger and had to pray a lot to forgive her parents. She told them again how she hoped the book I was writing might find its way to them and how Mark and

I were trying to help locate them as well.

"We will all help mother," Frances offered and the whole room agreed. Well except one.

"What was in the little grave mother," asked Kathy?

Until this minute I do not think Nana had asked herself that question. She looked at them and honestly replied with shrugged shoulders.

"I have no idea."

"That needs to be added to the list of things to do then," Annie said.

It was the first time she had made a sound. She had been there when Nana, Mark and I had made the list of things to do. Everyone seemed a little surprised that she had said anything. I am not sure some of them had even realized she was in the room.

"Absolutely," I said.

The questions continued for a while longer. At one point someone remembered all the paintings of the willow tree and the stream. We made our way to the library where all four of her children examined the paintings as they had never done before. They noticed some of the same things I had found after reading the journal. My mother had stayed in the living room, so I took the opportunity to talk to dad alone.

"Dad, I want to stay with Nana. I do not want to hurt you or mom, but I love it here. I am going to ask Nana if I can just stay here instead of at the dorm once classes start."

I waited to see if he would try to talk me out of it.

"I think that is a wonderful idea Alex. This place was always a happy place for me, and I know Nana will be so thrilled that you want to stay. You might wait and let me break that news to your mother after we get home," he said and winked.

"I love you dad."

"Same here kiddo."

When we came back to the living room Annie said she had made a variety of salads for anyone who might want a light dinner. A tossed green salad, pasta salad, three bean salad, and several others. There was some of the cake left and she had a fruit tray with watermelon, cantaloupe, grapes and some of the left-over strawberries. Once they had eaten Kathy, Steve, Susan and Philip were ready to leave. I was so happy to see them embrace Nana and encourage her to find Isaiah and Willow.

"Please keep us posted if you find anything. We can't wait to meet them," both sisters agreed.

Mother had not joined us for dinner. She had told Annie she had a terrible headache and would be upstairs lying down.

Frances was the only one that Nana considered showing the painting in her bedroom. She waited until dad was in conversation with Adam and took Frances by the hand.

"I want to show you something," she said and led her up the stairs.

I noticed and I guess because I am protective or maybe just nosy, I followed them into Nana's room. Frances had her head on Nana's shoulder and Nana had her arm around Frances and they were both quietly weeping. I decided to give them this time and stepped out, closing the door behind me.

I wanted to just go back downstairs but daughter guilt got the best of me and I knocked softly on my mother's door.

"Come in," she said weakly.

"Mother, are you alright?"

She proceeded to tell me how embarrassed she was at her behavior. And by my father's reprimand in front of everyone.

"I wasn't raised like your father was Alex. In my household growing up we were taught that anyone who is not like us was less. My parents both used slang words that are so offensive to different races. I always felt it was wrong but when it is embedded in you as a child it takes deep roots. Your father taught me so much after we married about acceptance and God's love for all who he created. I had not even thought of others as his creation. He asked me one day just where I thought they came from, if not from God. I know my behavior was horrible and I will apologize but something just came over me and I allowed it to control me."

"It's called hate mother. As a child you were taught to hate certain people for nothing they had done, but for the very fact that they existed at all."

She sat up and laid her head on my shoulder.

"You are a wise girl."

"So did dad ever tell you about the apples?"

She had to laugh.

"Yes, but maybe I need to hear it again."

Mother made her apologies as humble as is possible for her. She is a proud woman and eating crow does not wash down well for her, but I was proud of her for making the effort. We all said our goodbyes to Frances and Adam, and they told Nana they would be back soon to make plans for the wedding.

"Maybe in the fall when the leaves start to change color," Frances had suggested. "You have so many beautiful trees on your property and it would just be so pretty."

"Fall sounds perfect," Nana agreed.

My parents told me goodbye and good night at the same time.

"We will need to leave extremely early to get home at a decent time and there is no need for anyone to see us off. We will give out our hugs and kisses tonight."

Annie had already gone to bed. She was exhausted both physically and emotionally.

Nana said she was pleasantly exhausted.

"Thank you, Alex. I would have never been able to do this without you."

I decided this was as good a time as any to ask her about staying here instead of staying at the dorm. She did not even seem surprised at my request. She hugged me goodnight and as always, she kissed the top of my head.

"Well of course you're staying."

I could not help but think that had been her plan the whole time. Good plan I thought.

Before going to sleep I called Mark and told him about the day. I told him about everyone's reaction including my mothers. I told him about Adam and Frances. His reaction made me think that Annie may have talked to him already, but he let me talk it out anyway. I guess he knew I needed to tell it to process it all.

"So how do you think your mom will feel about us," he asked?

"I don't know," I said. "But I think dad can handle her."

After we hung up, I decided to go to work on the novel. I was tired but my mind was too full to sleep so I would put all the day's events down on paper while they were fresh.

I had been right this morning. This was a very eventful, scary, educational and wonderful day. I stood up when I was finished for the night and looked out my window toward the field behind the house. The moon was so big and bright it had the area lit up like a spotlight. I thought about Isaiah and Beulah.

Where could he be? And if we do find him… What then?

Chapter Seventeen

The Gazebo & the Guest List

For several months after Nana broke the news to her children, life seemed to flow smoothly. I worked every possible free minute on the novel. Each time I completed a chapter of the book I would have Nana proofread it. I wanted the book to be as true to the actual events as it could possibly be.

"Alex, it is as if you were there with me. You are feeling the same joy, the same fear, the same desire as I was. You are going to be an excellent writer. I love what you have done."

I was thrilled with Nana's praise. Her opinion was the only one that mattered. I must admit I hoped I would never feel this kind of pressure to get it right on anything else I might do.

The book would be close to completed by the time my classes started in September. My plan was to have it ready to send to several publishing companies before I started my freshman year but there was one thing that would keep that from happening. I could not end the book until we knew about Isaiah. We had not found anything on him yet. We had no way of knowing if he was still alive. Would he even be interested in seeing Nana again? Maybe he was married with grown children and grandchildren just like Nana and he did not want his wife to know about his first wife. The white girl he had fallen in love with. I would lay in my bed at night and run through all the possible scenarios. Would there be a happy ending to the book, or would it end as a sad tragedy? Could a love that had remained in my Nana's heart and dreams for 50 years have been one sided?

I know Nana was having some of the same concerns. As she had always done, she made her way to the stream and the willow tree on July 31st to wish Isaiah a happy anniversary. She had allowed me to walk with her to the clearing but had asked me to let her go to the tree alone. I really did try not to eavesdrop on her, but the sound carried more than she may have realized. I could hear her crying. I heard her talking to Isaiah or at least her memory of him and asking him if he still loved her. Did he still have feelings for her, and would he want to see her again if he knew she was searching for him? She had to be thinking that if neither he or Willow could be found or if they simply did not want to see her then she had told this secret to all of her loved ones for no reason. She had worked through embarrassment and fear of rejection and nothing would come of it.

"Nana, I just have to believe he will be happy when we find him. He will be thrilled because he still loves you too," I said to comfort her on our walk back to the house.

She merely patted my hand and gave me a half-hearted smile. This was always an emotional day for her but this year the emotions were probably tripled in size.

Mark was trying to search from the library on campus, but he was in the middle of a test for the end of his summer courses and would have only a two-week break before the fall quarter.

I had my classes lined up and had been lucky enough to schedule all of them in the mornings so I would not be out late. I also had no classes on Friday's. This would permit me to still spend time on the book and in helping Nana. It would also give me time with Mark if he were to come home on any given weekend.

My mother had not reacted negatively about my staying with Nana like I had feared she would. She said she was relieved knowing I would not be tempted to let social life pull me away from my studies. I had not told her and daddy about Mark. Nana agreed that there was no need in adding anything else to their plate until it became necessary.

Aunt Frances and Adam had decided that planning even a small wedding needed more time than they would have for a fall wedding. Frances decided that spring flowers would be even more beautiful than fall leaves. They decided that Saturday May 8, 1993 was the most perfect day for a wedding they could imagine. Nana had plenty of time so she insisted on having a gazebo built on the side of the house where the ceremony would take place and Mark would plant buttercups, tulips and Irises' in a pattern that would allow for an aisle for the bride to walk down.

The reception would be around the pool area. Of course, there would be a plan B if rain interfered with their plans. Wedding ceremony in the living room and reception in the formal dining room. The guest list was very small so either situation would work just fine. Adam came from a small family. He had no siblings and his father had passed so it would only be his mother and two of his cousins. He would invite his aunt and uncle, but they were not pleased with his choices and unless they changed their mind, they had refused to be a part of this ***shame of a marriage, as*** they put it. Frances would of course have her siblings and their spouses and children. Annie would be a guest as well.

Nana insisted she would hire someone to serve at the reception because Annie was family in this circumstance. Frances and Adam both had long time friends that would serve as their attendants. There would be a maid of honor and a best man. She had explained to her sisters that if she had them as bridesmaids and their husbands served as groomsmen there would be no one sitting in the chairs provided for the guests.

Nana's gift to her other children for their weddings had been portraits of the couple to hang in their new home. She had been busy every morning possible to have it completed before May.

I was glad she had this wedding as a distraction. The months just kept creeping by with no results from our searches. She had talked to her parents' lawyer. He was the son of their original lawyer. The man who had been privileged to their terrible secret. The man who helped with the deception about Willow and had even drawn up the agreement to give a lump sum to Millie for the child upon her grandfather's death, had been gone for years. He had died long before Nana's mother passed away. It was his son who had taken over all his clients and had delivered the letter to Nana that revealed the truth about Willow to her. He had never known her parents personally and knew nothing about where he may have sent Mille and grandmother all those years ago. After all he was just a child himself back then. He did promise to investigate his father's old records to see if he could find any clue as to where we might start our search.

Mark had tried the military approach. He had been unable to find anything so far about the plane crash or if Isaiah had been a prisoner of war. When he might have returned to the states and how he found Willie at the USO.

Nana had purchased a computer for the house in hopes that we could search on it for answers. It had not helped us come up with anything about Isaiah or Willow yet, but it was making my work on the book much easier. It would be a help for schoolwork also.

The months were quickly passing by. It seemed anyone who might have known Isaiah was no longer around. Mark and I had gone to the areas of town where people of color seemed to live to see if anyone knew the name. Maybe knew the family and could tell us where they might have moved to but no one remembered Millie, Isaiah or grandmother Mabel. We had called and ordered copies of phone books from Washington D.C. and when they arrived, we searched them from cover to cover to see if anything might lead us to them. We found nothing.

Mark and I had also used his two-week break to search the local library with no results but then it was time for both of us to start classes and we knew our searches would be limited.

Nana had applied for permission to dig up the tiny grave that she had visited for 50 years thinking it was her little daughter. It was not in any record as an actual grave but because it was practically on top of Nana's grandmother's grave, and in a cemetery owned by the church she couldn't dig it up. She would be digging her grandmother's grave up in the eyes of the law. She had filed all the paperwork and was just waiting for permission. She had promised me she would not go without me once she was granted that permission. Nana and I had also been searching through the attic thinking maybe a clue was buried up there in some box or something. We had returned to Millie's house to search as well. Maybe we would find a note or something letting us know where she and grandmother were taking Willow.

Nothing but dead ends. Hope was fading and with each passing month the light of hope in Nana seemed to grow more and more dim.

I had promised to go home for Thanksgiving and Annie had promised to go to her daughters for a week. Nana refused to go with me because she needed to work on the painting and she just was not in the mood to travel. I think she was trying to avoid my mother. She had accepted mother's apology and I felt I had truly forgiven her but there was still a thin wall between Nana and my mother and I think Nana just didn't want to let that ruin the holiday for my dad and me.

Mark came and stayed with Nana for Thanksgiving and kept her spirits up. Kathy, Susan and Frances had all been at the homes of their husbands and fiancé but came by later that day and insisted that Nana would go with them for Christmas shopping on the Friday and Saturday following Thanksgiving. A fun girl's trip of sorts.

On December 22, Nana received a letter from the courts letting her know she would need to appear before a judge on January 28th for the purpose of consideration for her request to exhume a grave. Another case of hurry up and wait. It was amazing to us how many hoops she had to jump through to dig up what was supposed to be nothing more than a hole in the ground.

When Christmas came all her children and grandchildren came to celebrate with her. It was the best gift she could have received. Instead of getting each other gifts we played dirty Christmas. A game where you do not know who brought which gift and you draw numbers to see whose turn it is to pick a gift. You also have the option of stealing a gift from someone if you like what they have. We all laughed and laughed. It was the most fun Nana had experienced in months. My parents had brought a little gift for me, but Nana had always encouraged her grown children to give to a charity or a needy family they knew about instead of giving her or each other gifts.

"I have everything I need materially. It is a true gift to me to see my children do good for others," Nana explained.

At the Christmas gathering Kathy's son Samuel started telling funny stories about his Papa Sam. Everyone quickly looked at Nana as if they expected her to be upset. She realized they were unsure of how to handle it under the circumstances so in response to them she started telling her own funny and happy memories of him. It was wonderful to remember him with such joy.

"I told you all about Isaiah because I felt it was time to be honest with you and to find my past. It takes nothing from my love for Samuel. He was as much a part of my heart as Isaiah ever was. I still think of him daily. I see little things that remind me of him, and I smile. Please do not ever doubt my love for your father. Or for your grandfather my dear Samuel."

Everyone seemed to feel greatly relieved at her statement that somehow gave them permission to still talk about him.

Mark and I decided to join in on Nana's suggestion rather than get each other gifts this year. He did however find time and enough money to take me on a special night out for New Year's Eve. When he kissed me at midnight, I could not help but remember the story of Papa Sam in her journal when he took Nana out for New Year's Eve.

I had noticed my mother looking at us when they were here for Christmas. She suspected I guess that something was going on between us and I knew from her expression she was not pleased about it. She was probably waiting to be sure before having a talk with me. Hate is such a deep-rooted thing. I hoped she would get to know Mark and accept him but if not… it would be her loss. If made to choose I would choose Mark.

Classes had resumed on January 10th. I still had a similar schedule, so I was able to attend the hearing with Nana on the 28th. The clerk called her case and asked her to step forward. Judge Manning was presiding that day. She read her notes, made a couple of marks on the paper and handed it to the court secretary to document it. She then looked at my Nana and said "granted" and hit her little hammer on the provided block on her podium.

It explained that she would be permitted to have the 'grave' exhumed but would need to have a member of the Sheriff's department and the medical examiner present at the time. They would also have to arrange for a grave digger to be there to do the actual digging.

So, on February 3rd at eight o'clock in the morning we all

gathered around the site of my great grandmother's grave to witness what may be nothing more than a pile of dirt. Or perhaps an empty box. Everyone was there except my parents because of the long drive. Nana of course. Annie, Mark and I. Kathy, Susan, Frances and the men in their lives. Even Kathy and Steve's son Samuel who was stationed in the states and was granted permission to take a two day leave to attend. We had promised my dad we would call him the minute we knew something.

It was Nana's 68th birthday. She said she hoped her wish would come true and there would be some information buried that would help her find her oldest child and her Isaiah.

Nana showed the grave digger exactly where the dirt had been disturbed those many years ago. There had never been a marker because it was supposedly a secret grave of a child her parents had not wanted anyone to know about. Nana could trace it out to the exact measurements because she had cried at least a million tears over it.

Mr. Gains, the grave digger, began to push his shovel into the ground. He scooped out two large shovels full of dirt but then after a couple of scoops he tried to be cautious with his digging just in case he was to come upon something. We all held our breath and watched intently. At about two or three feet deep he heard a scrapping of his shovel. He laid the shovel aside and got down on his knees to move dirt with his hands. He began to reveal a small metal box. We stepped back and began looking at each other in fear that maybe the story that Willow had not died was a lie. Why would they give me that gift of hope that my baby had not died if indeed she is in that box. Nana began to breath very fast and erratic. We helped her to sit down on the cold ground beside the grave and managed after several minutes to calm her down.

"Nana, it's not her. You saw the letter. She was sent away with Millie and Grandmother Mabel. Just take several deep breaths and calm yourself. Then we can open this box and see if maybe it holds the answers to where they took her."

Nana nodded her head at me and took two very slow deep cleansing breaths before she asked Mr. Gains to please open the box. He handed it off to the medical examiner… just in case. He looked at all of us for a second and then opened the little box and peered inside. After only a few seconds he turned the box around and handed it to Nana. She peered inside as we all looked on waiting to see just what had been placed there so long ago.

Isaiah's Bible lay inside wrapped in one of the little blankets Millie had made for Willow. Nana took it out so gently you would have thought it were a fragile baby. She ran her hand across it and the tears began to flow down her cheek.

"I had sent this home with Millie the last day I remember having Willow with me. I had recorded her birth in it and told Millie to keep it safe for me."

We all gave her a little while to lovingly remember all the hours she and Isaiah had spent reading it together. How they had used it to conduct their marriage with only Millie and God as witnesses. Finally, we could not take it another minute.

"Is there anything inside," several of us said simultaneously?

She seemed to jolt into reality and had us help her up off the ground. Her car was parked only a few feet away, so we all walked toward it and she lay the Bible on the hood. She opened it up to the first page. There were all her entries. The marriage on July 31st, 1941. A notation about the day the horrible letter about Isaiah presumed to be dead. And her last entry about the birth of her first child on April 30th, 1942. Kathy seemed to read the date at the same time Nana did and we heard her gasp.

"We share the same birthday?"

"Yes, Nana replied."

Both Nana and Kathy hugged and wept at that.

"I feel truly honored mama," Kathy choked out through her tears.

She continued to flip the pages one at a time. Isaiah had always underlined certain passages that he felt strongly about and had often made notations on the margins of the pages. Nothing really stood out to Nana until she came across the book of Ruth in the Old Testament. Ruth chapter one verse 16 had been highlighted with a yellow crayon or something. It was different from any marking she had ever seen in Isaiah's Bible.

16 And Ruth said, Entreat me not to leave thee, or to return from following after thee: for whither thou goest, I will go; and where thou lodgest, I will lodge: thy people shall be my people, and thy God my God:

In very small handwriting under the words 'I will go' was the word Tennessee. Nana squealed with excitement.

"She took her to Tennessee! Isaiah went there to meet up with his cousin and his friend before enlisting. I think he had some family there."

She looked at all of us with wide eyes.

"WE KNOW WHERE TO LOOK!"

Nana was practically ready to jump in her car and head

to Tennessee that very minute. It took us a while to talk her down.

"Mother, we know this is exciting news, but Tennessee is still a lot of ground to cover. We need to sit down and come up with a plan. We need a map of all the little towns. It could still take a while to locate them. Plus, that was fifty years ago. They could have relocated," Frances pointed out.

Nana looked as if we had all taken turns punching her in the stomach. She began to cry again. Mr. Gains, the sheriff and the medical examiner had filled the hole up and were loading up in the sheriff's car to head back to town. They glanced our way and the sheriff made a questioning face toward us as if asking if we needed assistance. We all shook our heads and tried to motion them to go ahead and leave. We would be fine.

"Mother, we don't mean to sound defeated. Please do not misunderstand what was said. This is fantastic news and is the first hopeful information we have found. I just want you to realize that it will still take time to locate them. At least now we know where to start looking," Susan soothed.

Once we were back at Nana's we talked her into laying down for a little while. The rest of us sat around the dining room table and tried to brainstorm.

We divided the state up in its three sections. East Tennessee would be for Kathy, Susan, Steve, Philip and Samuel. West Tennessee would be Frances, Adam and Nana and middle Tennessee would be my parents, Annie, Mark and me.

"This way we are not stumbling over each other's efforts and wasting time duplicating searches," Mark suggested.

"I agree but we need to keep each other posted on anything that sounds promising," said Steve.

We all promised to do a conference call once a week.

Somehow during this intense search, we also had to keep up our classes, do our jobs and of course prepare for a wedding that would take place in about thirteen weeks.

I called my dad and told him everything. He and mom would do as much searching as possible from their end and wanted to be included on the weekly call.

"We have just got to find them," I said.

"We will find them," he assured me. "I just hope finding them brings the happy ending we are all wishing for."

Chapter Eighteen

Let's Get You Married

It was the day of the wedding. Everyone tried to make sure Frances and Adam felt special. That this was their day, and no one was thinking about anyone except them. Apparently, Frances and Adam did not get the memo. Frances was so preoccupied with the search she could not stop talking about it. While her bridesmaid Monica worked on making sure her makeup was perfect and her dress was buttoned down her back without missing even one of the thirty buttons, all Frances could talk about was the search. She had told her lifelong friend about it and so we felt free discussing it around her, but we wanted Frances to enjoy her day.

When Nana came in to see how she was doing Frances bombarded her with questions on what each one had managed to find and gave a report on everything she and Adam had attempted.

"Frances," Nana said. "You are such a beautiful bride. I know what that means to a woman. This is the day you and Adam pledge your love to each other. The day you make promises to each other until you are separated by death. Please my love, let go of everything else today. Let this day be about you and the man you love. You are not only cheating yourself if you don't, but you are cheating Adam and your family. We think Adam is an amazing person and that he is amazingly lucky to be marrying you. Give all of us this special day."

Frances hugged her mother so tightly. "Thank you, mama. I love you so much."

"I love you too," she said and tenderly arranged her hair then kissed her cheek. "Now let's get you married,"

It was a beautiful ceremony and the weather was perfect. Cool enough to be comfortable but not cold. No breeze at all so things were not being blown off the tables. Mark had planted all the bulbs in the fall and the flowers came up perfectly in line to make the aisle pristine. Frances had taken several of the tulips and tied a ribbon around them as her bouquet and her bridesmaid carried just one perfect tulip. Frances wore white but it was a shorter dress with a full skirt.

It had a neckline that came down on the shoulders to accent her lovely long neck and the pearls she had borrowed from her mother. Instead of a veil she had chosen a white hat with a white ribbon around it. The look on Adams face as she walked down the aisle on my dads' arm made my heart swell. The love they felt for each other was so obvious. Adams' aunt and uncle had decided to come after all and his aunt and mother were absolutely blubbering. After the wedding they assured us that they were happy tears.

"The look on my son's face could not be denied. He loves Frances with his whole heart. It is so hard to find that kind of love in this world and to know he has found it will allow me to live happily the rest of my days," his mother said and his aunt just kept nodding her head with tears streaming.

The reception was a lot of fun. We had music and dancing. When it was time to cut the beautiful cake that Annie insisted on making as her gift, the bride and groom had to smear it in each other's face.

Everyone had brought gifts, but the highlight was when Nana lifted the covering from her painting. Everyone gasps at the beautiful likeness. Nana had outdone herself. Adam's mother was speechless… for about two seconds. Then she went on and on about it. Since they had met on a trip to Paris, she had them sitting at a café table with the background obviously the beautiful city where they had discovered each other. She had captured them so exactly. They were holding hands on top of the table and looking deep into each other's eyes.

"OH MAMA! It is so wonderful. I just love it. Adam, don't you just love it? We just love it," Frances said without waiting for an answer from Adam. He shook his head so vigorously when she was talking that there was no doubt he did love it.

I was dancing with Mark, lost in his arms. I had my head on his shoulder and we would occasionally kiss. It was so magical. It was as if we were the only two people there… that is until I noticed my entire family staring at us. My Nana and Annie were huddled together trying not to laugh because they could see exactly what was happening. My parents both had that look they get when I need to come up with an explanation fast. Mark had noticed my body tense and when he looked around at all the faces that were facing us, he whispered in my ear, "Busted."

Then without missing a beat he twirled me like a ballerina and then dipped me in a very classy dance move if I do say so myself. I was just so happy to do anything in response to the glaring eyes of my mother. I smiled at Mark and hugged him even more tightly. Everyone including my dad just kind of shrugged at us and went back to dancing. My mother looked angry. I was not sure if she was angry because I had not told her about us or if she was that upset about Mark's obvious black origin.

Annie noticed her glare and I knew if my mother said even one thing there could be a cat fight. I knew I would probably have to talk to my parents about this later but for now I just wanted to enjoy the moment. Dad pulled her in to dance and after a little whispering and teasing he had her smiling. Good ole dad. He would have my back and that was enough.

Frances and Adam had to leave for the airport because they were going to honeymoon in Italy. They thanked us all for making this such an unforgettable day, but they did whisper to Kathy that if anything happened, she had better call them.

Once everyone else had gone my mother asked me if we could talk in private. I assumed I was about to get the third degree. As soon as we entered my room I started to explain.

"Mom, I know I should have told you and daddy that I was dating Mark. I was just so afraid you would be upset. He is such a wonderful person and we are both taking things slow. Oh, mama please don't be upset," I rattled on and on but suddenly noticed she was trying to get me to listen.

"Yes dear, I am sure he is a nice young man. You are young and it is just a little crush. He certainly does dance well," and she waved it off as nothing.

"Now would you please sit down and listen to me. Before I say a word, I need you to promise me you will not scream. I do not want anyone to run up here to see what is going on. I haven't even told your father yet, but I promise I will once we are back home."

Suddenly I was worried. Was something wrong with her? She was acting very anxious and it occurred to me she could be ill. Maybe she needed to tell me something terrible and that was why she wasn't overreacting about Mark and I.

"Oh, mother, is everything alright? Are you ill? What is it?"

She grabbed up my hands and grinned at me.

"I may have found Willow."

I started to scream but she put her hand over my mouth.

"Where? How?"

"Well as you know I am a realtor and I thought that maybe there would be a listing in the middle Tennessee area where someone named Willow was either trying to buy or sell property. I knew it was a long shot but that is such an unusual name. There cannot possibly be a lot of people with that name. I found a listing from last year. The realtor that listed the property was Willow Hamilton. She works out of Memphis.

Now I know it is a long shot and I felt it was best not to tell anyone else until it could be checked out. I have all the information that was listed. She worked for Hamilton Realtor so either she has her own business or perhaps she is married to the owner of the company. I put the phone number associated with her. I don't know if it is her personal number or if it is the business number."

My mother was completely out of breath, but I could tell she was proud of the fact that she had found this information.

"Oh mama, this is wonderful. It is the first promising lead we have had. I can't wait to tell everyone."

"Alex, please wait until you know something for sure. This will make me feel as if I have made up for my horrible behavior when Nana told us her story. I do not want to get her hopes up only to pull the rug out from under her. Even if it is her daughter we don't know if she would want to meet her mother and we need to see if she will lead us to Isaiah."

"I need to at least tell Mark. If I go to Memphis to meet with her, I wouldn't want to go alone."

She agreed but wanted me to be sure Mark would keep it secret until we were sure.

When we walked down the stairs together everyone seemed to be trying to read us. I think everyone had assumed the same thing I had. That she was going to read me the right act about Mark. Once we reached the bottom of the stairs my mother approached Mark and put her hand out to shake his.

"Nice to officially meet you Mark."

My dad walked up and offered his hand to Mark as well. Mark shook both their hands and smiled but seemed to be waiting for the other boot to fall as they say.

Once everyone could tell there would be no fireworks, they resumed their goodbyes and within minutes everyone had left and Nana and Annie had gone to their rooms to rest before dinner. Nana had told Annie we would just have simple sandwiches for dinner and to please not make a fuss.

I asked Mark if he would like to go to the pool house and talk for a minute.

Once we were in his pool house and seated, he took a deep breath and looked at me with concern.

"Give it to me straight. What did your mom have to say?"

"She may have found Willow," I blurted out.

He had obviously not been expecting that and proceeded to tell me how he would not let me go no matter how much my mother objected. Then once it clicked what I had said…

"What? What did you just say?"

My mother may have found Willow. I then began telling him exactly what my mom had said and showed him the paper she gave me with all the information written out on it. I also told him that she felt it was best we do not tell anyone else until we checked it out. It may not be her and if it is, she may not be happy we found her. Until we know I do not want to give Nana any false hope.

"WOO HOO!" he yelled and jumped up to take me in his arms and twirl me around and around. "Road trip," he asked?

"Road trip," I confirmed, and we began to make our plans.

We looked it up to see how long it would take to drive it and it would take us eight hours at the least. We did not have the money needed to fly and since we did not want anyone to know what we were doing there was no one we could ask except my mother.

"Let me call her in the morning. She and daddy are driving home today, and I have to try and call when he isn't there to overhear."

We spent a while talking over what we might say to her

when we found her. The idea was making me so nervous. Mark decided to look up the Hamilton Realtors of Memphis Tennessee to see if we could get more information. The website had a picture of all the realtors that worked for them. There were several tiny photos of the people who worked there and there was a picture in the top left-hand corner with the name Willow Hamilton under it and the title of Owner under her name. She owned this business. That was impressive.

The picture was of a beautiful woman around the right age of what our Willow would be. Her hair was a caramel color. It was in a short loose FRO cut. It was just below her ear lobes and beautifully framed a very pretty face. It was hard to make out the color of her eyes in the small picture, but they didn't seem dark. Her skin was very pale for a black woman. It was brown but more like a smooth tan. Almost the color of coffee with a lot of cream in it. The memory of what Nana had said about her and Isaiah's body reminding her of cream being poured into coffee popped in my head. It was ironic that a child they had created would be the color of that coffee once the cream was mixed in.

I studied her eyes, her mouth, and her facial shape. This had to be Nana's daughter. Her features reminded me a great deal of Kathy, Susan and Francis. I could even see a little of my dad in her but not a lot. My dad looked just like Samuel Stone so it was not expected that she would favor him.

"Mark, it has to be her. The resemblance is uncanny. She looks kind. Her eyes are kind."

Mark knew I was trying to convince myself that she would be accepting and eager to come with us to see her mother. He walked me to the French doors and told me I must go straight to bed.

"You look like you could go to sleep standing up. We need to be alert tomorrow when we set our plan into motion."

He kissed me goodnight and then turned and walked away. I think he was the one who was too tired to think. Or maybe it was both of us. I barely remember making my way up to bed. The next thing I remembered was the sun shining through the gap in my curtains and then my first thought was of Willow Hamilton. I pray she will want to see Nana. It will break her heart all over again if she does not. It will feel as if she died a second time.

It was seven o'clock in the morning and I knew dad would be in the shower about now preparing to go to church. If nothing else my dad was consistent. You could plan your day by his actions. I called mom hoping we could talk before dad was finished with his shower.

"Hello," mom said across the miles.

"Mom, it's me Alex. Is dad in the shower so he won't hear us talking?"

"Well of course he is sweetie. It's Sunday morning."

Like I said you could plan your day by his precise schedule.

"It would take Mark and I a full eight hours to get to Memphis. Is there any way you could pay for two plan tickets so we can do this without Nana or Annie getting suspicious," I blurted out quickly?

"I told your father yesterday on our trip home. He was thrilled but did agree that no one should tell Nana until we know how Willow will react to the news. Let me talk it over with him and see if we can afford a couple of tickets and a rental car. I will call you back later today and let you know."

I tried to tell Mark what she said without his mom or my Nana overhearing. *Were they always this clingy?* The four of us had attended church and had lunch and had still not had a minute alone. I volunteered to clean up the kitchen after lunch in order to talk to him.

"You ladies need to just put your feet up after that busy day yesterday."

I had made a few bonus points with everyone but Mark who looked at me like I was nuts for offering to clean when we could have sat and watched a little television while cuddling on the couch. Once the ladies were in the den, I told him about talking to my mother. I had barely finished telling him when the cell phone Nana had given me began to ring.

Mama had talked to daddy and he was on board. It would be worth it to get the answers we all wanted for his mom. He would wire us the money for the tickets and the car. He said we may even have enough for a nice meal, and chuckled.

"Thanks dad. And thank mom for me. I love you both."

"We love you too sweetie. Call us as soon as you have news."

"I will. I promise."

We hated to lie to Nana or Annie, but we did not know what else to do. Mark just made sure to tell them both that he had a few things to do next weekend and he would not be home. This was not uncommon so no problem there. Now for me. I was always home. I finally blurted out my only idea.

"Mark, would you be okay with me coming down next

weekend? I can help you study."

All three of them looked at me and then Nana and Annie turned and looked at Mark for his answer.

"I would love that," he finally said. "I can really use the help."

It suddenly occurred to me why the three of them were looking at me so strangely. Mark had finished his end of semester test and was not due to start back for summer classes until June. I hated to think what they suspected we were up to. I tried to control my face, but it was out of my control and my cheeks flushed red. I could feel the heat. They probably think we are planning a wild weekend out of their supervision.

Mark is 22 and I am 19 so we were both adults, but I felt like the little girl who had lied in order to play hooky from school. It mattered to me what both thought of me. I would have to explain once this is over and we can tell them.

Once we left the room Mark started to laugh. I elbowed him and told him to shush before they heard him.

"It can't get much worse. They probably already think we are going to the cheapest motel we can find for a wild night together."

"Maybe they believed me," I defended myself.

"Alex, you do remember that I was supposed to be home for the next three weeks and I would have no place to live if I went back to school. The student apartments are being painted and cannot be occupied until June 12th."

I slapped my forehead and rolled my eyes in total amazement of just how bad my job of covering my tracks had been. I guess to their credit neither of them called me on it. I guess they decided that if what I was doing was important enough to tell such a ridiculous lie that they would give me my space.

I had trouble looking Nana and Annie in the face all week. I could not wait until Friday morning when I put my lie in action. Mark and I each tossed a little suitcase in his car and waved like we thought they believed what we had told them. We had gone to town on an errand for Nana a couple of days ago and it gave us the perfect opportunity to go pick up the money dad had wired to us. We had time to run by the airport Friday to purchase tickets to Memphis. They offered cheaper prices for one way and since we were not sure how long this would take; we would just purchase one-way tickets in Tennessee to return home.

It was amazing how the same trip that would have taken us no less than eight hours in his car took less than an hour to go by plane.

Once we landed, we rented a very small, very cheap car and asked directions to the area where we knew Willow worked. The closer we got to the realtor's office building the more nervous I became. When he parked and was standing outside the door, I was afraid I might vomit. Mark rubbed his hands up and down my arms and calmed me down.

"This is a good thing," he said. "We are doing this for Nana. Giving her back what was taken from her. Just remember that… and breathe."

I inhaled a deep breath and exhaled slowly.

"Okay, I'm good now. Let's do this."

We walked in and asked the woman at the front desk if Willow Hamilton was available.

"She is away for lunch. Can I give her a message," she

asked and we both just stared at her? "Or you are welcome to wait," she added.

We both just stood there and nodded. It is a miracle she didn't call the police and report two mental patients had escaped from a hospital and they needed to come get us.

We sat there for almost three hours. I was so hungry and needed to go to the bathroom desperately but was afraid she would come as soon as I left the room.

"Just go to the bathroom," Mark insisted. "If she comes, I will go in and stall till you come out."

When I came out of the bathroom she had just walked in and I almost ran into her. The lady at the front desk told her we had been waiting to see her for three hours.

"Oh well by all means come into my office."

Here goes nothing I thought and followed her into her small office.

There were pictures all over the walls of the many houses she was hoping to sell. She had a few pictures on her desk. One was of her and a man that I assumed was Mr. Hamilton. There was a picture of a younger man. Possibly her son I thought. And one of the three of them and an older gentleman. The older man was sitting beside the younger man with his arm around his shoulders. All of them had big smiles on their faces. Could that older gentleman be Isaiah? My whole body began to shake. This was the most important thing I had done in a long while and I was afraid I would not be able to speak. I could tell she was waiting for one of us to say something. After all we were the ones who had waited all this time to see her.

"Is there something I can do for you," she finally asked?

"My name is Alex Stone," I said. "And this is my friend Mark Armstrong. We are here to talk to you about my grandmother. Her name is Willamina… Willamina Beulah Stone."

The strangest look came over her face. It was not joy or shock or even uncertainty. It almost appeared to be anger.

"Is this a joke? Because if it is, I'm not amused."

Mark and I looked at each other a little unsure of how to proceed.

"We think you might be her daughter. She gave birth to a girl on April 30th, 1942."

I was about to say more but then Willow's next comment gave me reason to pause.

"Yes, she gave birth to me on that day... and then seven days later she sent me away. She was ashamed of me and wanted nothing more to do with me," she spat out with venom. "She felt if she paid off my cousin Millie and my grandmother she could just walk away and start her new life. Well I have done just fine thank you very much and I do not need her. I am a grown woman with a child of my own. You tell her to leave me alone."

"Oh no that isn't true. Please listen. She did want you and she loved you… still loves you very much."

"Then why didn't she try to find me. My poor father has grieved over her for all these years. He still thinks of himself as married to her. I have watched him struggle over the years looking at that picture she gave him and talking about his Beulah. How can I ever forgive her for what she did to him?"

I was in shock. For a few minutes I just sat there with my mouth gapped open. Then Mark nudged me.

"The letter. Show her the letter."

I had decided at the last minute to sneak the letter from the lawyer out of Nana's room. I also brought the few journals that told the story of how she loved Isaiah and how much she loved Willow. I hope Nana will not realize they are missing but I was very glad I had brought them now.

"Can I please show you something?"

She sat there with arms folded but she did not say no so I handed her the letter from the lawyer.

"She only received this letter about a year ago. She has been trying to find you since she received it."

I watched her read it and I saw the wall start to fade around her. She was still angry but seemed to be more willing to listen to us.

"She thought I was dead. You mean she did not give me to Millie to get rid of me?

I spent the next hour telling her everything. I also told her about digging up the grave and finding her father's Bible with the clue in it.

"That's how we finally found you. Millie had put a message so we would know where to look but she had thought you were buried in that tiny grave all these years. She has grieved over you all this time. I also told her how she had grieved over Isaiah for years until the incident at the USO club and she could not find him afterward.

I told her how she went to the willow tree every year to wish Isaiah a happy anniversary and would talk to him. Apparently, Nana's father had only gone in person to deliver the yearly check for a few years. Willow had no real memory of him. I had no way to be sure, but I did wonder if his decision to stop delivering it in person had something to do with Isaiah's return.

"I really need to think about this. I need to talk to my father about this. It is a lot to find out all of a sudden. To think one way my whole life and find out it wasn't anything like what I had believed."

It was the hardest thing I had ever done to walk away and wait to hear back from her. I was so afraid she would just not believe it. I asked her if she wanted to read the journals. She wanted to take them and show them to her father as well. She asks me how long we would be in town. I promised we would stay a couple of days if she needed that much time.

When Mark and I got back to the car I fell apart. He was trying to comfort me. He kept telling me I had done a wonderful job of explaining things to her. I should just give her a little time to process it. She is in shock. I knew he was right, but I was still hysterical. I could not go back and tell Nana that they did not want to see her.

"What if she never contacts us? What if Isaiah has been angry all this time? What if she does not even tell him we came? What if she never gives the journals back to us? Nana will never forgive me."

With each word that came out of my mouth I got louder and more upset. Poor Mark was not sure what to do. He just kept stroking my hand and trying to sooth me. Finally, I managed to calm down and after a few ragged breaths I stopped crying. He just held me for a long while.

"What do we do now," I asked. Do we have money to get a room to sleep in?"

"Not really," he said. "I saw a rest stop just past the airport. Maybe we can sleep in the car there. It has a restroom so we can use it to wash up."

I nodded. We really had no other choice. We stopped at a little market and purchased cheap snacks in order to save the money we did have. We pulled into the rest stop where most people just stopped to use the restroom and stretch before continuing with their travels. There were signs suggesting this was not a place to sleep but we were hoping no one noticed us. Mark parked in an area the farthest away from the lighted area. Maybe in the shadows no one would notice two people sleeping. Once we had eaten our snacks, we made our way to the main building to use the restroom and brushed our teeth.

I lay down in the back seat and used my purse as a pillow. Mark laid down in the front seat and within minutes we were both sound to sleep. We probably slept for about four hours when I heard something tapping on the driver's side window. I continued to lay very still but Mark rolled down the window and began talking to someone. It was the guard for the rest stop. He pointed out to Mark that he had been sleeping in his car most of the night and that it was not a place for loitering.

"I'll have to ask you to move on sir."

Mark figured the best thing to do was to leave quickly before he noticed me in the back. He may think we were doing something wrong or that I was there against my will or something. He could call the police. We drove around for a little while, but we didn't want to just burn gas for no good reason. Finally, he parked in a church parking lot. We were just so tired that we drifted off to sleep again.

After another couple of hours passed where we were able to sleep, I heard the tapping at the window again. I feared it would be the police this time. Mark rolled down the window and I heard a kind voice ask if we needed anything. Were we okay? I raised up and noticed the man standing at the car window looked just like the man in Willow's picture. Isaiah Reed was standing not two feet from me. I called out his name.

"Isaiah?"

"Yes child," he replied.

"Beulah is looking for you."

Chapter Nineteen

The Bible That Never Reached Her

No one will ever be able to convince me that God had not sent us to that very church parking lot. I mean what were the chances that out of all the parking lots in a city as large as Memphis, Tennessee that we would park in this exact parking lot.

We followed Isaiah into the church building. He was apparently a man of many trades. He informed us that he not only filled in for the regular preacher from time to time but was the custodian for the large building. He had been retired from a job with a well-known car manufacturer for about five years and this was something he did to feel useful. He also told us that he lived with his daughter nearby.

"Her husband passed away from cancer two years ago and her son is grown and lives in Florida where he is a computer engineer of some kind. I don't understand all the new electronic stuff," he laughed. "She told me about your visit to her office. She showed me the letter and we spent most of last night reading the journals. I was shocked to find out she still felt that way. That after all this time my love for her was not as one-sided as I had believed."

His eyes seemed wet as if he were close to tears. He was

lost in a memory, but I needed to keep this conversation going forward. This was my chance. Possible my only chance to convince Isaiah to come back to her. And in turn to convince Willow that her mother truly loved her and would have never left her.

"Mr. Reed."

"Isaiah," he corrected me. "Please call me Isaiah."

"Isaiah, why did you leave that song at the USO club and then not try to see her? Why did you not find her and explain where you had been. She thought you were dead. Had died in a plane crash. She has never stopped loving you sir."

"Oh, child it seems that my Beulah and I have been victims of a lot of wrong information."

He sat and thought for a while as if planning his words very carefully. I remembered Nana telling me he tended to do that.

"When I left my new bride to join the army it was the hardest thing I had ever done. I almost turned around several times. But things back then were so different. If we had made our love public, it could have cost me my life and possibly her life as well. So, in order to protect her and myself I kept moving. I was in physical pain it hurt so much to leave her.

I thought that the fact that black men would be fighting alongside white men in this war would make a difference in how we were portrayed. I was wrong. When my plane went down most of the men on board were killed. Me and two other men were all that survived. One of those men died two days later while we waited for help to come. The other man and I were injured enough that we couldn't travel, and we were almost sure we were going to starve to death or die from lack of water to drink. A local man found us and hid us for several months. It took us a while to heal and then we had to stay hidden for a long while because enemy troops had moved into the area and we had nothing to defend ourselves with. If they found us not only would they kill us but probably would kill our kind friend for helping us. It was almost two years before we could make ourselves known to an American troop in the area and received help getting us out of there and back home. Of course, the wheels turn slowly when the government is involved so it took another half a year to brief us and determine we had not deserted but had been hidden for our safety. As soon as I was free to go, I started looking for my wife and daughter.

I came back to our stream first thing. I discovered my grandmother's house had long been deserted and according to Mr. Carlton, the man I had worked for all those years ago, all three of the Pettigrew girls had moved off. The only place I knew to look for Millie and grandmother was Tennessee. That was the only place they would have family to lean on. I was thrilled to find not only them but my baby girl," he smiled with a great deal of pride at that.

"She was almost four years old by then. I asked Millie how she ended up with her. Where is Willamina?

Apparently, Mr. Pettigrew had shown up one night and told them that his daughter had decided to give the baby to the Negros so she could be raised by them. He told them that Willamina knew that the whites would never accept her as white and her life would be full of cruelty and shame. He offered a great deal of money to Millie to take her and raise her as her own but that it had to be where no one would associate her with Willamina. People might see a resemblance if they were in the same area. He made it sound as if he and his wife were merely helping Willie with her decision.

Millie had her doubts. She said no way would Miss. Willamina gave up her baby. That is why she put the clue in my old Bible. She left it in the cabin for her to find but I am guessing Mr. Pettigrew found it instead. He may not have known about the clue, but he wanted to hide anything that had to do with me."

I could tell that he was getting upset telling that part. He knew now that Nana had gone to the little house looking for them only days after they had left. If the Bible had been left, she would have seen the clue. She would have found them, and they could have raised their daughter together.

"Why did you leave the song for her?"

He shook his head and looked up as if asking God to help him.

"When they told me she had abandoned our child I didn't believe it. The girl I loved and married would not do that. I had to see for myself. I found out she had just recently moved back to her old house. Her father had died and left it to her. I was going to go see her there but the night I arrived I saw her get into a car and it pulled away. I was parked nearby and followed at a distance. At first, I lost sight of the car and was not sure where it had gone. I drove around until I spotted it in front of the USO club."

He looked down and shook his head and I noticed a tear run down his cheek.

"I still wasn't allowed to go in after her. I had fought and almost died in the war, but the club meant for veterans was segregated and blacks could not enter unless they were working in some capacity. I had not spotted her yet through the window, but I knew she was in there. I found a young boy outside and I paid him to take the sheet music to "Beulah's Song" to the band leader and I gave him money to give the singer hoping he would sing it. I waited outside across the street under a streetlight so she could find me once she heard it and knew I was there. The boy came back and said they would be playing it next.

I finally spotted her in front of the window just before they played the song. She was dancing with a man she obviously cared for. She had her arms around his neck and her head on his shoulder. She even kissed him gently. Then when the song they were dancing to ended and she stepped away to clap I realized she was very pregnant. This had to be her husband. I came to the conclusion that she had not only abandoned Willow but she had stopped loving me and replaced me with another. I left before she ever heard the song."

Isaiah was obviously upset after finding out the truth. He sat with his head down and his face in his hands. I reached over and placed a hand on his shoulder. I gave him time to gain his composure. I had a hundred more questions but the only one I really wanted to ask him was. *Will you come back to her?*

"Isaiah, what do you want to do now that you know the truth?"

"Things are different now all these years later but there are still those who hate it when different races marry. Even now that a law passed as far back as June of 1967 saying it is legal for blacks and whites to marry. There are those who will never accept it. I just kept hoping things would change and it would be safe for us to finally be together. Maybe that is why I believed the worst when I saw her. I wasn't just jealous because she was with another man, but I was jealous that she could love him so openly."

I knew I had to convince him to come back to her. I could not go home and tell her we had found him, but he was not willing to come back to her. I would give it my best effort. Then it would be up to him. I said a little prayer silently in my head and said what was on my heart.

"Isaiah, I can't imagine what it has been like for you or for Willow in this world. I have never faced the things that you have. I know that no matter what you decide it will not change the fact that some people will hate you just for the color of your skin and maybe some will stop talking to my Nana because of who she loves and who her daughter is. But one thing she taught me, and I feel she learned from you is that hate is from evil. It belongs to Satan and can only be a part of a person if they let it in. Hate is taught. No one is born to hate another. She tells me that God is no respecter of persons. That he created us all and he loves us all. That his son died for us all and his salvation is equal to all."

"You are correct Miss. Alexandria Stone. Your grandmother has taught you well," he smiled.

"I know this much. Willamina has loved you deeply all these years. Not despite the fact that you are black or because you are black, but she has loved you for who you are. A kind, loving, wonderful, spiritual MAN. Just a man who is loved by just a woman. She has never felt shame for her love and wants more than anything for you to come back to her. She wants to meet the daughter that was stolen from her so long ago. So, what I need to know sir is will you come back with me to Georgia to be with your Beulah?

"Child, I have considered myself married all these years. Many times, I would be so lonely and so in need of companionship that I would consider finding another. But I could never allow myself to look for love again because in my heart I was still married to her. I knew she had married another but still I could not accept that she wasn't mine. My wife till death would part us.

I know now that she only married another because she thought she was free to do so. She was convinced I had died and would never come back to her. I have to forgive her and accept that she never meant to hurt me."

Suddenly he just stopped talking. He sat there in deep thought for the longest time not saying a word. I was trying so hard to stay calm but my whole body was jerking with each beat of my heart. I was not sure what he was thinking. He had proclaimed his love for her and all but admitted he had to forgive her because she did not know the truth. Now I just needed to hear the words. He took a ragged breath and looked up at me. He gave me the sweetest smile and took my hand in his.

"Can you meet me here again tomorrow? I need to talk to my daughter before I can give you an answer."

I had called my parents, my aunts and uncles and my cousins to tell them Mark and I would be returning home late in the afternoon.

My aunt Frances had used a business phone to do it like a conference call. That way I only had to tell it once. Mark would call his mother once we landed so she could be the one to pick us up at the airport and we could fill her in with all the details on the drive home.

I told them the whole story. How we had found Willow through a clue mom had found and how dad had paid for our trip so we could keep it from Nana. I told them how angry Willow had been with her mother all these years because she had been told that Nana had just wanted to get rid of her. I told them about dear Isaiah and how he had seen her in the window of the club with Papa Sam and could tell that she was in love with the man that held her so lovingly. How he had assumed he must have been a fleeting fancy soon forgotten when she found love with another. I told them how he had always thought of her as his wife and had never allowed himself to love another.

I told them that Millie had passed away just last year and sadly never knew she was right about Willamina all along.

I told them that Willow had lost her husband to cancer and had a grown son that lived in Florida which meant Nana had another grandson she did not know about. I went on and on about our quick but informative visit to Memphis. Then I got quiet and just waited. After a few seconds of silence everyone on the phone started asking together….

"WELL, WHAT DID THEY DECIDE?"

Chapter Twenty

Too Full to Talk

When we went to the church the next day Isaiah and Willow were waiting for us. We did not tell them we had slept in the car for a second night and had gone to the rest stop this morning to clean up and change our clothes. We did not tell them we were so hungry our stomachs were hurting or that we had no money left other than what we needed for the plane tickets home. We simply walked up and gave each of them a hug and a smile. We sat on one of the pews in the church and they sat on the one in front of us so they could turn and face us.

I had a grip on Mark's hand that had to be painful but to his credit he did not pull away. All I could do was pray they would give me the answer I hoped for. I was trying not to look desperate, but I kept thinking about my poor Nana and what it would do to her if they said no. If they were done with that part of their life and wished never to return to it. Never to see her again. How would I ever break that news to her?

"I talked it over with Willow last night," Isaiah finally said. "As much as I want to see my Beulah again, I would not go without Willow. As you know we had both been misinformed about some things and Willow has dealt with a lot of anger over the years. There were times when I would try to talk to her about her mother and she would get enraged and storm from the room. Being a child of mixed races growing up was hard on her. She never seemed to fit in on either side. White people would never accept her as white and black people never completely accepted her as black. She was always in between. Maybe if her mama and I could have raised her together it would have made it easier on her."

Isaiah paused for a while and smiled at what was probably his ongoing dream of what that would have been like. I was guessing he pictured Nana and himself sitting together watching their little girl play.

"She has thankfully forgiven her mother now that she knows Millie had been telling her the truth all those years. She would tell her all the time about how much her mother loved her and that they had to have lied to her or she would have turned the world upside down to find her. Of course, I didn't help matters when I returned from going to find her. I returned thinking she had forgotten me and moved on. I was very angry when I came back home. Hurt to my soul and grieving the loss of what I thought had been nothing to her. I said things that did not help Willow think better of her mother. I have asked her to forgive me."

They were smiling at each other while holding hands. I was trying to read them. Did this mean they were coming or not? It took all my restraint not to yell at them for their answer. Mark apparently was just as frustrated.

"WELL? What did you decide," Mark asked?

Isaiah and Willow both laughed and together nodded.

"Yes, we are coming to Payne, Georgia. It will be a few days because we must take care of things here. Willow will have to put things in storage and close her house up for now. She will need to make arrangements for her business. She can do many things online and the realtors that work for her are very capable. She has employees she trusts to keep it going."

I was thrilled beyond words. Mark and I both were. But I had noticed that Isaiah had done all the talking. I looked at Willow. Looked into those beautiful eyes and wondered if she was completely sure this is what she wanted. She had not appeared to be the quiet type when we were in her office, so it surprised me that she was so silent now.

"Willow, how do you feel about all this? Have you truly forgiven your mother for what you thought was the truth all these years?"

She bowed her head for a few minutes much like Isaiah seemed to do when preparing to answer a question. I watched her soft curls move and knew she was probably crying. Finally, she looked up and I noticed that tears had indeed made her cheeks a little wet.

"Alex… Mark… I admit I have held hate in my heart for most of my life. I could not let myself forgive a mother who would give me away. It made me feel worthless and unwanted. My sweet cousin Millie, who was more like a mother to me, taught me about forgiveness and would tell me stories about her Miss Willamina. About the young girl who loved to paint and draw. About the girl who loved my daddy with all her heart. '***No one could doubt it if they saw them together,***' she would say. I have always wanted it to be true but would never let my heart believe it. If I had known she loved me and just didn't know I was alive it would have been hard to bear. Finding out that she thought I had died as an infant. Knowing she has visited my grave all these years and has grieved over what she thought was the death of her child. I can easily forgive her and more importantly I can forgive myself for all those years of bitterness. I am so excited to finally meet my mother. It is a dream come true for me.

I called my son, Robert Isaiah, last night and told him everything that had happened. He is so happy for me. He knows the pain this has caused me. He will come to visit once we are settled. He cannot wait to meet everyone.

"Robert Isaiah," I repeated?

"Yes, named after the two most wonderful men in this world. My husband and his father Robert Hamilton and my dear daddy Isaiah. He has had a lot of names to live up to," she laughed. "And he has done a wonderful job. I am very proud of him."

We talked for a while longer and Isaiah asked us if he could buy us lunch before we left. Mark and I looked at each other and said emphatically "YES PLEASE."

Isaiah and Willow both laughed and admitted they had heard our stomachs protesting and figured we had not eaten. We went to a wonderful Bar B Q restaurant near the home of Elvis Presley. It was ***so*** good, and I ate until I was almost sick. We finalized plans before leaving for the airport. With tight hugs we told them we would see them soon.

On the plane we slept. Too exhausted and too full to even talk. Once we landed, we called to ask Annie if she could come and pick us up. She would have to come up with an excuse for leaving so Nana would not become suspicious. We knew things would be crazy once we got home but we knew Nana had no idea what was going on. We would tell Annie on the trip from the airport to home and we would decide how best to tell Nana. I think everyone wanted to be there when she got the news so they would all start arriving tomorrow afternoon. Keeping my mouth shut until everyone was there would be so hard to do.

I had avoided Nana as much as possible once we were home. She knew something was up because of the lame excuse I had given for being gone over the weekend. She probably thought Mark and I had spent the weekend in some cheap motel because she knew his test was over and his apartment was not available for several weeks while all the student apartments were being painted and carpets cleaned. I hated lying to her and I hated even more that she might be thinking bad of me but it would all be worth it once we told her the '**why**' of it all.

Tuesday afternoon she informed us she had a hair appointment and a dinner date with a client who wanted a painting of her two year old child. Nana usually just took pictures of babies and toddlers to go by because getting them to sit still and pose was impossible. We looked so happy at her news she stopped to ask us what was going on. Why did we look so thrilled she would be gone the rest of the afternoon?

"What are you up to," she asked me while giving me a very stern look.

"Nothing Nana. I am just glad you have new customers."

Could I have sounded any lamer. And I am sure I was smiling like the cat that ate the canary. She just gave out a breathy *Hmm* and went out the door.

My parents arrived around 2 p.m. and we called the others to let them know it was safe to come over. Frances and Adam were there in about an hour and the others arrived within fifteen minutes of each other. They all parked their cars in the back hoping she would park on the side of the house as she often did. We were busy talking among ourselves about how wonderful it was, how surprised she would be, how excited we were for her. With all the noise and chatter we had not heard her pull up or walk into the house.

Apparently, the client only wanted a quick drink and made arrangements, so dinner was not part of the deal. We were laughing and planning right up to the minute we spotted her standing there looking at us as if someone had just knocked the wind out of her. We all got quiet and just looked at her.

"You found them," she asked in a cracked weepy voice. "You found Isaiah and my daughter?'

We all rushed to her because she honestly looked as if she might pass out. All of us were talking at once and I am sure no one could have understood a word that was being said because we were talking over each other. She just sat there looking stunned for a while but finally she held up her arm like a teacher trying to instruct her class to be quiet. We all stopped talking and just stood there looking at each other for a clue as to what we should do next.

"Alex," she finally said. "I am going to assume this has something to do with your mystery trip this weekend with Mark. So, if you would please tell me what is going on… from the beginning."

Everyone took a seat. We filled up the entire dining room and kitchen. Nana sat on one of three stools at the island in the middle of the kitchen. Mark and I sat on the other two facing her. I took her hand and smiled at her. With tears in my eyes I took a deep breath and opened my mouth.

"Nana, we found them."

I heard her suck in a big breath and she then proceeded to cry almost uncontrollable. We knew that she had so much built up on the inside, so no one spoke and we just let her cry.

I imagined she was crying for the love who left her the day after they wed. She was crying for the news that he was lost at war. She was crying because she believed their only child conceived on their wedding night had died at just a few days old. She was crying because of the lies she had been told. She cried for her lover's return too late and the news that she had missed out on her child that had been stolen from her by her own parents.

She cried so long and so bitterly that I knew she had held in so much pain for all those years and now she was finally letting it all out. I put my arms around her, and she lay her head on my shoulder and sobbed. My shirt was wet with her tears, but I didn't care. My own tears were falling and as I looked around the room, I realized every man and woman in this room was crying.

We were a mess!

This went on for at least ten full minutes. Once she seemed to cry out. She got up and went to the refrigerator for a bottle of water. She grabbed a tissue and wiped her face. Then she blew her nose. Once she was done, she handed the tissue box to the table where her children sat and with a weak smile, she said…

"You look frightened. You need these more than I do."

We all had to give a little laugh of relief. Mark got bottles of water for everyone else in the room and Nana sat back down across from me and took my hands in hers.

"I'm ready," she said.

And so, I began. I told her everything. I wanted to be sure and give my mom the credit for our original clue on Willow. I thought it would sooth old wounds. I told her about how bitter Willow was at first. How she had thought she was not wanted and given away by a mother who did not love her. I could tell this hurt her deeply, but I quickly added that we had told her what really happened.

I told her about Isaiah and what he had originally thought when he saw her at the USO club. How sweet Millie had defended her all these years but sadly did not live to know how right she had been. I told her that all had been forgiven and that they could not wait to see her. That they would be arriving in a couple of days after they made a few arrangements.

I also told her about her grandson Robert Isaiah Hamilton who lived in Florida and would be coming for a visit soon. I told her he was so happy about the fact that we found them and that his mom finally knows the truth and is going to meet her mom.

Apparently, he was extremely close to Millie who was like a grandmother to him. She had always told him stories about his real grandmother and how sure she was that Miss. Willamina would be so proud of him.

I think I talked nonstop for an hour. Maybe longer. I wanted to be sure I didn't leave anything out. Nana sat there for a long time with her hands folded together in front of her mouth. Her fingers were interlocked but it still looked like she was posed to pray. Her eyes were like the most pitiful puppy dog. Wet and tear streaked cheeks told the story of how much pain and joy she was in at the same time. She was dealing with an inward turmoil but when I had finished, she hugged me tightly and just kept saying;

"Thank you, thank you everyone, thank you so much."

Once she had herself composed, we spent time talking about what we would do once they arrived. Annie was talking about the food she would prepare. My parents were going to stay and help with preparations. Everyone else lived close enough that they could go home and come back the day Isaiah and Willow were to arrive. Mark would go pick them up at the airport. The room was buzzing with excitement but suddenly we realized Nana had grown very quiet. She was sitting at the table and looked upset.

"Nana, what is wrong? Aren't you excited?"

"What if he is disappointed when he sees me? I do not exactly look the same as I did the last time he saw me. Maybe he will take one look at me and want to go back to Tennessee."

"Nana, you know that is not going to happen. He has loved you for all these years. Do you feel differently about him? I mean you know he is not the young virile man he was the day he left for war. He has aged just like you have. But I have to say, he is still very handsome," I said with a grin and a raised eyebrow.

She had to laugh.

"Really? So, he is still as sexy as ever?"

"Well Nana, I don't know what you think is sexy. I mean yeah, he is a nice-looking man and he seems to have stayed fit. You know, no pot belly or bald head. I guess he could be considered sexy to an older lady such as yourself," I rambled.

Nana burst out laughing. She had been teasing me about the sexy thing.

"I will still love him if he has a pot belly or a bald head.

Our love for each other was never based on the outside. Yes, I thought he was a beautiful man. I was attracted to the way he looked at first. But as we got to know each other we both fell in love with the person inside. I loved his kindness, his spiritual strength, and his sweet nature. And his talent. Have I told you about how beautifully he sang? He had the voice of an angel."

"Yes, Nana you told us," we all agreed.

It was so much fun sitting together and planning. Nana was getting excited. Once everyone had left and my parents had gone to bed. Nana decided to go to her room. I gave Mark a good night kiss. Well, I gave him several.

"Thank you for going with me. I don't know what I would have done without you."

He kissed me a few more times before responding.

"I hope you never want to find out how it would be without me. I love you."

"I love you too," I added and knew I meant it.

Once he finally went to the pool house, I made my way upstairs. I heard Nana talking from her room and wondered what was going on. I knocked lightly and opened the door. Nana was standing in front of the portrait on her wall. The one of a young Isaiah and Beulah as they stood in an embrace in the stream near the willow tree.

"I can't believe how nervous I am," she admitted.

"It is going to be fine," I promised.

I gave her one more hug and went to bed.

The next two days we cleaned the house from top to bottom. Got all the guest rooms clean with fresh sheets and towels in the guest bathroom. After we finished cleaning,

Annie went to the grocery to make sure the refrigerator was well stocked, and her menu items were available. Poor Annie was exhausted. I was exhausted and Nana was exhausted and nervous. Their flight was supposed to arrive at one o'clock in the afternoon and Mark was all lined up and ready to go.

Mark left at noon to head to the airport and all my aunts and uncles arrived just as he was leaving. The anticipation was building and building as we waited for Mark to pull up in the car with Isaiah and Willow.

At one fifteen the house phone rang. Annie rushed to answer it with her usual cheerful *"Stone residence."*

We all noticed her facial expression went from all smiles to a look of total panic. It was Mark calling to let us know that they did not get off the plane. We were listening nervously to Annie's side of the phone conversation from Mark when my cell phone rang. I looked at the name that popped up.

"It's Willow," I said and then answered it.

I listened as she explained why they were not on the flight. As my eyes grew larger with the news everyone drew closer to me to wait for the end of the call and the explanation that would be coming. Nana looked like she was about to lose it so I took her hand to form a connection and worked hard not to let my face give away how panicked I was. As soon as I hung up the phone, I led her to the couch and asked her to please sit down. Everyone gathered close to listen but also tried to give Nana a little space.

"Nana, Willow said that this morning while they were getting ready to go to the airport Isaiah started acting strange. He was suddenly confused, and his speech seemed slurred. She tried to tell him maybe they should wait to come another time and he could go see his doctor. But before she could get the words out, he passed out and she called an ambulance. She is at the hospital with him now, but they have her in the family waiting room until the doctor can come out to talk to her. She doesn't know exactly what has happened but the physician in the emergency room mentioned a possible stroke."

I waited for her to come apart. Expected tears and hysteria. But Nana stood and walked toward the stairs. She climbed up the stairs and went straight to her room. We all looked at each other a little unsure of what to do. Mark came in the door about that time and we told him why they missed the flight. As we all stood around waiting for another phone call, Nana came down the stairs with a small suitcase in her hand.

"Alex, go pack your bag. You too Mark. We are going to Memphis."

There was not a drop of hesitation in her voice. She had made up her mind and no one dared to try and talk her out of leaving. Every one of her children offered to go with her but she pointed out that we had already been there. We knew where to go, and Willow would feel more comfortable with them because they had met her already. It made sense and everyone understood her choice. But all of them wanted to be there so they told us that once we were up in the air safely, they would rent a van and follow us to Memphis. Yes, it would take at least 8 hours, possible more but maybe by the time they arrived we would have answers about Isaiah. Mark and I packed with record breaking speed and as we joined Nana at the door to leave, she stopped and turned to face her family. She looked at each of them making sure each realized when she was ac knowledging them. Once she had taken the time to make eye contact with each of them, she smiled and said…

"I have always loved all of you. I have always been proud of you. I have never for even one second regretted the wonderful gift that each of you gave me and your father. Despite the way things happened I hope you all believe I have never regretted meeting Samuel Stone and spending a big part of my life with him."

She swallowed hard, took a ragged breath and a tear ran down her cheek.

"But I have never been so proud of the people you have become than I am at this moment. I want you all to know I love you deeply and nothing will ever change that."

They all nodded acknowledgment and agreement. Hugs were passed around. And we walked out the door on our way to Memphis, Tennessee. On our way to Isaiah.

Nana was quiet on the flight. I could tell by the way her lips were moving that she was praying for Isaiah. She continued to pray for the forty-five minutes we were in the air. As soon as we landed, we had a taxi take us to the hospital. We knew we could not carry our suitcases around with us all day and possibly into the night, so we went to the hotel closest to the hospital and rented a room with two double beds. We would work out arrangements if it became necessary but for now, we just needed somewhere to park our things. We made our way to the floor he was supposed to be on, and Nana went straight to the nurse's station and asked what room he was in.

"I'm sorry ma'am but only family can go in and he is in ICU so even then you have to wait until the next allotted time for a short visit."

I could tell Nana was frustrated. She was not sure what to say. Could she say she was his wife? After all their marriage was never a legal one as far as man was concerned. She had no license to show as proof. The nurse had assumed that because Isaiah was a black man and Nana was a white woman who happened to have a different last name, she would have no rights to go into his room.

"You don't understand. I must see him. You have to let me in."

The nurse was unrelenting. She would not even look up at Nana in response. She was not moved by the pleading of this elderly woman to see someone who for all we knew could be dying. I was about to say something to her myself when we heard a voice behind us that sounded very irritated.

"She is family," it proclaimed. "That's my mother."

It was Willow.

Chapter Twenty-One

The Wall Falls

Willow and Nana stood for several minutes just looking at each other. Both amazed to finally be seeing the other. Both obviously overcome with emotion by this reunion so longed for.

Nana had thought her child had died days after birth and only last year found out the truth. That her child had been stolen by cruel parents who allowed their own prejudice and shame to override the happiness of their daughter or their granddaughter.

Willow had lived a life filled with hatred and spite toward a mother who she believed had willingly abandoned her in order to live the life she wanted. She had thought for all her 52 years that her mother had easily let her go and never looked back.

Now they both knew the truth. That their relationship had been interrupted by fate and now was their second chance. They had an opportunity to build on the time they might have left. They also both knew that the main connection between them lay in a bed in a room down the hall and could be leaving them alone to find their way. The one thing they had in common was that they loved Isaiah Franklin Reed with every fiber of their being and both would feel lost if he were to die now so close to the reunion he had dreamt about for so long.

Both seemed unsure of what to do. Both afraid to make the first move. I felt desperate to move them toward each other. To break that wall down they both feared to go over.

"Nana, this is Willow Hamilton."

That was all it took. Before I had time to complete the word Hamilton they were wrapped in each other's arms sobbing. Both saying over and over how sorry they were. Both telling the other how wonderful it was to finally see them.

"I have grieved over you for all these years. I thought I had lost you when you were only days old. I cannot believe it's you. I am begging you to forgive me. I would have found you somehow If I had known you were alive. Oh Willow, my sweet girl, you are so beautiful."

"Of course, I forgive you. I need your forgiveness for thinking you could be so cruel or spiteful. For believing the worst about you and never trying to find you."

They spent the next few minutes apologizing to each other for anything that might be upsetting to the other.

Nana was overcome with emotion over meeting her first born. Willow was also sobbing. She had her face buried in Nana's neck. She was slightly taller than Nana but there were so many ways they favored. Both were slim and fit looking. Their eyes were different colors but shaped much the same. I had noticed in the past that when Nana hugged you, she would tighten her grip and loosen it several times. Willow was doing that very thing now to Nana. Once they finally parted from the tear-filled hugs, they moved to a corner of the family waiting room of the hospital.

As they sat there, they constantly had to touch. They would hold hands. Pat each other on the shoulder or leg.

Once I witnessed Nana reach up and touch Willow's hair. Playing with a soft curl just behind her ear. Later Willow reached up to wipe a tear away on Nana's cheek.

We had another twenty minutes before anyone could go in and visit Isaiah. This gave the two ladies time to really talk about their lives. Nana told Willow about her birth in the attic. That Millie had come just in time to help with the delivery. She told her about the day her parents told her that her baby daughter had died. They had even implied I might have rolled over on you and you could not breathe.

Willow told her mother all about her life. How Isaiah had come back when she was a young child and how he spoiled her and loved her more than she could express.

"I honestly think there were times he would see you in me. Some way I would speak or argue would make him think of your time together. I know some of my features reminded him of you. He would smile at me but I would notice the heart ache in his eyes," Willow explained.

Mark and I just sat back and quietly observed. I felt a little invisible at first but then I just sat with my head on Mark's shoulder and witnessed this beautiful scene as mother and daughter became family at last.

We heard the soft bell that was used to announce that the families could go see their loved one. Willow told Nana to go.

"I'll go the next time. Usually they give us twenty minutes so people can trade out to go back and visit but this first one needs to be all you," she smiled.

Nana wasted no time. She was told where she could find him. The patients were not in the actual hospital room. They each had a cubicle type room with dividers between them. Most of the patients in this area were not responsive to their families. As she walked down the hall and peeked into the different cubicles, she saw many of the same people she had noticed in the waiting room. Many of them were clinging to their loved ones. A few were awkwardly trying to 'visit' their loved one but did not know what to say to a person hooked up to several noisy machines and not responding. Finally, at the end of the row of cubicles she saw him. She knew instantly it was Isaiah.

She went in and took his hand into hers. She talked to him as if he were sitting across from her at the stream and they were just having a conversation. She stroked his cheek; she stroked his hair which had a little gray in the temple area now. She examined all the machines that seemed to be his lifeline. A tube down his throat, oxygen going into his nose, and an IV in his left hand and a monitor hooked up to keep record of his heartbeat. She had noticed at the nurses' station there were twelve screens. Each room had a camera pointing to the patient so they would know if any of the people in their care were in distress. They also had the ability to look at stats from the station. A nurse came in while she was there and checked everything. Made a few notes on his chart and told her to talk to him.

"He still hears you. Let him know you are here," she smiled.

Once she left Nana did as she had said.

"Isaiah, it's me. It is your Beulah. It's your wife," she said weakly not sure if she still had the right to call herself that. "Open your eyes darling. I saw Willow in the waiting room. She has forgiven me, Isaiah. I have finally found my little girl."

She talked nonstop until the soft bell sounded letting the

family know they had to return to the waiting area. Before leaving the room, she kissed him on his head and kissed his hand.

"I'll be back as soon as I can my love."

When she came back from her short visit all three of us jumped up and walked swiftly toward her.

"Was he surprised to see you," Willow asked.

"How's he doing," Mark asked.

"Nana are you okay," I asked.

She looked up at us and as tears fell, she shook her head back and forth fast.

"He never opened his eyes. I don't think he ever knew I was there."

We once again started the waiting game. The room was full of family members with that same sad, desperate look on their faces. Everyone looked so very tired. It appeared some had been there day and night for days. Under each seat the person who occupied that chair would have a stash of soda cups and snacks. Some had books to read or puzzle books to challenge their minds. One lady had her knitting and spent hours clicking the needles and wrapping the yarn. She was making a beautiful afghan. It looked like it might be for a baby's room. There was a television in two different corners of the room. Both had the same local station playing. The sound was low, but the words ran across the bottom of the screen. There was a coffee maker with disposable cups, packs of sugar or artificial sweetener and a large container of powdered creamer. There were two vending machines in a room next door to the waiting room. One with soda or water and the other with snacks like chips or candy bars. Also, there were restrooms at each end of the hall. Women to the left when leaving the room and Men to the right. There were also signs posted to let family members know the hours of operation for the hospital cafeteria and gift shop.

Around six o'clock the doctors made rounds. Most had an office to see patients and had to wait till their office had closed before meeting with the families. They assured us they had been in constant communication with the staff here and had ordered tests or prescribed medication as needed throughout the day. There were four small rooms provided for the doctors to talk to families privately. Isaiah's doctor stood in front of one of the doors and called out., "Family of Isaiah Reed."

All three of us piled into the small room along with the doctor. He sat behind a small desk and placed his file on the desk. Willow and I sat in the two chairs provided and Mark stood behind us.

"We have run a test on Mr. Reed. I am convinced he has had a stroke," he blurted out very matter of fact. "His records show that many years ago he was injured when his plane crashed during the war. I am thinking the head injury he sustained then caused scar tissue to form over the years. It appears the scar tissue allowed a blood clot to form and sit unmoving for several years. For some reason it finally came loose this morning and well basically exploded in his brain. This caused him to react strangely and to finally pass out. I will be honest with you. I am astonished that he lived through it. For whatever reason he is still with us. It has to be pure determination. He may improve with time but there is also a possibility that he will remain in this state indefinitely. We will keep him here for a few days to be sure he is stable but then we will have to make other arrangements."

He stood and gathered his papers. He reached out and shook all our hands and readied himself to leave.

"I'm sorry the news wasn't better."

We stayed in the little room for a few minutes feeling a little shell shocked. But then we noticed other families were waiting for the room, so we filed out and went back to our seats.

About eight o'clock my phone rang. It was my mom. She asked where we were staying, and did we know anything. I was not ready to talk about the report on Isaiah, so I just told her to get rooms at the hotel we had left our luggage at.

The soft bell sounded again to mark the last visit session. Willow went to visit this time. When the visit was over, she came back feeling very discouraged. We realized we had not eaten all day and most of the places inside the hospital were closed. Thankfully, there was a change machine next to the vending machines and we managed to get peanut butter and crackers for all of us. We also had some nasty machine coffee and I wanted a chocolate bar. This was our nourishing meal for the day.

My mom called back and asked if we wanted to come to the lobby, so the large group didn't overwhelm the waiting room so late at night. We did exactly that. We had been allowed all the visits we would get for the day. They did not continue the visits through the night.

We introduced Willow to everyone. It should have been such a wonderful meeting but we were sad and exhausted, so it was very low key. Once we had filled everyone in on the news we decided to go to the hotel and get a couple of hours of sleep. We invited Willow to come along and told her we would pay for the room but she said she still had a couch in her house that she had not bothered to store and it would work fine for a night or two. She would meet us in the morning at a pancake house two blocks from the hospital.

Once we had all settled in our rooms for the night Nana lay on the side of the bed nearest to the bathroom. She told me to use the other side of the bed and that Mark could have the other bed to himself. I was fine with that. I just wanted to get a little sleep. There was very little space between the two beds. Just enough to fit the shared bed side table with its lamp and phone. I set the alarm on my phone on the unlikely possibility that any of us would sleep that late. I knew we had to be ready to meet everyone at the restaurant at six thirty in the morning because the first visit was at eight and we wanted to be sure we were there. Mark and I held hands on top of the nightstand just looking at each other in the dim lighting of the room. Not one word was said by any of us and we simply drifted off into restless sleep. I heard Nana call out for Isaiah a few times during the night. I was not sure what was happening in her dream, but she sounded like she couldn't find him and was calling his name. Each time I would reach over and pat her shoulder. I would whisper softly that everything was okay, and she needed to sleep. She would settle for a while, but this played out numerous times.

The next morning, we all dragged into the Pancake Heaven Restaurant and started out with the most wonderful cup of coffee I had ever had. I'm not sure if it was really that good or just in comparison to the machine coffee combined with our exhaustion it just seemed that good. I allowed the waitress to refill my cup twice. The food was good, but we were very robotic in our eating. Just putting nourishment into our bodies to make it through the day.

The day was long and repetitive. Willow and Nana took turns going back to visit Isaiah. The rest of us were there for support but never wanted to take a turn from either of these women. They were talking to Isaiah each time they went back but the longer it went without a response from him the more discouraged we all became. This same scenario continued for two more days. We would sleep a few hours at night, eat at the same restaurant twice a day and spend the day waiting for the time to visit.

They argued at first, but we finally talked the rest of them into going home.

"We will keep you posted," I promised. "There is no reason for all of us to be here sitting in the waiting room all day. I promise I will take care of Nana."

Reluctantly they agreed to leave us after two full days. Each of them gave us hugs. They all hugged Willow and again told her how wonderful it was to meet their newly discovered sister. Before they left Mark asked if he could please have a prayer. I almost broke into tears at that suggestion. I was so proud of him. Willow smiled and said that was exactly what Isaiah would have done. We joined hands in a large circle and Mark asked God to bless each of us. To please heal Isaiah and to give everyone a safe journey. It was a beautiful prayer and the tension that we had all struggled with seemed to pour out of us like water. The minute we turned it over to God it just felt so different. Nana and Willow both thanked him and gave him a hug.

The four couples piled into the van they had rented and headed for home. It was about seven thirty on the third day. I knew if all went well, they would be home by six o'clock tonight.

The doctor was making morning rounds when we got to the waiting area and asked us to go to the little room again so he could talk to us.

"Mr. Reed has made no changes. He has good brain activity and his heart and lungs seem strong. It is as if he does not want to wake up. I ordered the nurses to remove the vent tube last night to see how he would do breathing on his own. He is stable and doing well without it. Today when you ladies go in, I need you to encourage him to wake up. Give him whatever reason he needs to push through."

We agreed to do our best. It was Willow's turn first and we alternated all day. After each visit we would compare notes as to what we had said and how he did not seem to react to anything.

"Maybe he hasn't forgiven me. Maybe he does not want to see me," Nana reasoned.

"No," we both told her.

"Nana, he loves you and I feel he will come back to you if he can."

"I have watched him for years trying to find a way back to you. You have been his only love. There is no way he will not come back. I think he is fighting his way out of this and we have to be patient," Willow added.

The day ticked by and it was Nana's turn. It would be the last visit of the day. The doctor had mentioned at the second meeting of the day that we might have to consider putting him in a nursing facility.

"We aren't really doing anything to medically treat him now. It's all dependent on his desire to wake up."

Those words rang in her ears as Nana marched down the

hall to his cubicle. She stood there with her fist clinched and suddenly she was filled with anger. Filled with rage. How could he do this to her? She had grieved her loss of him for over 50 years and now that she had found him… now that they could be together again, he was going to turn tail and run from her.

"Now you listen to me Isaiah Franklin Reed," she spat at him while poking him in the chest. "You left me under that tree all those years ago. You promised you would come back to me and we would be together. Yes, it hasn't exactly been the original plan, but I have found you and you will not leave me. DO YOU HEAR ME?"

One of the nurses peeked into the cubicle. She was about to say something, and another nurse took her by the arm and shook her head. She smiled at Nana as if to say… ***You go ahead sweetie. Give him what for and make him wake up.***

Nana stood there just looking at him and her rage suddenly turned to heartbreak.

"Isaiah, I have loved you since I was fifteen years old. I loved you from that tree limb even before you knew I was a girl," she gave a weak laugh. "I love you to my very soul and to your soul too. You are my first love. You taught me about God, and you baptized me. You taught me that love is inward and not what is outside. You taught me about intimacy. About how a good man will be gentle and tender and love his wife completely. I mean you gave me my own song Isaiah. How can I live without you? How can you leave me when I have finally found you?"

She was sitting at the side of his bed pleading with him. She laid her head on his chest and soaked his blanket with her tears. She knew the twenty minutes was almost up and she had failed to make him want to stay. She took in a breath to quieten herself. She would just walk out and prepare to face the rest of her life without him. She had made it this long and at least now she had her daughter.

She heard a soft raspy sound. A voice as low as a whisper but gravelly like one would sound with a sore throat. At first, she did not even recognize what it was but then she knew. It was her song. She heard the tender loving words as he had given them to her on their wedding night. She felt his hand on her head stroking her hair. It was just as he had the last time, they had made love. When she had asked him to sing it one more time. She looked up and saw those beautiful eyes looking back at her. He gave her a weak smile.

"I'll never leave you again," he promised.

Isaiah had found his way back to his Beulah.

Chapter Twenty-Two

Color Blind Eyes

As we sat there waiting for Nana to finish her visit a nurse called us to the desk.

"Are all of you here for Mr. Reed," she asked?

We all nodded in agreement and waited for instructions from her.

"Follow me please," she continued and turned to go down the long corridor.

We followed swiftly but cautiously after her. We kept looking at each other questioning with our eyes as to what this could mean. Had Isaiah taken a turn for the worse and they were calling in all the family to say goodbye? Had something happened to Nana? We were all imagining the worst possible scenarios as was obvious by the panic on our faces.

The nurse came to an abrupt halt just this side of the curtain that divided his cubicle from the other man next to him and we noticed his doctor and another doctor standing in the opening. Another nurse noticed us standing there looking anxious and motioned us to come over. We could get no hint from their faces as to what we might see when we moved over close enough to see inside the area.

We all looked in together and could not help but shout at what we saw. Nana was sitting on the side of the bed next to Isaiah and they were wrapped in each other's arms. Isaiah was stroking her hair and whispering sweetly to her as if calming her. He looked up at us and as soon as he spotted Willow he grinned as big as you please.

"She found me. My sweet Beulah found me, and I have promised her I will never leave her again."

There were just no words to be said after that. We all stood around embracing each other and smiling. Even the doctors and nurses seemed to be at a loss for words. They did say there was no medical explanation for his surviving the stroke so completely. We did not need a medical explanation. It was God. That is all we needed to know.

Isaiah was moved to a private room for observation until the following afternoon and was then released from the hospital. We had arranged to go from the hospital to the airport since it was so close, and it made no sense to make him stay in an uncomfortable hotel room when the rooms at Nana's were ready and waiting.

Mark called Annie before we boarded the plane and I called my mother. It would be up to them to inform the rest. Since we had no cars at home big enough for all of us, we had an airport taxi to take us to Nana's once we landed. The tension had been thick in the plane and continued to be in the taxi. It was not a bad tension. No fright or even feeling uncomfortable but just the nervous excitement of this new situation. Willow, Isaiah and Nana just kept looking at each other and smiling at each other. They talked among themselves trying to catch up and connect the dots. Occasionally one of them would try to include us in the conversation because they did not want us to feel left out. But we did not mind at all. Mark and I just sat there watching this miracle reunion unfold in front of our very eyes. The joy each of them displayed was contagious and we both found ourselves smiling to the point that our cheeks were sore just from our own happiness over their love for each other.

When we pulled up to the house Isaiah seemed surprised. "You still live here in the same house," he asked Nana.

"I inherited it from my father. An atonement for his sins, I think. I asked Samuel if we could live in it."

Suddenly Nana looked embarrassed.

"I guess I wasn't fair to him. He only wanted to give me everything I asked for. I used that kindness to stay near our stream and the willow tree just in case you ever came back. That makes me sound like such a horrible person," she said and looked at me in a way that implied she was apologizing.

"Nana, we know you loved Papa Sam. We don't doubt it at all."

"I love you no less because of the things that happened to keep us apart. I am grateful you found someone who cared so much for you. I have admitted my first reaction was not exactly reflective of that but in hindsight I can say I am thankful to Samuel Stone for giving you what I could not have. We both know that the world was not ready to accept us as a couple when I returned. Sadly, there are some who still will not be willing. But if we wait until everyone accepts us, we would never be together. Growing old has taught me many things. One truth is you need only please God and yourself because those are the only ones you must answer to. Hate will always be with us. It will be around long after we have gone home to our reward. I dare say it will be here until the end of time. But hopefully if we teach our children and they teach their children the hate will lesson, people can learn to accept people for who they are with color blind eyes."

Annie came rushing out to greet the taxi. She was beside herself with excitement. She shook Willow's hand and then Isaiah's then she hugged them both while talking at full speed the entire time. This was just how our Annie was and Mark, Nana and I were laughing at her as she shuttled them into the house. We had anticipated this and thankfully had warned them in advance.

"My mom, you got to love her," Mark said. And we all did…

Nana had told Annie to prepare the one guest room that was downstairs for Isaiah. She did not want to hover, but she was still concerned with his health and did not want him climbing stairs yet. She insisted he go lay down for a little while before the rest of the family arrived.

"We are having a celebration dinner tonight and you need to rest after your trip," Annie commanded.

Isaiah looked at us for help but we all just shrugged our shoulders and made faces that let him know he had better do as she said.

"Yes ma'am," he finally responded to Annie's delight.

While Isaiah took a nap, Nana took Willow for the tour. She started with the library across the hall from Isaiah's room. Willow was amazed at all the paintings on display in the room. It almost seemed silly to call it a library. It only had a small bookcase with books and part of them were albums of family photographs. It had been Papa Sam's office until he retired from running the newspaper and Nana had slowly taken it over for her paintings. A few of the paintings were from recent commissions and were only there temporarily until the customer had time to pick it up. But most of them were Nana's large collection of the stream and the willow tree.

"Are these of the willow tree my father told me about?"

She looked amazed. She walked around and examined each one much like I had after reading the journals. Isaiah may not have written journals, but he had told her about this time in his life. And of course, I had allowed Willow and Isaiah to read several of the journals in order to convince her that her mother had not given her away. She seemed to need to touch them. I could almost tell the minute she noticed the corner of the quilt sticking out from under the willow tree skirt. It was so discreet that only those of us who had heard the story would ever notice it. After she finished looking at all the paintings, she hugged her mother and kissed her cheek. Nana looked so completely blissful.

She took her through the French doors at the end of the hall and pointed toward the field to let her know that was the path to the stream.

"I'll take you there soon," she promised.

She also took her upstairs and pointed out where Willow's room would be. Just down from Nana's and across the hall from mine. Maybe I spoke out of turn, but Nana seemed to be happy when I told Willow there was one more painting in Nana's room. Willow stood and looked at the young couple that embraced in the stream.

"There is no way I can ever doubt you love my father if it shows so strongly in this painting. The love is so obvious it almost causes you to blush when you look at it. As if you just walked up on the young couple at a time meant to be private."

"EXACTLY," I exclaimed. "I blushed the first few times I looked at it."

They both laughed at me and we continued down the hall. Nana had Willow follow her up the stairs to the attic. Once she turned on the lights that allowed full view of the attic she pointed at the bed and dresser at the opposite end of the room.

"That is where you were born Willow. That was where I first lay eyes on my perfect little daughter and where I looked upon you for the last time until a few days ago. Willow did not really say anything. She walked over to the small bed and sat on it just looking around and taking it all in. Nana sat next to her and put her arm around her. They sat there just holding each other and soaking in the feelings that surrounded them. I decided to ease out and back downstairs. I felt they needed time alone.

I walked into the kitchen to find Mark, my parents, Frances and Adam and Annie. Poor Annie was working hard to prepare a feast and Frances and mother were attempting to help but when Annie is in her crazy zone it is best to just stay out of her way. Mark walked up behind me and put his arms around me.

"You okay?"

"I'm fine," I replied. "Just gave them some space to get re-acquainted with each other. It just all seems so surreal. I got to know all these people by reading the journals and it is just such an odd feeling for them to be walking around now as if they stepped out of the pages."

Mark smiled and rubbed my shoulders as if trying to massage away the tension. It was not really tension I was feeling. It was a bottled up expression pushing me from the inside. I needed to go up to my room and work on the novel. It was compelling me and nothing else would rid me of this almost electric feeling. I asked Mark if he would mind if I went to work on my novel for a little while. He knows what this means to me and has always been supportive of my desire and need to write.

"I'll come get you when it's time to eat," he said and turned me in the direction of the stairs.

I typed so fast once I started, I thought my fingers might knot up. I wanted to get caught up from where I had left off a few weeks ago. So much had happened. So many new developments and new characters to introduce. I did two full chapters before Mark knocked at my door. At some point I would have to find an ending to my story… To the story of Isaiah and Beulah. Once I could put an ending to the story of them, I could present it to a few publishers in hopes one will want to publish it. But not yet. There would be more to this story. I knew it was not time. But soon.

Mark told me that once Isaiah woke from his nap that Nana had given him the same tour. He had cried over the paintings. Not all sad tears. Some were sad because of regret. Others were joyful memories and overwhelming love. Nana argued with him about the stairs. She felt it was too soon. She finally agreed to show him the painting in her room because of how much Willow had talked about it but she made him promise he would not try to climb the stairs to the attic just yet.

"To be honest I don't think I can climb them again today. I'm exhausted," she said.

That was all it took to get him to promise. As had been true then and still true now… he wanted to take care of his girl.

The dinner was a big success. There was so much chatter going on it was hard to keep up with all the conversations. Nana had insisted that Annie put it all out buffet style and let everyone serve themselves. "

You will eat with the rest of us and I won't hear of an argument on the matter," Nana insisted.

Annie was moved and thrilled to be included. She was seated on one side of Mark and I was on the other side. Nana and Isaiah sat side by side at the head of our massive dining room table. Willow was next to Nana and without really meaning to the rest of her children were sitting in a row on the same side of the table in order of their ages. When she noticed it, she asked me to take several pictures with her camera from the den. I did and took a few of she and Isaiah. I somehow assumed that there would be a painting somewhere in the future commiserating this event.

We had gotten so loud that we almost did not notice when Isaiah stood and clinked his water glass with his fork. Once we did realize it, we all grew silent and waited to see what this dear gentleman had to say. I could tell neither Nana or Willow were in on it because they both looked as surprised as the rest of us when he did speak.

"Today is June 30, 1994. In thirty-one days, Beulah and I will celebrate our marriage of fifty-three years. I know this marriage will never be recognized by most because our only witness for the event was my sweet cousin Millie and God above."

At the mention of Millie both Willow and Nana reached out and gave the other's hand a squeeze.

"I know I should get down on one knee for this and have a beautiful ring, but neither is the case. I only have a humble heart filled overflowing with love for this woman. Willamina Beulah Stone, will you do me the honor of marrying me again on July 31st beside the stream like we did so long ago."

You could have heard a pin drop. Nana had both hands over her mouth and tears streaming down her face. Annie was fanning herself and grinning from ear to ear. Willow was looking at everyone in the room as if to try and read our reactions, and the rest of us were just kind of shocked and waiting for that pin to drop. Finally, the silence was broken when my dad could not take it another minute.

"The man asks you a question, mother. I think you need to give him an answer."

Nana looked at her wonderful children all seated in a row side by side. All five of them now nodded their heads as if to encourage her to respond with a positive answer. All smiling and looking hopeful. Her heart was about to burst with joy.

"Yes, Isaiah Franklin Reed, I will marry you beside the stream just like before."

The next few weeks flew by. We were all busy doing our assigned jobs to prepare for the wedding. We had the gazebo that had been built for Frances and Adam's wedding moved to the clearing beside the stream. And in connection with that move we had the path leading to the clearing widened and gavel put down. We wanted it to stay as true to the way it had always been as possible, but we also wanted to be able to drive Nana and Isaiah to the area.

Willow was to be Nana's maid of honor and Isaiah's grandson Robert was going to be his best man. We were all excited to meet him. He would arrive a few days early in order to meet everyone. The biggest surprise was that Mark had gone through the things needed to be ordained so he could legally perform their marriage ceremony. Nana was absolutely thrilled.

We were only inviting family but that was a big crowd on its own. Nana's five children along with the spouses of four of them. Her five grandchildren. Annie and Mark. Her two sisters Georgia and Carolina. That was twenty people and for that tiny spot beside the stream that was a lot. The only ones invited that were not able to attend were Carolina's children and their families.

No friends had been invited. Most of Nana's long-time friends were also friends with Samuel when he was alive, and she felt it would be too awkward for them. Plus, she did not have time to explain her whole story to them. They all knew she had not been dating anyone since Samuels passing and her sudden announcement that she was getting married would send her social circle into a whirlwind. She was hoping they would all respect her privacy until the book was published and they could all read her story and come to their own decision as to how they felt about it. About Isaiah and Willow. She had to smile thinking how shocked they would be when they read the part of the story telling about her being held prisoner in the attic and giving birth. She said she could imagine them as they tried to picture the stairs they had seen when visiting the house. Wondering what kind of secrets this house must hold. Some would think it was all a made-up fantasy to sell a book. Some would elaborate and embellish until the story was more horrific than anyone could have lived through.

"I want this day to be shared with those who I love and who love me. I want it to be so joyful and celebrated. The other time we married only Millie was a witness to our marriage and she was not happy about it," she smiled. "And only God was asked to accept our pledge, but we could not share our news with anyone. This time we will have many witnesses and a certificate that allows us to celebrate. To shout it from the rooftops if we want to."

I had not shared it with Nana, but I had used this marriage as the conclusion to my novel. I had come to a few assumptions as to how it would play out and sent the finished copy to several publishers to be considered for publication. I knew there would be an editing process if they did and I could make changes if needed later. I knew the chances of a response before the wedding was almost zero but maybe by the time they returned from a short honeymoon I could give her the good news.

They were going to go to Arizona for a few days. The artist in Nana wanted to see the Grand Canyon. I could just imagine the beautiful paintings she would glean from that visit.

In the days before the wedding Isaiah and Willow had both become as much of our family as any other member. My dad had at first acted like the big brother and was giving Willow advice on how to handle her business in Memphis while so far away. He also would give her lessons on our family history or give her insight on their mother. But as soon as my Aunts arrived, they set him straight real fast. They reminded him he was the 'baby' of the family and not to get too high and mighty with their sister. Willow was loving it. She seemed to love nothing more than for the five siblings to sit around the kitchen and brainstorm over any and everything. Especially the wedding.

Robert arrived Thursday before the wedding. We were all excited to meet him but none more than Nana. She had talked to him on the phone a few times, but she wanted to wrap her arms around him and hug him tight. That is exactly what she did when he arrived. We all stared at him for a few minutes. He looked just like the younger pictures of Isaiah except for skin tone. He was not as dark, and his eyes were a lighter brown, but the resemblance was uncanny. Willow joined in and they just hugged and laughed and cried and enjoyed this magnificent long-awaited reunion. As much as we all wanted to greet him, we stepped back and gave them their time. Isaiah had walked up to join in on this group hug but the rest of us would wait.

Before we knew it, July 31st was upon us and the big day was under way. Isaiah and Nana had been ordered to stay away from each other until the ceremony. We had done our best to make Nana's dress much like the one she had worn that day. Because of her age it was more tailored than when she was 15. She wore baby's breath in her hair and carried a small bouquet of daisies and some wildflowers. Willow would be in a mint colored sundress with a lace overlay on the skirt. She carried only wildflowers. Both Isaiah and Robert wore black slacks and white shirts with mint green ties. No jackets because let's face it. It's hot outside in Georgia in July. We had decided because of the heat we would go back to the house after the ceremony and have a pool party reception. The cake and refreshments would be in the air-conditioned pool house so it would stay cool. Mark had been more than happy to move all his belongings to the back of the pool house to allow room. I had to laugh when I saw him stuffing a lot of his things in the back of his car and in the garage so we could make the pool house look festive and beautiful for the newlyweds.

Everything was ready to go. I knew that all the family would make their way to the clearing at 5:45 p.m. except for me, Willow and Nana. Mark, Isaiah and Robert would follow behind them in the golf cart to take their places and I would drive Nana and Willow to the designated spot to await their musical cue at 6:00.

Everything seemed so perfect. I expected Nana to be nervous, but she was calm and as content as I had ever seen her. Willow was giddy with excitement but not nervous. I was a wreck. I was shaking in my boots. Well in my sandals. I wanted this to be everything she had ever dreamed of. I guess Nana noticed because once we got out of the car and got in place, she took my hand and kissed it.

"I am so very happy Alex. Thank you for making this possible for me." I could not speak. I was so close to crying but had promised myself I would not cry. "I will not cry" I whispered to myself as I made my way to the seat left empty for me.

Mark looked so handsome as he stood center stage on the gazebo that had been adorned with ribbons and flowers. Isaiah stood next to him. Because the space was limited in the gazebo Robert stood just outside of the opening just in front of his grandfather. Willow would take her place opposite of Robert once she came up the makeshift aisle and Nana would step up and join Isaiah on the gazebo.

It was time. I had finally calmed myself and was wondering about the music. No one had mentioned the music and it occurred to me I had no idea where it would be coming from. I looked around for a cassette player when I heard the sweetest voice begin to sing out. Very low at first and then louder and stronger than I would have imagined possible. It was Isaiah. He was singing Beulah's song. The words were so beautiful and the story they told so inspired, so sensual and loving. Willow began to walk down the path made by chairs and flowers to take her place.

Then Nana started toward him. I could tell Isaiah was having trouble because he was so overwhelmed by the sight of his beautiful bride that he was unable to continue singing. We looked at Nana who had stopped walking unsure if she needed to continue her walk or give Isaiah a chance to gain control. But suddenly we heard the singing resume stronger than ever. Nana smiled and continued to walk toward him and as we turned to face the gazebo again, we noticed Isaiah was not singing.

He was still weeping with joy as he watched her approach. Instead the song was coming from Robert. His grandfather had sung that song to him many times over the years and he knew it by heart. As he continued to sing, he walked down the aisle toward Nana and escorted her the rest of the way and helped her climb the step to the place where Isaiah stood.

Okay my promise not to cry was totally broken but to my defense everyone else seemed to have wet cheeks too.

Mark stood there just smiling for a minute and took a deep breath.

"Nana, you look absolutely beautiful."

Everyone nodded and smiled in agreement as Nana blushed from the compliment.

"Isaiah, you look beautiful too. That goes without saying."

At this we all laughed. Mark has a great way of putting people at ease. He asks that we all bow our heads and he leads a prayer asking for God's blessing on this family and this union.

"In our lives we always seem to seek out others. Others that can fill a void or complete us as people. We seek out the familiar but are often attracted to the unique and total opposite of what we started out looking for. Willamina was a very young impressionable girl when she first saw Isaiah. No one would have thought they would be right for each other. Too many differences and too complicated to ever work out. And for a long time, it seemed that was exactly the case.

Their union was short lived and traumatic and for a long time it seemed it was just not meant to be. But as we can witness today… their love has stood the test of time. Their love has endured and because of that God has granted them another chance at happiness."

Mark placed his Bible on the podium we had provided and opened it to the Old Testament.

"I would like to read Ecclesiastes 4: 9 thru 12.

Two are better than one, because they have a good reward for their labor. For if they fall, one will lift his companion. But woe to him who is alone when he falls, for he has no one to help him up. Again, if two lay down together, they will keep warm; But how can one be warm alone? Though one may be overpowered by another, two can withstand him. And a threefold cord is not quickly broken.

I think the threefold cord the writer talks about is the

couple joining with God. That combination of three cords can stand strong. And that is why Isaiah and Willamina have stayed strong and will continue to do so. They have always looked to God as their help and strength.

Proverbs 18: 22 says; He who finds a wife finds a good thing. I think Isaiah feels the same way so at this time I would like to ask him a very important question: "Isaiah, do you take this woman that stands next to you holding your hand to be your lawfully wedded wife? Do you promise to love her and cherish her through all circumstances until you are separated by death?"

"Oh, I most assuredly do," Isaiah announced while smiling broadly.

He repeated the question to Nana, and she was just as enthusiastic with her response. Mark took the rings from Willow and Robert and had another prayer while holding them. He then allowed them to place the rings on the other's finger. Simple gold bands that meant this time it was right with God and man.

"By the authority granted me by the state of Georgia I pronounce that you are husband and wife. What God has joined let no man put asunder. Isaiah you man kiss your bride."

Once the kiss had broken apart, which was longer than you might imagine for their ages, Mark had them turn and face us.

"I would like to introduce Mr. and Mrs. Isaiah Franklin Reed."

We burst into applause and whistles and yelling for joy. It had taken a long time to get to this place. But Isaiah finally had his Beulah back and they were ready to begin the life that had been stolen from them so long ago.

The reception had lasted late into the night. Lots of pictures and hugs and cake. Mark and I danced several times, but we also tried to mingle. He danced with Willow, Georgia, Carolina, and of course his mother.

"I guess when a party has so many single ladies and so few men you have to do your part," Mark offered.

My dad tried to help as well and so did Robert, who turned out to be a very good dancer. Beautiful singing voice, talented dancer and all-around nice guy. I started thinking of friends I should introduce him to, but Mark said I needed to back off.

"I somehow think he can find girls on his own. You need to be concentrating on this man," he gestured and smiled.

"Oh I am. Believe me I am keeping my eyes on you sir. And I like what I see."

We knew school started back in only a few days for both of us and we would see little of each other for a long while, but we were enjoying this time together as much as possible.

The party was winding down and Nana and Isaiah had a late flight to catch. Robert was returning to Florida because of his job obligations and had arranged to take a flight that would allow him to see them off. They would leave the car in the provided parking at the airport and would drive themselves home when they returned.

The hugs went on and on as if we did not expect to see any of them again. It was especially hard on Willow. She missed her son so much and with Isaiah leaving for a week she felt a little abandoned. I would have to make an extra effort to spend time with her this week. A spa day and a nice meal at my favorite restaurant would be in order.

My parents were planning to return home early in the

morning and gave me ample hugs and instructions before going to their room for a few hours rest. The rest of my Aunts and Uncles left as soon as the newlyweds were out of sight. Annie started cleaning up and I told her to stop and go to bed. We would tackle this mess together in the morning. Willow agreed and she and Annie drug themselves to bed.

Mark and I decided to sit around the pool and enjoy a few minutes alone.

"You did such an excellent job on the ceremony. I was so touched by your words and by your prayer."

"It was easy to find the right verses. I just thought of how I feel about you," he said while looking into my eyes.

I blushed and a tear escaped to roll down my cheek. He kissed the tear and then kissed above both eyes as if soothing my tears. Then his mouth found mine and the rest was a blur. I woke up in the lounge chair where I had fallen asleep in his arms. This had become a too familiar occurrence, but I could not think of any place I would rather wake up than in his arms.

Chapter Twenty-Three

Her Story, My Words

As hard as it was to believe Isaiah and Beulah had been married for a year and a half. So much had happened in those eighteen months. I had heard from a publisher just six months after the wedding and a publisher out of Atlanta Georgia wanted to publish the book. I was overjoyed. We had gone back and forth with edits and more edits. Revisions and decisions on the cover. I had Nana's permission to use a copy of the picture she had given to Isaiah as the front of the book.

I had her do a drawing of the willow tree as the back cover. The final edit has been sent in and now I wait. I had not realized what a long process it was to publish a book. After twelve long months it was finished, and I was told I would receive the copies I had requested as soon as they were satisfied with the final copy. I watched daily for the big box.

I was getting so close to graduating from the university. This was my final year and it was half over. Mark was now a resident in a large hospital in Macon and was specializing in Geriatrics. Nana and Pops, as we now called Isaiah because that was Robert's name for him, would tease Mark telling him he chose that field because he had so many patients already. We are all so proud of him.

We became officially engaged when he graduated medical school and we plan to marry next year once I have finished and he is at the halfway point in his residency. He had proposed to me at the get together we had given him after his graduation from medical school. He had already talked to my parents and so they were in on it. My mother was not thrilled at first, but she had gotten to know Mark and realized he was a wonderful person. She was really working hard to erase the hate she had been taught as a child.

We had all eaten and were just having fun around the pool. Annie came out with a tray of home-made ice cream in fancy sundae cups. All of them were plain except for one that was covered in sprinkles and had a little plastic ring on top of it. I was beginning to think I had the rudest family ever as they all pushed in front of me to take one of the plan cups. Once I finally got to the tray and took the one cup with the sprinkles, I commented that I got a prize for being patient and pulled the ring from the ice cream intending on placing it on my finger. Mark walked up and took the ring from me. Got down on one knee and held out a beautiful diamond engagement ring.

"I hope you will accept this ring instead," he said while holding my hand. "Alex you are my best friend, you are my dreams at night and my joy in the morning. I cannot imagine going through life without you beside me. Will you be my wife? Will you marry me?"

I was so thrilled and so surprised I all but tackled him in a hug as he was beginning to stand up and said; "YES, Oh

Mark yes" as we lost our balance and fell into the pool ice cream and all. At least he did not lose his grip on the ring and when we surfaced, he placed it on my finger, and we kissed as the others applauded.

Willow had decided after several months with us that she wanted to make the move to Georgia permanent. She just could not see going back to Memphis without any family there. She had the realtors she had worked with to put her house on the market and had offered them a great deal on the building her business had been located in. She spent several weeks there getting everything from storage she wanted to keep and donated the rest. She would rent a truck to bring it all back in. She didn't bother to keep a lot from the business because everything would have the wrong address on it, but she kept some personal things from her office to use once she opened a new business in Georgia.

As much as she loved her mother and father, she wanted to find a place of her own. She moved to Macon because it was so close yet big enough to support a realtor. She found a nice house with a large room up front that could be used as an office. For now, she would work and live in the same house. She came to visit often, and once Mark and I are married she is going to help us find the perfect starter home.

Robert was still in Florida for now but his job re-located people all the time. He had let it be known that if a position became available in Georgia he would love to be considered. I know Willow will be much happier if he can re-locate to Macon or at least Georgia.

Watching Nana and Pops was one of my favorite pastimes. They seemed so very happy. In the mornings Nana would work on some special painting that no one except Isaiah could see. If we dare to try to peek, she will set us straight fast. It was the only thing she was working on now. She said it was because she did not have time or energy to paint for others with a tight timeline to go by. She would only paint for pleasure from now on.

I had heard her telling Annie that some of her friends had become distant. She had invited two ladies that had been her friend the longest for lunch so they could meet Isaiah, and both had found excuses more than once. She was hurt but had not been surprised. We both knew that once the book came out there would be more old acquaintances that would fade from her life.

"I can do without that type of friend," she had protested when Isaiah showed concern.

She would paint and Isaiah would sit and read to her from his Bible or just talk about any and everything. Some mornings when she did not want to paint, they would take a stroll that usually landed them at the willow tree. They would often sit under the gazebo on the bench we had added after the wedding. There had been one time when they had been gone for an extremely long time. I became concerned and walked up there to check on them. I did not see them anywhere and called out to them. I heard a giggle in the direction of the willow tree.

"Nana, are you under the tree?"

"Yes dear, we are under here."

"Are you okay?"

"Oh, we are doing just fine," she said in an almost giddy tone. And I heard a low laugh from Isaiah.

I just realized what I had probably interrupted. I was so embarrassed.

"Oh Nana, Isaiah I am so sorry. I had no idea. I was just worried because you were gone so long."

Again, Nana had to chuckle just a little.

"Just remember dear," she paused for effect or to laugh, not sure which. "If the tree skirt is shaking its love we are making."

Isaiah laughed again and I walked home with my head low and my face a brilliant scarlet. When I returned to the house Mark and Annie both asked me if I found them. They both had to notice I was a little put out.

"Are you okay," Mark asked? "Are they okay?"

"Fine they are just fine. They are more than fine. They were shaking the tree skirt."

I could not look either of them in the eyes. I think it occurred to both at the same time because they both grinned and shook their heads.

"Ohhhhhh," they said together.

I rolled my eyes and went to the den to calm down from my humiliation.

As I sat there fuming about how I had allowed myself to once again be so visually embarrassed I heard a knock at the front door. I answered the door and there stood a delivery truck driver waiting for me to sign for a large box. A large box from the publishing company in Atlanta. The books were here. Inside this heavy box was 110 copies of her published novel. The publisher had told her if she purchased at least 100 copies at the discounted price afforded to the author that she would receive 10 free copies to share with friends and family if she so desired. The suggestion was that the other 100 copies be sold to bookstores and used for book signings to promote her first published novel. She had dreamed of this experience for years, but the subject matter was not what she had expected her first attempt at writing to be. Her heart pounded in her chest as she sat in the middle of the living room floor with the large box planted between her legs and a knife in hand to cut the tape. This had been a labor of love bringing this story to these pages. Her first novel but so much more.

She opened it and took the first copy out to examine it. The picture on the front cover was of a beautiful young girl with long auburn hair and pale blue eyes. Willamina was the name of the bravest person she had met to this day. How honored she felt to tell her story but also afraid of the fall out that was sure to come as a result of the secrets kept for so long.

This book had been a well-kept secret from the family, and she had feared some of them would be very upset that a secret kept from them would now become public knowledge. She thought some would be embarrassed and some would be insulted or maybe angry at the truth; but the ones that mattered had been accepting and supportive. Now, as she held up the first pristine copy only deep pride filled her heart. "Willamina… a young girls journal" by Alexandria Stone.

I turned the book over and examined the back cover. There was a picture of the beautiful willow tree where the story began and on the inside of the back cover my own face stared back at me. I read about myself as if confirming it was really me. Alexandria Stone attended the Mercer University of Macon, Georgia where she studied Journalism and received her bachelor degree in Liberal Arts and Sciences.

I had explained to them that I would not graduate until December, but they said to go ahead and put it as part of my description. I was close enough.

I had begged my Nana to put her own name as the author or to at least co-author so she would get credit for her own story, but she had insisted it be my book. Her story was told in my words.

Mark and Annie walked into the room and found me sitting on the floor surrounded by paper and books.

"There here," I cried. "The books are here." Nana and Pop walked in through the French doors and I could not help it. I screamed at the top of my voice.

"Nana the books came!"

They rushed in and everyone was looking at copies.

"They are beautiful Alex. You can be so proud," Nana said.

Everyone in the room was flipping through the book. Running their hands over the cover and pointing out things they thought would really catch the reader's eye.

We had to celebrate. The entire family gathered the following weekend for a party to not only celebrate my first novel but to celebrate Nana and Isaiah and the journey that had led to now. Robert even came in for the weekend which especially thrilled Willow who had not seen him in several months. Nana and Pop had gone for a quick trip to see him a few weeks ago, but Willow was so busy trying to build her new business and could not spare the time just yet.

We planned on how to best promote the book. I would take a few copies to both bookstores in Payne. Willow would take several copies and work on bookstores and specialty shops in Macon. Mark and I had planned a trip to Atlanta to try and promote them also. Maybe line up a book signing. I gave a signed copy to Willow, my parents, my Aunts, Nana's sisters, and Annie. Oh and of course one to Nana. I kept one for myself and told Mark I would sign it for him, and it would be in our home when we married. All other copies would be for promotion and book signings. It was also available on a few online markets and electronic readers.

As is true with all new authors I had high hopes for a fast and furious rise to fame. I just knew the book would be so well accepted that it would be made into a movie. I guess that is what all new authors hope for. The truth is it was loved by some, hated by others and never became a movie.

The reviews were very mixed among those who knew us. In our small town, people who had known Nana when she was married to Papa Sam the book seemed scandalous or just wrong. To others it seemed like a great fantasy romance. The fact that people did not know her, or Isaiah made it hard to impress them if they even believed it was true.

Some were curious for a short time. They would drive by pointing to the top of the house at the round windows in the attic and even take pictures.

I sold all the copies I had ordered originally and even placed a second order for copies. I still have about ten of them left.

I received royalty checks for those sold online and managed to sell an additional one hundred copies in online orders over a years' time.

"I'm sorry Nana," I said one day out of the blue. "I'm sorry the book wasn't a success."

She looked at me shocked by my comment.

"Not a success? How can you say such a thing? That book was a magnificent success. I don't know how much money you made or how many copies you sold, but it gave me my Alex," she said and put her arm around my shoulders.

"Before the journals you hardly knew me. You most likely would not have stayed here for more than the few weeks required if that.

It gave me back my Isaiah and my beautiful daughter Willow. It gave me the courage to tell my children about my past and it allowed me to meet my grandson Robert that I had not known existed.

It showed me who my true friends were, and it showed me the ones who were superficial.

Alex, I know you had high hopes that your first novel would skyrocket to the top of the charts and make you a millionaire. I have read books before that were at the top and made the author a rich person, but to be honest I could not figure out why.

You must **never** measure success by profit, or by popularity. Those are false signs of success. You wrote a beautiful book. As the person the story was about let me assure you that you captured my feelings so beautifully, I felt them fresh again. My goal was to tell my story. To no longer hide the truth of who I was and how I became this person. That is what I had asked you to do, isn't it?"

"Yes Nana, that is what you said you wanted. But…"

"***But nothing***. You gave me what I wanted. You gave me what I asked for and more. In my eyes and in my heart, you produced a most wonderful first novel and I am proud of it and I am so very proud of you. And you gained insight and knowledge that will help you with your next novel and the one after that and the one after that.

Alex, when I was young, and I would paint or draw people would sometimes laugh at my work. Sometimes they would ridicule or make fun of something I had done. But I just saw it as my expression of something. It was beautiful to me. As I have grown and have learned from my mistakes, have perfected my methods I have become better in the eyes of others. But it is still just me enjoying my gift. You need to enjoy writing. If you become a world-famous author or even if it never goes farther than this. Do it for yourself Alex. You should do it for the love of writing.

As always, my sweet Nana had put it all in perspective. She thinks her talent is being able to paint. Her true talent is how she makes the people in her life feel so special and so loved. How she can calm a worried spirit and make you see things in a different light.

She may be right. I may publish many more books. I know I will try because it is a passion of mine. But no matter where it leads me, I will always be the proudest of this first novel. The story of the bravest woman I know.

CHAPTER TWENTY FOUR

Twenty-Three Years of Us

My favorite place to be these days is the gazebo next to the stream. Mark and I walk here together most afternoons that weather permits but I also love to come by myself. I sit and think about all that these trees have witnessed. I talk out loud to the willow tree and the beautiful spirits that now rest under its protective skirt.

Beulah and Isaiah had 23 years together. They spent all their time enjoying what life offered. In the beginning they traveled often. They would garden and take walks. They would sit and talk as if they had not seen each other in years but you seldom saw them apart. In their final years together both Isaiah and Nana had been ill. They were weaker and in need of assistance for almost everything so we moved their room downstairs across from the library. The steps leading upstairs had become too much for their advanced ages.

Mark and I had married and lived in Macon for almost eighteen years. He had a successful practice and I had worked the first few years of our marriage at a newspaper just like my Papa Sam. I had also managed to publish several more novels all of which had been well received but none had reached the level of success I had once dreamed of. Mostly I was busy raising our three children. Our son, Slaid, who was now sixteen and our twin girls Nova and Kayla, who had just turned twelve.

About four years before they passed away, we had made the decision to move back in the house with them. Annie had retired and gone to live with her daughter. We had hired housekeepers for a few years but none were family like Annie and we just felt that Nana and Isaiah needed family with them. I enjoyed our home in Macon but I had to admit that coming back to this house was my dream come true.

This house had been home to me more than my parents' home I grew up in and more than any house Mark and I had shared. This house was alive with memories and love. Not just the house I suppose but the property surrounding the house. To know I could visit the stream and the willow tree any time I wanted gave me security and a joy I can't really put in words.

We decided I would help care for them along with their own personal physician in residence. Mark kept a close watch on them and when he could tell their time was growing short, he tried to prepare me. He said he was very surprised that Isaiah had held on so long but he seemed to be waiting on his Beulah. Both of them had made us promise they would remain in this house until their time to 'go home'. Of course, we understood what they meant until they died and went home to be with God.

Willow would come and stay when we needed to be out of town or just to give me a break. She loves staying at the house and taking care of her parents. We knew it was the fulfillment of a dream from her childhood. To be a family of three. Her mom and dad with their daughter. You would have never guessed that Nana had not raised her from birth when they were together. Willow loved her more than I think she ever thought possible. No sign of the anger or resentment remained.

Willow's son Robert had moved to Macon about two years after Willow had settled there and was now married to a sweet girl he met at church. Her name is Carrie and they have a beautiful little girl, Zaniyah, who is six years old. Willow is a loving grandmother and was spoiling her as much as they allowed her to. Often, she would bring Zaniyah with her when she spent the weekend with her parents. Zaniyah would sit and visit with them for long periods of time and Nana was teaching her to paint. Her Pops would sing with her until he grew hoarse and I must admit she had a beautiful voice for one so young.

Willow had dated some but never seemed to find someone she cared about enough to get serious. I asked her once why she thought she hadn't found someone. She said when she compared them to her dad and Nana they just never seemed to measure up. She felt like she had already had her one true love when she found her husband Robert.

The day my Nana and her Isaiah passed was August 1st, 2019. This was probably the first year they had not gone to the stream for their anniversary. She was 93 years old. Isaiah was 96.

It had seemed like any other day except they had not

opened the door to signal they were ready for us to help them to breakfast. I knocked on the door and knew the minute I walked in that she was gone. Mark rushed to her side and confirmed what I knew. He said he could tell she had only passed minutes before we came into the room. We looked over at Isaiah who was still holding her hand. He looked at her so lovingly and I saw a tear travel down his cheek. He looked up at us and said,

"I told her I would never leave her again. I was just waiting for her."

At that he closed his eyes and exhaled. Mark rushed over to see if he could do anything, but he was gone. They had died within minutes of each other.

We struggled with where Nana should be buried. As much as they loved Isaiah, her children wanted her buried next to Papa Sam. When he had passed the headstone had included Willamina's information and date of birth. They would only have to add the date of death. This was a very common practice in southern states.

Willow wanted her next to Isaiah. This was her mother and she wanted her parents' side by side as much as my dad and aunts wanted their parents' side by side. We came up with the only solution we could think of. We had them cremated. We put part of her ashes on the top of Papa Sam's grave and had the date of her death placed on the headstone. The remainder of her ashes were mixed in with Isaiah's ashes. I wasn't really sure how the others felt about it but my opinion was that the body left behind is like an abandoned house.

The person that lived inside that house had vacated it and moved to another location. In my faith that location was heaven. I compared it to this example. If this house we all love so much were to burn to the ground and we could no longer see it. We could no longer visit it. We would have wonderful memories of this house but it would be the people who lived inside that would matter. As long as we knew those people were in a safe location and they were happy we could deal with the loss of the house. I knew in my heart that Nana, Pops and Papa Sam were happy wherever they were living now. I didn't know how God would arrange things but I was sure all was well. That is what I had learned from them. God has a plan and as long as we give him control of our life all will work out for good in the end.

We kept them in an urn in the library surrounded by her paintings until the following year. On July 31st on what would have been their 24th anniversary or their 79th anniversary depending on how you look at it; our family gathered at the stream and had a sort of memorial for them. We dug a small hole under the willow tree and placed the urn containing their ashes in the hole. We had placed a plague on the trunk of the tree with their names and birth and death dates. It only seemed right that they rested under their tree as they had so many times.

The house had been left to Mark and I. I had spent a lot of time after they passed arranging to put some of her paintings on display. The reason she had wanted the book written was to show others her story and I felt like these pictures would do the same thing. Even if a person didn't know the story, the paintings were beautiful. But for those who had read the book or heard the story from others the paintings would come to life.

I had rented a small building in Macon that Willow found and we had made it a gallery to honor her work and to honor their memory. I had placed a copy of my book in the gallery so anyone who had read it or heard the story would make the connection between the paintings and the love story between Isaiah and Beulah. I also had a recorded message giving a brief rundown of the history of these paintings and the lesson she had wanted people to learn from her story. Anyone who wanted to listen needed only push the button on the podium provided. The message was also printed out and placed under glass on top of that same podium. In the background a rendition of Beulah's Song played softly over and over.

Isaiah's grandson Robert had recorded it for us. He sounded so much like Isaiah and you could tell the song meant a lot to him because Isaiah had taught it to him when he was a young man. Some people seemed not to notice the song. Others would catch on after hearing it a few times and you would see the moment they realized what the song was about by the expression on their faces. Then there were those who had read the book or perhaps knew the couple and as they walked through, they would weep at the beautiful message of the song. The words were felt so passionately by Isaiah as he pinned them for his bride.

Many made offers to buy the paintings but we refused to sell them. They would be on display for a while and then divided among her children. Her final painting was at the center of the display. It was the largest of all the paintings and she had told us that it would be hung in the living room of the house once she was gone. She had worked on it up until the final year of her life. We had tried many times to sneak a peek at it as she worked on it but she would not allow it. She would tell us it was a work in progress. She did however let Isaiah watch her paint. I would watch through the window at them and notice him pointing at it and talking in a low voice to Nana as if giving suggestions. I don't think she would have let anyone else on this earth tell her what to paint or how to paint but this apparently was a joint project. A message they both believed in strongly that the painting would portray.

The day after they had passed away our entire family had gathered at the house to make all those dreaded decisions and one of the first things we all agreed on was it was time to see the mystery painting. Once Nana had finished it, she had it moved to her and Isaiah's bedroom and kept it covered so we could not see it until she was ready. We moved it to the living room for the big reveal. Mark lifted the sheet and there was a group gasp and a mixture of sounds of appreciation and admiration. This would hang in a place of honor. This moment with all of us gathered together was probably the most healing. More than any funeral or memorial to come. We all cried and hugged and shared memories of these two-lovely people.

It was a painting of Beulah and Isaiah sitting in rocking chairs on the porch of Millie and grandmother's old house. In Isaiah's lap was his old Bible. They were young and obviously very happy. As odd as it seems Papa Sam was sitting on the edge of the porch on the other side of Nana. He was smiling up at her. Out in the yard and near the stream were all the children playing and laughing. Willow, Kathy, Susan, Frances and William. The painting also included Nana's parents and sisters.

Alex and Mark with their children. Robert and his family. Millie and grandmother. It also had Steve, and Philip talking with Annie's husband. Nana's other grandchildren and their families were mingled within the picture. The willow tree and the stream were in the picture and the big old tree with the seat that Willie had sat in to draw. She had even included Mr. Carlson waving from the field across from the stream and he was smiling at them as if they were all old friends.

In the picture everyone was happy. She had deliberately paired up where they seemed equally divided. Her father was talking and smiling with Robert. Her mother was holding hands with Willow. No one seemed out of place and everyone belonged. The message of the painting was as clear as a bell… to us at least. She and Isaiah had tried to teach the lesson that all are equal in the eyes of God who created us all. That we love others because of what is inside of them. We should never like or dislike someone because of their outside covering. I had to smile when I noticed a piece of paper taped to the bottom of the canvas and I knew she meant for this to be the title of the painting.

We opened the gallery one week after we had placed them under the willow tree. Willow had found the perfect place to share these precious gifts and I was so excited to place her last painting on the back wall of the largest room in the gallery. By the time a person made their way to this painting they would know the story. Each painting had a little plaque under it explaining some about the origin of the painting and even gave a reference to where in the book they could find more detail if they desired.

I admit this did help my sales for a short time but that wasn't my reason for doing it. I wanted to do what they had wanted all along. To help people to understand that love is limitless and a true gift. The title of the painting was on a golden plaque along the bottom of the painting. It was entitled, *APPLES*